D1178649

50 Years of Notable Books

Reference and
Adult Services Division
American Library Association

Booklist Publications
American Library Association
1996

ISBN 0-8389-7836-3

Table of Contents

Foreword

The title notwithstanding, this compilation actually contains 52 years of Notable Books. Think of this dating irregularity as a way of honoring the enduring success of Notable Books. After all, anyone who survives in good health for more than half a century deserves the right to shave a couple of years off his or her age. In a sense, too, our title reflects a pattern of dating peculiarities. Up until 1989, the date of the list reflected the year of publication of the books on it. In 1989, it was decided to date the list with the year the books were selected and the list published. Thus, there is no list dated 1989; books published in 1989 are on the 1990 list.

The lists are arranged here by year, from the most recent selection, 1996, to the earliest, 1944. The original bibliographic information for the titles on some of the early lists is very limited; no publisher was given, for example. We checked every one of these titles against *Books in Print Plus* and either noted it to be out of print ([o.p.]) or listed the current publisher, price, and ISBN. If the original hardcover edition is out of print, we have put the current publisher, price, and ISBN in brackets. Some of these books are available in many formats—hardcover, trade paper, mass market. If there were both trade paper and mass-market editions, we listed the trade paper edition. A mass-market edition is listed when it was the only one available. Some of these books are also available in large-print and audio versions, which we have not noted.

For some nonfiction titles, the edition listed is not the original but a revised one. Most of the collections of poetry selected as Notable Books are now out of print. However, in many cases, the complete works of the poet have since been published.

Thirty-four percent of the titles selected in 1946 are still available, usually in a reprinted edition. Fifty percent of the titles from 1956, 48 percent of the books from 1966, 66 percent of the titles from 1976, and 68 percent of the titles from 1986 are still in print. While a surprising percentage of the titles, even the oldest ones, are still in print, libraries perform a valuable service to our culture by continuing to stock books that are no longer available through the book trade. We hope you will use this book to review your collection for gaps and to mount exhibits for your users.

Throughout the history of Notable Books, the lists have appeared in *Booklist* in their entirety, and for many years *Booklist* staff members have served as consultants to the council.

Thanks to Kim Dillon of the *Booklist* staff for creating the electronic files that made publication of this book possible.

—*Sandy Whiteley*, Editor

Introduction

Purpose

The annual list of Notable Books is compiled for use by the general reader and for librarians who work with adult readers. Its purpose is to call attention to titles published during the year that are significant to the world of books.

Selection Criteria

The following criteria are used to select books for inclusion on the list:

1. A book may be selected as notable for any of the following reasons: it possesses exceptional literary merit; it expands the horizons of human knowledge; it makes a specialized body of knowledge accessible to the nonspecialist; it promises to contribute significantly to the solution of a contemporary problem.

2. Each book is considered in relation to the general adult reader and will not be excluded on the basis of its unsuitability for younger readers. Books of limited interest and books requiring specialized knowledge for their use are not eligible.

3. Each book shall have been published between November 1 of the preceding year and October 31 of the current year.

History, 1944–96

The Notable Books list evolved from an activity begun by the Lending Round Table of the American Library Association in 1944. During the intervening half-century, this annual selection of outstanding books has been achieved using a variety of methods under the auspices of different groups of the ALA.

Initially called "Outstanding Books," the list was compiled with the assistance of membership votes. By 1947, the division of Public Libraries assumed responsibility and changed the name to "Notable Books." The Notable Books Committee was expanded in 1955 to become a 12-member Council, and three years later was transferred to the Adult Services Division (ASD). In 1959, the ASD Board of Directors adopted a mission statement for the Council, and with the merger in 1972 of the ASD and the Reference Services Division, the Notable Books Council became a committee of the Reference and Adult Services Division.

In recent years, a publicity subcommittee has been formed to promote the prestige of the list. Publishers, both major trade and small press, now include the Notable Books designation in book blurbs, authors' biographies, and press releases.

"Literary Tastes: A Notable Books Breakfast" has become a regular event at the ALA Annual Conference. The breakfast is one of the few ALA programs that brings together librarians, writers, and publishers of books for the adult market.

Today, the 12 members of the Notable Books Council represent a variety of library constituencies from all parts of the country. Appointed to an initial two-year term, they meet twice a year to discuss the more than 500 titles being considered for inclusion on the list. Making informed recommendations and encouraging people to read books of merit continue to be the goals for the Council with the release of each new list.

Tom H. Ray,
Virginia State Library Archives,
Notable Books Council Chair,
1993–94

Notable Books of the 1990s

Notable Books, 1996

Fiction

Camus, Albert. The First Man. Knopf, $23 (0-679-43937-4).
A vivid and deeply moving novel based on Camus' impoverished childhood in Algiers.

D'Ambrosio, Charles. The Point. Little, Brown, $19.95 (0-316-17144-1).
In this powerful debut collection, D'Ambrosio's characters move toward knowledge and hope in a desolate and confusing world.

Dexter, Pete. The Paperboy. Random, $23 (0-679-42175-0).
Murder brings a big-city reporter back to the Florida swamps of his childhood home in this riveting novel.

Ishiguro, Kazuo. The Unconsoled. Knopf, $25 (0-679-40425-2).
A famous pianist journeys to a European city in a fascinating story of angst and uncertainty. Is it all a dream?

Lee, Chang-Rae. Native Speaker. Riverhead, $21.95 (1-57322-001-9).
The power of language underlies this elegant portrayal of Korean American Henry Park, spurned husband and unhappy spy.

Maxwell, William. All the Days and Nights. Knopf, $25 (0-679-43829-7); Random, paper, $13 (0-679-76102-2).
Set in small midwestern communities and New York City apartments, these are the graceful, subtle tales of a short-story master.

Nordan, Lewis. The Sharpshooter Blues. Algonquin, $17.95 (1-56512-083-3).
Hydro Raney and his father are two of the unforgettable characters in this darkly comic novel of love and violent death on the Mississippi Delta.

O'Nan, Stewart. Snow Angels. Doubleday, $20 (0-385-47574-8); Penguin, paper, $10.95 (0-14-025096-4).
A woman killed by her estranged husband and a boy facing his parents' breakup—two interwoven stories—drive this masterfully written first novel.

Schumacher, Julie. The Body Is Water. Soho; dist. by Farrar, $21 (1-56947-042-1).
Jane, a pregnant, unmarried schoolteacher, returns to her father's house to confront her future—and her past.

Wiggins, Marianne. Eveless Eden. HarperCollins, $22 (0-06-016951-6).
International crises frame this compelling story of obsessive love, narrated by journalist Noah John.

1

Poetry

Doty, Mark. Atlantis. HarperCollins, $22 (0-06-055362-6).
Doty engages the senses with stunning verse about salt marsh and imagining, partnership and caring, AIDS and dying.

Hughes, Langston. The Collected Poems of Langston Hughes. Knopf, $30 (0-679-42631-0); Random, paper, $16 (0-679-76408-9).
African American life within five tumultuous decades flows through this definitive collection.

Kunitz, Stanley. Passing Through. Norton, $18.95 (0-393-03870-X).
From his youthful poems to those of his old age, Kunitz's voice remains sure, strong, and celebratory.

Nonfiction

Allende, Isabel. Paula. HarperCollins, $24 (0-06-017253-3); paper, $12.50 (0-06-092720-8).
Sitting by the bedside of her comatose daughter, the Chilean novelist spins true stories about their magical family and their country's turbulent history.

Brooks, Geraldine. Nine Parts of Desire. Doubleday/Anchor, $22.95 (0-385-47576-4); paper, $12.95 (0-385-47577-2).
Journalist Brooks examines the impact of fundamentalism on the lives of Islamic women today.

Covington, Dennis. Salvation on Sand Mountain. Addison-Wesley, $20 (0-201-62292-0).
Covington becomes caught up in the passions of a snake-handling sect while covering a murder trial in the rural South.

Donald, David Herbert. Lincoln. Simon & Schuster, $35 (0-684-80846-3).
In a scholarly and readable biography, Donald relies on primary sources to create a fresh and human image of Lincoln.

Douglas, Ann. Terrible Honesty. Farrar, $22 (0-374-11620-2).
A portrait of the generation, from Dorothy Parker to Duke Ellington, that made jazz age New York the capital of American culture.

Frey, Darcy. The Last Shot: City Streets, Basketball Dreams. Houghton, $19.95 (0-395-59770-6); paper, $11 (0-684-81509-5).
Frey examines how the hoop dreams of inner-city high-school athletes are exploited by the college recruitment system.

Gjelten, Tom. Sarajevo Daily. HarperCollins, $22 (0-06-019052-3); paper, $13 (0-06-092662-7).
Public radio correspondent Gjelten personalizes the destruction of a multiethnic city, explaining how the Bosnian war happened.

Hockenberry, John. Moving Violations. Hyperion; dist. by Little, Brown, $24.95 (0-7868-6078-2); paper, $14.95 (0-7868-8162-3).

An angry, passionate, humorous autobiography of the self-described crippled reporter who refuses to let his disability slow him down.

Karr, Mary. The Liar's Club. Viking, $22.95 (0-670-85053-5); Penguin, paper, $16.95 (0-14-086308-7).

Unraveling the mystery of her family's breakdown, Karr poetically reflects on a troubled yet triumphant childhood.

Kozol, Jonathan. Amazing Grace. Crown, $23 (0-517-79999-5).

The stark face of urban poverty comes alive in this haunting portrait of a South Bronx neighborhood.

Little, Charles E. The Dying of the Trees. Viking, $22.95 (0-670-84135-8).

In this startling wake-up call, Little describes the alarming decline of North American forests with frightening clarity.

Postman, Neil. The End of Education. Knopf, $22 (0-679-43006-7).

Postman addresses the dehumanizing impact of technology on teaching in this provocative look at the state of America's schools.

Reynolds, David S. Walt Whitman's America. Knopf, $35 (0-394-58023-0); Random, paper, $19 (0-679-76709-6).

A poet's life and a country's history are skillfully interwoven, illuminating each other in new ways.

Notable Books, 1995

Fiction

Alvarez, Julia. In the Time of the Butterflies. Algonquin, $21.95 (1-56512-038-8); NAL, paper, $11.95 (0-452-27442-7).

This powerful novel, based on the lives of three sisters from the Dominican Republic murdered by dictator Trujillo's men, captures the humanity of the women's lives and the terror that political repression engenders.

Bainbridge, Beryl. The Birthday Boys. Carroll & Graf, $18.95 (0-7867-0071-8); paper, $9.95 (0-7867-0207-9).

The beauty and danger of Antarctica are described in the words of Robert Scott and his four companions as their 1910 expedition comes to a disastrous end.

Betts, Doris. Souls Raised from the Dead. Knopf, $23 (0-679-42621-3); Simon & Schuster, paper, $12 (0-684-80104-3).

In this wise and affecting novel, a child's illness compels a father to face the fact that, despite his love for his daughter, he is unable to save her.

Drury, Tom. The End of Vandalism. Houghton, $21.95 (0-395-62151-8); Fawcett, paper, $11 (0-449-90982-4).
Louise, her ex-husband (a thief), and her new husband (a county sheriff) make a far-from-ordinary triangle in this tender, funny first novel set in rural Iowa.

Ignatieff, Michael. Scar Tissue. Farrar, $20 (0-374-25428-1).
This beautifully crafted novel details the tragedy of a woman's descent into Alzheimer's disease and its paralyzing effect on her philosopher son.

Maitland, Sara. Ancestral Truths. Holt, $22.50 (0-8050-2536-7); paper, $12 (0-8050-3779-9).
The question of whether Clare Kerslake murdered her lover is framed within an exploration of family ties, religious faith, and the mysteries of disability and loss.

Munro, Alice. Open Secrets. Knopf, $23 (0-679-43575-1); Random, paper, $13 (0-679-75562-4).
Eight complex, fully developed stories explore elements of secrecy in the lives of women.

Norman, Howard. The Bird Artist. Farrar, $20 (0-374-11330-0); St. Martin's, paper, $13 (0-312-13027-9).
Fabian Vas, a bird artist and murderer, tells eccentric tales of mystery and morality in Witless Bay, Newfoundland, in the early 1900s.

O'Brien, Tim. In the Lake of the Woods. Houghton, $21.95 (0-395-48889-3).
The Vietnam War is brought home in this richly textured novel about a politician whose past participation in wartime atrocities is suddenly revealed.

Paley, Grace. The Collected Stories. Farrar, $27.50 (0-374-12636-4); paper, $14 (0-374-52431-9).
This treasury, brimming with city life and quirky women, brings together all of the stories of a master of the form.

Power, Susan. The Grass Dancer. Putnam, $22.95 (0-399-13911-7); Berkley, paper, $5.99 (0-425-14962-5).
The resilience of the North Dakota Sioux is skillfully depicted in a magical first novel that moves backward through layers of history and time.

Schulman, Audrey. The Cage. Algonquin, $17.95 (0-56512-035-9); Avon, paper, $5.99 (0-380-72473-1).
Lost in the Arctic, members of a photographic expedition confront two enemies—the fierce, intense cold and the polar bears.

Poetry

Bierds, Linda. The Ghost Trio. Holt, $20 (0-8050-3485-4); paper, $12.95 (0-8050-3486-2).
The ghosts of Bierds' poems are historical personages captured in moments of imaginative activity and realized in rich and nuanced language.

Clampitt, Amy. A Silence Opens. Knopf, $20 (0-679-42997-2).
What lies hidden and silent in the world around us is given voice in these elegant poems.

Nonfiction

Beals, Melba Pattillo. Warriors Don't Cry: A Searing Memoir of the Battle to Integrate Little Rock's Central High. Pocket, $22 (0-671-86638-9); paper, $10 (0-671-86639-7).
Beals dramatically recounts how she and eight other students courageously faced mob violence when they became the first African Americans to attend Central High School in 1957.

Chaikin, Andrew. A Man on the Moon: The Voyages of the Apollo Astronauts. Viking, $27.95 (0-670-81446-6); Penguin, paper, $15.95 (0-14-009706-6).
Based on in-depth interviews, this insightful account reveals the intense personal dedication, professional competitiveness, and remarkable teamwork of the Apollo astronauts.

Cohen, Leah Hager. Train Go Sorry: Inside a Deaf World. Houghton, $22.95 (0-395-63625-6); Random, paper, $13 (0-679-76165-9).
Having grown up at the Lexington School for the Deaf, a hearing woman sensitively describes issues central to the deaf community.

Gates, Henry Louis. Colored People: A Memoir. Knopf, $22 (0-679-42179-3); Random, paper, $11 (0-679-73919-X).
Warm memories of extended family and close community infuse this account of growing up "colored" in a West Virginia town during the early days of the civil rights movement.

Gilmore, Mikal. Shot in the Heart. Doubleday, $24.95 (0-385-42293-8); paper, $14.95 (0-385-47800-3).
Painful and honest, this haunting record of a family devastated by abuse and violence shows that life is most difficult for the survivors.

Goodwin, Doris Kearns. No Ordinary Time: Franklin and Eleanor Roosevelt: The Homefront in World War II. Simon & Schuster, $30 (0-671-64240-5); paper, $16 (0-684-80448-4).
This engaging narrative combines biography and social history in a compelling vision of what the nation was then and what we are now.

Martin, Russell. Out of Silence: A Journey into Language. Holt, $22.50 (0-8050-1998-7); Penguin, paper, $11.95 (0-14-024701-7).
Martin's account of his family's heartbreaking efforts to communicate with his autistic nephew explores the nature of language and the resilience of parental hope.

Nuland, Sherwin B. How We Die: Reflections on Life's Final Chapter. Knopf, $24 (0-679-41461-4).
Nuland's compassionate, wry look at the treatment of death in modern America is medically informative and oddly reassuring.

Price, Reynolds. A Whole New Life. Atheneum, $20 (0-689-12197-0).
Price's candid memoir portrays his valiant struggle to overcome the effects of spinal cancer and to return to a productive life.

Weiner, Jonathan. The Beak of the Finch: A Story of Evolution in Our Time. Knopf, $25 (0-679-40003-6).
Weiner's absorbing account of scientific dedication, observation, and measurement makes Darwin's theory of natural selection relevant to contemporary readers.

Winerip, Michael. 9 Highland Road. Pantheon, $25 (0-679-40724-3); Random, paper, $13 (0-679-76160-8).
Journalist Winerip chronicles the personal and political struggles and triumphs in a group home for the mentally ill.

Wolff, Tobias. In Pharaoh's Army: Memoirs of the Lost War. Knopf, $23 (0-679-40217-9); paper, $12 (0-679-76023-7).
Written in spare, understated language, Wolff's depiction of his tour of duty in Vietnam is, startlingly, more humdrum than horrible.

Notable Books, 1994

Fiction

Coyle, Beverly. In Troubled Waters. Ticknor & Fields, $19.95 (0-395-57437-4); Penguin, paper, $9.95 (0-14-023301-6).
The story of a small-town Florida family, this moving and funny novel explores timely issues of racial conflict and community harmony.

Eugenides, Jeffrey. The Virgin Suicides. Farrar, $18 (0-374-28438-5); Warner, paper, $10.99 (0-446-67025-1)].
In an evocative and mysterious first novel, the suicides of five teenage sisters assume mythic proportions for the now middle-aged men who observed their deaths.

Gaines, Ernest J. A Lesson before Dying. Knopf, $21 (0-679-41477-0); paper, $11 (0-679-74166-6)].
A young, illiterate black man condemned to death for a crime he did not commit finds his voice in this story about racism in 1940s Louisiana.

Jones, Thom. The Pugilist at Rest. Little, Brown, $18.95 (0-316-47302-2); paper, $9.95 (0-316-47304-9).
These strong debut stories encompass both the unsavory and the ordinary in settings ranging from Vietnam to hospital wards.

Klima, Ivan. Judge on Trial. Tr. by A. G. Brian. Knopf, $25 (0-394-58977-7); paper, $14 (0-679-73756-1).
A major Czechoslovakian novelist examines the moral dilemma of a judge struggling to survive within a totalitarian state.

Malouf, David. Remembering Babylon. Pantheon, $20 (0-679-42724-4); Random, paper, $10 (0-679-74951-9).
   When a young castaway reared by Australian Aboriginals appears in a colonial settlement, the British inhabitants confront the fears his strangeness provokes.

McCracken, Elizabeth. Here's Your Hat, What's Your Hurry. Random/Turtle Bay, $20 (0-679-40026-5).
   Quirky characters make the best of their eccentricities in these exuberant, life-affirming stories.

Nordan, Lewis. Wolf Whistle. Algonquin, $16.95 (1-56512-028-0); paper, $9.95 (1-56512-110-4).
   The Emmett Till lynching and trial in 1955 Mississippi is the inspiration for Nordan's haunting novel told in a tragicomic style.

Proulx, E. Annie. The Shipping News. Scribner, $20 (0-684-19337-X); Simon & Schuster, paper, $12 (0-671-51005-3).
   Offbeat characters manage life's ups and downs in a novel imbued with Newfoundland local color.

Russo, Richard. Nobody's Fool. Random, $23 (0-394-57778-7); paper, $13 (0-679-75333-8).
   Sully—60, down on his luck but a born survivor—is central to this humorous and compassionate novel set in upstate New York.

Watson, Larry. Montana 1948. Milkweed Editions, $17.95 (0-915943-13-1).
   The abuse of power, trust, and family loyalty creates a catastrophic dilemma for a small-town sheriff, his wife, and his son.

Poetry

Fiser, Karen. Words Like Fate and Pain. Zoland, paper, $9.95 (0-944072-23-2).
   Incisive poems explore physical disability and moments of grace.

Van Duyn, Mona. If It Be Not I: Collected Poems, 1959–1982. Knopf, $25 (0-679-41902-0); paper, $15 (0-679-75281-1).
   This powerful collection renders the complexities of ordinary life in precise, transforming language.

Nonfiction

Arenas, Reinaldo. Before Night Falls. Viking, $25 (0-670-84078-5); paper, $11.95 (0-14-015765-4).
   In fierce, often poetic language, Arenas describes his struggle to transcend childhood poverty and to survive as a gay man in Castro's Cuba.

Chernow, Ron. The Warburgs. Random, $30 (0-679-41823-7); paper, $16 (0-679-74359-6).
   Meticulous research and gifted storytelling combine in this historical biography of a German Jewish banking family whose destiny is changed by the Holocaust.

Delany, Sarah and **Delany, A. Elizabeth**. Having Our Say: The Delany Sisters' First 100 Years. Kodansha, $20 (1-56836-010-X); Dell, paper, $5.99 (0-440-22042-4).

With humor and forthrightness, Sadie and Bessie Delany speak their minds after living for more than 100 years as sisters, career women, and socially responsive African Americans.

Drakulic, Slavenka. The Balkan Express: Fragments from the Other Side of War. Norton, $19.95 (0-393-03496-8); HarperCollins, paper, $11 (0-06-097608-X).

A Croatian journalist's acute essays give the ongoing Balkan War an individual face and document Yugoslavia's slide into chaos.

Kaplan, Robert. Balkan Ghosts: A Journey through History. St. Martin's, $22.95 (0-312-08701-2); Random, paper, $12 (0-679-74981-0).

Travel essays provide the historical context for the long-standing blood feuds of the Balkan Peninsula.

Kaysen, Susanna. Girl, Interrupted. Random/Turtle Bay, $17 (0-679-42366-4); paper, $10 (0-679-74604-8).

Kaysen looks back with a sharp eye at the two teenage years she spent in a psychiatric hospital.

Kelly, Michael. Martyrs' Day: Chronicle of a Small War. Random, $23 (0-679-41122-4); paper, $12 (0-679-75014-2).

A journalist's eyewitness account of the Persian Gulf War makes clear the horrific cost of hatred.

Kennedy, Paul. Preparing for the Twenty-first Century. Random, $25 (0-394-58443-0); paper, $14 (0-679-74705-2).

Major trends in and implications of socioeconomic developments provide guidance to understanding technological challenges and global changes.

Mills, Kay. This Little Light of Mine: The Life of Fannie Lou Hamer. Dutton, $24 (0-525-93501-0); paper, $12.95 (0-452-27052-9).

Less-known details of the civil rights movement emerge in this lively biography of Fannie Lou Hamer.

Prejean, Helen. Dead Man Walking: An Eyewitness Account of the Death Penalty in the United States. Random, $21 (0-679-40358-2); paper, $12 (0-679-75131-9).

A Catholic nun, spiritual adviser to men on death row, presents strong testimony against capital punishment for its cruelty and injustice to all victims.

Remnick, David. Lenin's Tomb: The Last Days of the Soviet Empire. Random, $25 (0-679-42376-1); paper, $14 (0-679-75125-4).

A sweeping narrative filled with vivid scenes and strong individuals chronicles the ending of the Soviet regime and the beginning of an uncertain future.

Schaller, George B. The Last Panda. Univ. of Chicago, $24.95 (0-226-73628-8); paper, $13.95 (0-226-73269-6).

This account of an expedition to observe the giant panda describes the joys, frustrations, and griefs of studying an endangered species in its native habitat.

Vidal, Gore. United States: Essays, 1952–1992. Random, $37.50 (0-679-41489-4); paper, $22 (0-679-75572-1).
Intelligent, witty, and astute essays on literature, art, and politics span 40 years of U.S. history.

Notable Books, 1993

Auster, Paul. Leviathan. Viking, $21 (0-670-84676-7); paper, $11 (0-14-017813-9).
In this suspenseful and complex novel, a writer ponders the death of a friend and fellow writer and pieces together the events that defined his life.

Brown, Rosellen. Before and After. Farrar, $21 (0-374-10999-0); Bantam, paper, $5.99 (0-440-21654-0).
A family's love and loyalty are sorely tested when the teenage son is accused of murdering his girlfriend.

Budbill, David. Judevine: The Complete Poems, 1970–1990. Chelsea Green, $24.95 (0-930031-47-4); paper, $14.95 (0-930031-48-2).
Poems of dignity and passion spin a tale of rural folk in a poor Vermont town.

Butler, Robert Olen. A Good Scent from a Strange Mountain. Holt, $19.95 ((0-8050-1986-3); Penguin, paper, $10 (0-14-017664-0).
These short stories evoke past trauma and express the contemporary vulnerability and joy of Vietnamese living in Louisiana.

Cook, Blanche Wiesen. Eleanor Roosevelt: A Life, v.1, 1884–1933. Viking, $30 (0-670-80486-X); Penguin, paper, $14 (0-14-009460-1).
A distinguished and lively biography that examines the evolution of Eleanor Roosevelt from an insecure wife into a committed activist.

Duncan, David James. The Brothers K. Doubleday, $22.50 (0-385-24003-1); Bantam, paper, $10.95 (0-553-37849-X).
This novel set in the 1960s depicts a family torn by its two religions—baseball and Christianity.

Gallagher, Tess. Moon Crossing Bridge. Graywolf, $17 (1-55597-156-3); paper, $12 (1-55597-175-X).
Poet Gallagher confronts the immediacy and intimacy of grief at the death of her husband, Raymond Carver.

Galvin, James. The Meadow. Holt, $19.95 (0-8050-1684-8); paper, $12 (0-8050-2703-3).
A moving tribute to the courage and endurance of four ranchers in a deserted, hauntingly beautiful meadow on the Colorado-Wyoming border.

Greider, William B. Who Will Tell the People: The Betrayal of American Democracy. Simon & Schuster, $25 (0-671-68891-X); paper, $13 (0-671-86740-7).
   An inquiry into the ways members of the power elite undermine the American democratic process.

Hoffman, Alice. Turtle Moon. Putnam, $21.95 (0-399-13720-3); Berkley, paper, $6.50 (0-425-13699-X).
   Danger and love await Lucy Rosen and her son, Keith, as they begin a new life in the magical world of Verity, Florida.

Kenan, Randall. Let the Dead Bury Their Dead and Other Stories. HBJ, $19.95 (0-15-149886-5); paper, $10.95 (0-15-650515-0).
   Inventive stories of the inhabitants of a place called Tims Creek, North Carolina, explore the emotional, sexual, and racial limits of human character.

Maclean, Norman. Young Men & Fire. Univ. of Chicago, $19.95 (0-226-50061-6); paper, $10.95 (0-226-50062-4).
   A beautifully written record of the struggle to subdue the tragic 1949 Mann Gulch forest fire in Montana.

Maxwell, William. Billie Dyer and Other Stories. Knopf, $17.50 (0-679-40832-0); Plume, paper, $8 (0-452-26950-4).
   Charming stories of Lincoln, Illinois, in the early 1900s blend fiction and memoir.

McCarthy, Cormac. All the Pretty Horses. Knopf, $21 (0-394-57474-5); paper, $12 (0-679-74439-8).
   This evocative and exuberant novel describes John Grady Cole's coming-of-age in Mexico during the 1940s.

McCullough, David. Truman. Simon & Schuster, $30 (0-671-45654-7); paper, $15 (0-671-86920-5).
   An engaging and carefully researched study of the life and times of former president Harry Truman by the eminent historian.

Minatoya, Lydia Yuri. Talking to High Monks in the Snow: An Asian American Odyssey. HarperCollins, $20 (0-06-016809-9); paper, $11 (0-06-092372-5).
   A young Japanese American's search for her family's past as well as her ethnic and personal identity takes her from New York to Asia.

Monette, Paul. Becoming a Man: Half a Life Story. HBJ, $19.95 (0-15-111519-2); Harper San Francisco, paper, $12 (0-06-250724-9)].
   In this strikingly honest memoir, the author reveals the pain of growing up gay and not acknowledging it even to himself.

Moore, Alison. Small Spaces between Emergencies. Mercury House, $18.95 (1-56279-022-6).
   Compelling short stories of everyday life capture moments of rediscovery that provide hope in the midst of despair.

Morrison, Toni. Jazz. Knopf, $21 (0-679-41167-4); Dutton, paper, $10.95 (0-452-26965-2).
Harlem in the 1920s, with its syncopation and excitement, provides the backdrop to this portrait of a marriage gone sour and the perverse behaviors love can engender.

Naylor, Gloria. Bailey's Cafe. HBJ, $19.95 (0-15-110450-6); Random, paper, $11 (0-679-74821-0).
Wry portraits of the habitués of a Harlem eatery combine the mythic and the mundane.

Ondaatje, Michael. The English Patient. Knopf, $22 (0-679-41678-1); paper, $10.50 (0-394-28013-X).
Four wounded spirits come together in a deserted Italian villa during the final days of World War II. Three will begin a kind of healing.

Patchett, Ann. The Patron Saint of Liars. Houghton, $21 (0-395-61306-X); Ivy, paper, $5.99 (0-8041-1151-0).
Sustained by lies, wonderfully realized characters come to terms with the mysteries of love and loss.

Postman, Neil. Technopoly. Knopf, $22 (0-394-58272-1); Random, paper, $11 (0-679-74540-8).
Illuminating examination of technology's pervasive corruption of contemporary society.

Selzer, Richard. Down from Troy: A Doctor Comes of Age. Morrow, $20 (0-688-09715-4); Little, Brown, paper, $10.95 (0-316-78065-0).
With warm gratitude to his physician father and artist mother, this surgeon-turned-writer re-creates his youth during the Depression in Troy, New York.

Shelton, Richard. Going Back to Bisbee. Univ. of Arizona, $35 (0-8165-1302-3); paper, $15.95 (0-8165-1289-2).
A humorous, meandering road trip through the southern Arizona desert, rich with description and local history.

Smiley, Jane. A Thousand Acres. Knopf, $25 (0-394-57773-6); Fawcett, paper, $12 (0-449-90748-1).
In this contemporary tragedy, the lives of members of an Iowa farm family unravel as a dark secret is revealed.

Wills, Garry. Lincoln at Gettysburg: The Words That Remade America. Simon & Schuster, $23 (0-671-76956-1); paper, $12 (0-671-86742-3).
This insightful analysis breathes new vigor and clarity into the rhetoric, context, and ultimate meaning of the Gettysburg Address.

Notable Books, 1992

Alvarez, Julia. How the Garcia Girls Lost Their Accents. Algonquin, $16.95 (0-945575-57-2); Plume, paper, $10 (0-452-26806-0).
   Fifteen interconnected stories portray with warmth and humor the assimilation of a Dominican doctor's family into urban American culture.

Banks, Russell. The Sweet Hereafter. HarperCollins, $20 (0-06-016703-3); paper, $11 (0-06-092324-5).
   Communal bereavement unites an Adirondack village after a tragic school-bus accident.

Before Freedom Came: African-American Life in the Antebellum South. Ed. by Edward D. C. Campbell and Kym S. Rice. Univ. Press of Virginia/Museum of the Confederacy, paper, $19.95 (0-8139-1322-2).
   A richly researched and illustrated compendium brings to attention previously underreported aspects of slavery in the pre–Civil War South.

Bly, Carol. The Tomcat's Wife and Other Stories. HarperCollins, $19.95 (0-06-016504-9); paper, $9 (0-06-092264-8).
   Portrayals of Minnesota women who are bound by the narrowness of their lives and the expectations of their communities.

Brown, Larry. Joe. Algonquin, $19.95 (0-945575-61-0); Warner, paper, $9.99 (0-446-39438-6).
   An abandoned youth and a floundering middle-aged man rescue each other from desperate situations in rural Mississippi.

Carles, Emilie and **Destanque, Robert.** A Life of Her Own: A Countrywoman in Twentieth-Century France. Tr. by Avriel H. Goldberger. Rutgers, $19.95 (0-8135-1641-2); Penguin, paper, $12 (0-14-016965-2).
   A humane and wise woman tells the poignant stories of her life in a harsh, isolated peasant community in provincial France.

Cary, Lorene. Black Ice. Knopf, $24 (0-394-57465-6); McKay, paper, $10 (0-87923-948-4).
   Cary recounts with piercing honesty her experiences as a young black woman attending an elite New Hampshire boarding school in the early 1970s.

Dubus, Andre. Broken Vessels. Godine, $19.95 (0-87923-885-2); paper, $11.95 (0-87923-948-4).
   An acclaimed story writer turns his attention to essays, some of which detail his physical and spiritual struggle to survive a disabling accident.

Faludi, Susan. Backlash: The Undeclared War against American Women. Crown, $24 (0-517-57698-8); Doubleday, paper, $12.95 (0-385-42507-4).
   An eye-opening, well-researched analysis of the status of women in contemporary American society documents the antifeminist backlash of our time.

Greene, Melissa Fay. Praying for Sheetrock. Addison-Wesley, $21.95 (0-201-55048-2); Fawcett, paper, $10 (0-449-90753-8).

The eloquent and sometimes humorous story of official corruption in McIntosh County, Georgia, and the belated political awakening of its black population.

Griffith, Patricia Browning. The World around Midnight. Putnam. [Pocket, paper, $8 (0-671-75950-7)].

The beleaguered editor of a newspaper in the small town of Midnight, Texas, triumphs over adversity with irrepressible humor in Griffith's delightful novel.

Klinkenborg, Verlyn. The Last Fine Time. Knopf, $19.95 (0-394-57195-9); paper, $10 (0-679-73718-9).

This story of a family-owned neighborhood bar in Buffalo, New York, beautifully combines poignant memoir and subtle social history.

Kotlowitz, Alex. There Are No Children Here. Doubleday, $21.95 (0-385-26526-3); paper, $12.95 (0-385-26556-5).

This significant and heartbreaking account focuses on the struggle of two young boys to survive life in a Chicago housing project.

Kozol, Jonathan. Savage Inequalities: Children in America's Schools. Crown, $20 (0-517-58221-X); HarperCollins, paper, $13 (0-06-097499-0).

Vivid descriptions of the nation's poorest and wealthiest public schools illustrate how the quality of a child's education is determined by race and social class.

Lemann, Nicholas. The Promised Land: The Great Black Migration and How It Changed America. Knopf, $24.95 (0-394-56004-3); paper, $14 (0-394-26967-5).

Absorbing narrative of the African American migration from the newly mechanized farms in the Mississippi Delta to inner-city Chicago and of the failure of the government's war on poverty.

Levine, Philip. What Work Is. Knopf, $19 (0-679-40166-0); McKay, paper, $12 (0-679-74058-9).

The basics of life and labor, portrayed in terse, realistic, unembellished poems.

Lewis, R. W. B. The Jameses: A Family Narrative. Farrar, $35 (0-374-17861-5); Doubleday, paper, $15 (0-385-42495-7).

Collective biography of a distinguished American family that included psychologist William, novelist Henry, and diarist Alice, set within the framework of nineteenth-century intellectual life.

Lucas, Russell. Evenings at Mongini's and Other Stories. Summit [o.p.].

By turns erotic, humorous, chilling, and exciting, 10 short stories provide a view of Bombay, India, during the decline of the British raj.

Malone, Michael. Foolscap. Little, Brown, $19.95 (0-316-54527-9); Pocket, paper, $10 (0-671-78857-4).

A clever, exhilarating comic novel about the adventures and quests of Theo Ryan, a complacent academic whose life is transformed by his friendship with a bizarre, drunken playwright.

Morris, Mary McGarry. A Dangerous Woman. Viking, $19.95 (0-670-83699-0); Penguin, paper, $10 (0-14-016764-1).

An emotionally disturbed young woman struggles to gain control of her life in spite of traumatic experiences and rejection by friends, classmates, and guardians.

Nordan, Lewis. Music of the Swamp. Algonquin, $16.95 (0-945575-76-9); paper, $7.95 (1-56512-016-7).

In this comic and haunting novel set in a poor Mississippi Delta community, a young boy's stories illuminate both magic and horror in his family's life.

Parks, Tim. Goodness. Grove, $18.95 (0-8021-1390-7); paper, $9.95 (0-8021-3304-5).

In this tragic yet darkly humorous novel, the birth of a severely handicapped daughter forces George Crawley to rise above the pieties of his family to make a real moral choice.

Porter, Connie. All-Bright Court. Houghton, $19.95 (0-395-53271-X).

Steel mills near Buffalo draw black families north, and a vibrant community is established in the rapidly deteriorating housing of All-Bright Court.

Radestky, Peter. The Invisible Invaders: The Story of the Emerging Age of Viruses. Little, Brown, $22.95 (0-316-73216-8); paper, $14.95 (0-316-73217-6).

An account of scientific detection in the fight against disease reveals the genetic basis of life and emphasizes the importance of research.

Roth, Philip. Patrimony: A True Story. Simon & Schuster, $19.95 (0-671-70375-7); Random, paper, $12 (0-679-75293-5).

The moving, sometimes comic memoir of novelist Roth's reconciliation with his dying, irascible father.

Tan, Amy. The Kitchen God's Wife. Putnam, $29.95 (0-399-13578-2); Random, paper, $12 (0-679-74808-3).

Tan's second novel explores the dynamics of a Chinese American family through the long-suppressed secrets a mother and daughter ultimately reveal to each other.

Notable Books, 1991

Fiction

Bell, Christine. The Pérez Family. Norton, $19.95 (0-393-02798-8); HarperCollins, paper, $11 (0-06-097401-X).

A witty, almost surreal, portrait of Cuban exiles in Miami.

Boyle, T. Coraghessan. East Is West. Viking, $19.95 (0-670-83220-0); Penguin, paper, $10 (0-14-013167-1).

A Japanese seaman jumps ship off the Georgia coast in this tragicomic novel of cultural dislocation.

Byatt, A. S. Possession: A Romance. Random, $22.95 (0-394-58623-9); paper, $12 (0-679-73590-9).
Two contemporary scholars discover evidence of a clandestine affair between major Victorian poets and unravel a mystery that alters all previous interpretations of their writings.

Coetzee, J. M. Age of Iron. Random, $18.95 (0-394-58859-2).
A haunting lament by a white South African woman, forced at the end of her life to feel the full rage and horror of apartheid.

Hoffman, Alice. Seventh Heaven. Putnam, $19.95 (0-399-13535-9); Fawcett, paper, $5.99 (0-449-22018-4).
A 1950s suburban neighborhood is transformed with the arrival of a divorced mother in this deft blend of magic realism and subtle character portrayal.

Kingsolver, Barbara. Animal Dreams. HarperCollins, $19.95 (0-06-016350-X); paper, $13 (0-06-092114-5).
The multiethnic background of the Southwest provides the setting for a young woman's struggle to understand and accept herself and her family.

Lively, Penelope. Passing On. Grove, $16.95 (0-8021-1155-6); HarperCollins, paper, $11 (0-06-097370-6).
After years of repression by a domineering mother, an unmarried English woman and her bachelor brother try independence.

Mahfouz, Naguib. Palace Walk. Doubleday, $22.95 (0-385-26465-8); paper, $11 (0-385-26466-6).
The richly detailed account of daily life in a traditional Muslim family only dimly aware of the outside world in British-occupied Cairo in 1917.

Miller, Sue. Family Pictures. HarperCollins, $19.95 (0-06-016397-6); paper, $5.99 (0-06-109925-2).
A perceptive portrayal of the impact of an autistic child on a particular family, revealing universal truths about complex human relationships.

Munro, Alice. Friend of My Youth. Knopf, $18.95 (0-394-58442-2); paper, $11 (0-679-72957-7).
Flawless stories that juxtapose the intricacies of personal relationships and the curious circumstances of ordinary lives against bleak landscapes.

O'Brien, Tim. The Things They Carried. Houghton, $19.95 (0-395-51598-X); Penguin, paper, $10.95 (0-14-014773-X).
Stories, like a series of battle flares, link the psychological and physical burdens Americans carried in Vietnam to the emotional baggage they brought home.

Popham, Melinda Worth. Skywater. Graywolf, $17.95 (1-55597-127-X); Ballantine, paper, $4.95 (0-345-37150-X).
This first novel about a coyote's quest for water and peace evokes the beauty and spirituality of the endangered Sonoran desert.

Smith, Lee. Me and My Baby View the Eclipse. Putnam, $18.95 (0-399-13507-3); Ballantine, paper, $4.99 (0-345-36873-8).
Intimate stories of the New South embody the determined resolve of women, young and old, to survive.

Stegner, Wallace. Collected Stories of Wallace Stegner. Random, $21.95 (0-394-58409-0); Penguin, paper, $12.95 (0-14-014774-8).
Six decades of superb stories by one of America's most distinguished writers.

Tilghman, Christopher. In a Father's Place. Farrar, $18.95 (0-374-17558-6).
Seven seamless stories, diverse in voice and setting, form a remarkable first collection.

Poetry

Wright, James. Above the River: The Complete Poems. Farrar, $25 (0-374-12749-2); paper, $15 (0-374-52282-0).
A legacy of lyrical American language and imagery celebrates life with youthful humor, mature elegiac meditations, and evocative prose poems.

Nonfiction

Ackerman, Diane. The Natural History of the Senses. Random, $22 (0-394-57335-8); paper, $12 (0-394-26953-5).
An award-winning poet skillfully combines science, literature, history, and cultural commentary in a sensuous celebration of our ability to smell, taste, hear, touch, and see.

Bishop, Jerry E. and **Waldholz, Michael.** Genome: The Story of the Most Astonishing Scientific Adventure of Our Time—the Attempt to Map All the Genes in the Human Body. Simon & Schuster [o.p.].
An engaging account of genetic research and the ethical dilemmas it poses.

Chestnut, J. L. and **Cass, Julia.** Black in Selma: The Uncommon Life of J. L. Chestnut, Jr. Farrar, $22.95 (0-374-11404-8); Doubleday, paper, $13 (0-385-41938-4).
The first black attorney in the historic southern city is candid about the shortcomings of his segregated community and disarmingly humble about his own achievements.

Freedman, Samuel G. Small Victories: The Real World of a Teacher, Her Students & Their High School. HarperCollins, $22.95 (0-06-016254-6); paper, $13 (0-06-092087-4).
A detailed portrait of Jessica Siegel, a dedicated teacher at Seward Park High School in Manhattan, who really makes a difference in the lives of her students.

Goodall, Jane. Through a Window: My Thirty Years with the Chimpanzees of Gombe. Houghton, $22.95 (0-395-50081-8); paper, $9.95 (0-395-59925-3).

Continues the engrossing and intimate behavioral account of the principal residents of the Tanzanian Reserve by their compassionate protector, historian, and friend.

Lord, Bette Bao. Legacies: A Chinese Mosaic. Knopf, $19.95 (0-394-58325-6); Fawcett, paper, $10 (0-449-90620-5).
Narratives of the Chinese experience of the last half century—up to Tiananmen Square—reported by a woman who returned to her native land as the wife of the U.S. ambassador.

Malan, Rian. My Traitor's Heart: A South African Exile Returns to Face His Country, His Tribe, and His Conscience. Atlantic Monthly; dist. by Little, Brown, $19.95 (0-87113-229-X); Random, paper, $12 (0-679-73215-2).
A journalist, whose Boer ancestors were founders of apartheid, expresses hope for eventual racial reconciliation.

Szarkowski, John. Photography until Now. Museum of Modern Art; dist. by Little, Brown/Bulfinch, $60 (0-87070-573-3); paper, $35 (0-87070-574-1).
This history of the pioneers and processes in the development of photography questions the nature of art: how we see, document, and imagine.

Wills, Garry. Under God: Religion and American Politics. Simon & Schuster, $22.95 (0-671-65705-4); paper, $12 (0-671-74746-0).
Exploring the depth and variety of religious beliefs among Americans, Wills shows how this crucial element is largely overlooked by political analysts in the media.

Notable Books, 1990

Fiction

Atwood, Margaret. Cat's Eye. Doubleday, $18.95 (0-385-26007-5); Bantam, paper, $6.50 (0-553-28247-6).
An artist's retrospective of childhood love and cruelty is exhibited and unified in the landscape of her past and present.

Bausch, Richard. Mr. Field's Daughter. Linden, $18.95 (0-671-64051-8); Macmillan, paper, $8.95 (0-02-028145-5).
A single father, desperate when his only daughter elopes with a drug addict, learns that possessiveness carried too far can have tragic consequences.

Boyle, T. Coraghessan. If the River Was Whiskey. Viking, $17.95 (0-670-82690-1); Penguin, paper, $8.95 (0-14-011950-7).
These lively, insightful stories portray thoroughly contemporary characters with pathos, irony, and humor.

Burgess, Anthony. Any Old Iron. Random, $19.95 (0-394-57484-2); paper, $5.95 (0-671-72708-7).

A colorful multigenerational tapestry of rich myth and history, with flashes of comedy, extends the Excalibur legend into the twentieth century.

Busch, Frederick. Absent Friends. Knopf, $18.95 (0-394-57426-5); New Directions, paper, $11.95 (0-8112-1175-4)].
Bleak vistas and a sense of estrangement are common to these 14 stories, so finely wrought that they resonate in memory.

Casey, John. Spartina. Knopf, $18.95 (0-394-50098-9); Avon, paper, $11 (0-380-71104-4).
A rare combination of lyrical prose and stark realism reveals the complex relationships governing a New England fisherman's life.

Desai, Anita. Baumgartner's Bombay. Knopf, $18.95 (0-394-57229-7); Viking, paper, $9 (0-14-013176-0).
Fleeing fast from Nazi Germany and again from Calcutta during partition, Baumgartner establishes a contented, though eccentric, existence in Bombay— until fate intervenes again.

Gordon, Mary. The Other Side. Viking, $19.95 (0-670-82566-2); paper, $10.95 (0-14-014408-0).
As the stories of the gathering generations rise in her house, the dying matriarch, stone strong and inarticulate, waits for her husband's promise to be kept.

Hamill, Pete. Loving Women: A Novel of the Fifties. Random, $19.95 (0-394-57528-8); Pinnacle, paper, $5.50 (1-55817-385-4).
A fast-paced novel of a young man's coming-of-age in the 1950s. Love and loss, racism and brotherhood are among its central themes.

Irving, John. A Prayer for Owen Meany. Morrow, $23 (0-688-07708-0); Ballantine, paper, $6.99 (0-345-36179-2).
Diminutive Owen Meany, believing himself to be God's instrument, unlocks life's mysteries for his closest friend in this imaginative mix of humor and tragedy.

Ishiguro, Kazuo. The Remains of the Day. Knopf, $18.95 (0-394-57343-9); paper, $11 (0-394-25134-2).
A journey of brilliant insight into British class and culture in which Stevens, an English butler, faces the truth about himself and comes to terms with his own fallacies.

Kingsolver, Barbara. Homeland. Harper, $16.95 (0-06-016112-4); paper, $13 (0-06-091701-6).
Family ties and the optimism that enables people to endure life's struggles are explored in this memorable collection of stories.

Ozick, Cynthia. The Shawl. Knopf, $12.95 (0-394-57976-3); paper, $7.95 (0-679-72926-7).
Two stories—artfully and powerfully related—tell the horror of an infant's murder in a Nazi concentration camp and its haunting effects years later in Miami Beach.

Schaeffer, Susan Fromberg. Buffalo Afternoon. Knopf, $19.95 (0-394-57178-9); Ivy, paper, $5.95 (0-8041-0580-4).

The psychic aftermath of the Vietnam War, graphically depicted in a narrative blend of realism and surrealism.

Tan, Amy. The Joy Luck Club. Putnam, $18.95 (0-399-13420-4); Random, paper, $10 (0-679-72768-X).

Common threads of chance and fate are woven intricately through stories of four Chinese mothers and their American daughters, revealing their struggle for assimilation into American culture.

Wilson, Robley. Terrible Kisses. Simon & Schuster [o.p.].

These charming stories remind us that love can be expressed in many unexpected ways. Sometimes it is unwelcome, often memorable, and occasionally, even indelible.

Yehoshua, A. B. Five Seasons. Tr. by Hillel Halkin. Doubleday [o.p.].

A complex story, set in Israel and Germany, concerning a man's struggle to reclaim his ordinary life after the death of his wife.

Poetry

Carver, Raymond. A New Path to the Waterfall. Atlantic Monthly; dist. by Little, Brown, $15.95 (0-87113-280-X); Grove, paper, $10.95 (0-87113-374-1).

A moving collection of poems in which one of America's foremost short-story writers struggles to accept his imminent death.

An Ear to the Ground: An Anthology of Contemporary American Poetry. Ed. by Marie Harris and Kathleen Aguero. Univ. of Georgia, $30 (0-8203-1122-7); paper, $14.95 (0-8203-1123-5).

This anthology brings together the work of poets who represent the diverse backgrounds and voices of a multicultural nation.

Poets for Life: Seventy-six Poets Respond to AIDS. Ed. by Michael Klein. Crown, $18.95 (0-517-57242-7); Persea, paper, $11.95 (0-89255-170-4).

Communicating a surprising range of emotions, these carefully selected poems celebrate the human spirit confronting the reality of AIDS.

Nonfiction

Bentsen, Cheryl. Maasai Days. Summit [o.p.].

An unsentimental portrait of the Maasai by an American woman who lived in Kenya for six years and became aquainted with members of the tribe.

Branch, Taylor. Parting the Waters: America in the King Years, 1954–63. Simon & Schuster, $24.45 (0-671-46097-8); paper, $16 (0-671-68742-5).

An exhaustively researched, eloquently written account that captures the social upheaval and powerful personalities of the early civil rights movement.

Conway, Jill Ker. The Road from Coorain. Knopf, $18.95 (0-394-57456-7); paper, $11 (0-679-72436-2).

Historian Conway's childhood and youth are inextricably bound to the Australian landscape as she faces personal tragedies and cultural barriers that lead her to leave her homeland.

Dorris, Michael. The Broken Cord. Harper, $18.95 (0-06-016071-3); paper, $12 (0-06-091682-6).

The author's adopted son, irreversibly damaged by his birth-mother's drinking, is the focus of this profoundly moving personal investigation of fetal alcohol syndrome.

Duberman, Martin Bauml. Paul Robeson. Knopf. [New Press, $17.95 (1-56584-288-X)].

Long ignored because of his Communist politics and the pervasive racism of American society, Robeson emerges from this detailed and well-rounded biography as a larger-than-life twentieth-century Renaissance man.

Friedman, Thomas L. From Beirut to Jerusalem. Farrar, $19.95 (0-374-15894-0); Doubleday, paper, $12.95 (0-385-41372-6).

An intelligent analysis of the Middle East by a journalist who draws on his personal experiences and historical insights.

Hirsch, Kathleen. Songs from the Alley. Ticknor & Fields, $22.95 (0-89919-488-5); Doubleday, paper, $10.95 (0-385-41277-0).

Compassionate portraits of two young homeless women alternate with Boston social history, demonstrating that homelessness is much more than having no place to live.

Kidder, Tracy. Among Schoolchildren. Houghton, $21.95 (0-395-47591-0); Avon, paper, $11 (0-380-71089-7).

Observing a year in the life of a fifth-grade teacher, Kidder provides a picture of American education in microcosm.

Klüver, Billy and **Martin, Julie.** Ki Ki's Paris: Artists and Lovers, 1900–1930. Abrams, $39.95 (0-8109-1210-4); paper, $19.95 (0-8109-2591-5).

Elegant black-and-white photographs capture the reality of the fabled world of Ki Ki's Montparnasse.

Takaki, Ronald. Strangers from a Different Shore: A History of Asian Americans. Little, Brown, $22.95 (0-316-83109-3); Penguin, paper, $13.95 (0-14-013885-4).

A vivid, popular historical account of the hopes, hardships, and frustrations of Asians immigrating to the U.S. during the past century and a half.

Notable Books of the 1980s

Notable Books, 1989

While the work of the Notable Books Committee continued without interruption, the dating of these lists was changed. Up until this point, the date of the list reflected the publication date of the books on it. In 1990, it was decided to use the year the books were selected, rather than the year the books on the list were published. Therefore, books published in 1989 are on the 1990 Notable Books List.

Notable Books, 1988

Fiction

Allende, Isabel. Eva Luna. Knopf. [Macmillan, $18.95 (0-689-12102-4); Bantam, paper, $6.99 (0-553-57535-X)].
Eva Luna travels the distance from illiteracy to telenovelist and learns along the way that her strength lies in being able to choose the meaning of her own story. [BKL S 1 88]

Carver, Raymond. Where I'm Calling From: New and Selected Stories. Atlantic Monthly, $19.95; Random, paper, $12 (0-679-72231-9).
These 37 stories of everyday life and human experience, told in Carver's pared-down prose, transform the reader's perception. [BKL Mr 15 88]

DeLillo, Don. Libra. Viking. [Penguin, paper, $10.95 (0-14-015604-6)].
In a fascinating reconstruction of what was and what might have been, DeLillo delves into the assassination of President Kennedy and the mind of Lee Harvey Oswald. [BKL Je 1 88]

Dexter, Pete. Paris Trout. Random, $17.95 (0-394-56370-0); Penguin, paper, $11.95 (0-14-012206-0).
Racism and class distinction make a mockery of justice in this compelling tale of a psychopath in 1950s Georgia.

Dubus, Andre. Selected Stories. Godine. [Random, paper, $12 (0-679-72533-4)].
Short-story master Dubus scrutinizes the quotidian drama of ordinary people's lives. A memorable and well-balanced collection. [BKL S 15 88]

Erdrich, Louise. Tracks. Holt, $22.50 (0-8050-0895-0); Harper, paper, $12 (0-06-097245-9).
An eloquent novel dealing with the effect of disintegrating tribal life on a group of North Dakota Indians in the early decades of the twentieth century. [BKL Jl 88]

García Márquez, Gabriel. Love in the Time of Cholera. Knopf, $27.50 (0-394-56161-9); Penguin, paper, $12.95 (0-14-011990-6).
The legendary author speaks to each of us in an all-encompassing story of devotion and love that spans a half century. [BKL F 1 88]

Greenberg, Joanne. Of Such Small Differences. Holt. [o.p.].
The isolation, vulnerability, and daily frustrations of a deaf and blind young poet are insightfully portrayed through his struggle to function within a "normal" society. [BKL Je 15 88]

Lessing, Doris. The Fifth Child. Knopf, $16.95 (0-394-57105-3); paper, $9 (0-679-72182-7).
A tale of violence and chaos made manifest in a brutish animal-child and his profoundly conflicted mother who can neither nourish him nor deny him life. [BKL Ja 15 88]

Mukherjee, Bharati. The Middleman and Other Stories. Grove. [Fawcett, paper, $5.99 (0-449-21718-3)].
Stories about "new" Americans in which immigrants and refugees from the Third World are skillfully juxtaposed against the condos, barbecue pits, and shopping malls of the New World. [BKL S 1 88]

Naylor, Gloria. Mama Day. Ticknor & Fields. [Random, paper, $11 (0-679-72181-9)].
Straddling the real worlds of New York City and an imaginary island off the South Atlantic Coast, Naylor's story creates unforgettable characters caught in a web of love and violence. [BKL D 15 87]

Powers, J. F. Wheat That Springeth Green. Knopf, $18.95 (0-394-49609-4).
A witty and literate book about the life of Father Joe Hackett, a priest who makes a mature but not altogether successful accommodation to his youthful idealism. [BKL Jl 88]

Sexton, Linda Gray. Points of Light. Little, Brown, $16.95 (0-316-78200-9); Avon, paper, $4.50 (0-380-70684-9).
After a tragedy, a mother and artist withdraws from her family and seeks refuge in her work. A lyrical novel of grief and loss redeemed by love and memory. [BKL O 15 87]

Smith, Lee. Fair and Tender Ladies. Putnam. [Ballantine, paper, $10 (0-345-38399-0)].
An epistolary novel that chronicles several decades in the life of Ivy Rowe, a poor, hardworking woman and born storyteller from the mountains of Virginia.

Spark, Muriel. A Far Cry from Kensington. Houghton. [Avon, paper, $7.95 (0-380-70786-1)].
Through the eyes of a warmhearted young war widow, Spark elevates the modest private lives of several London neighbors and colleagues into fine art and hilarious entertainment. [BKL Je 1 88]

Tyler, Anne. Breathing Lessons. Knopf, $25 (0-394-57234-3); Berkley, paper, $6.99 (0-425-11774-X).

A funny, perceptive exploration of family relationships, this novel depicts one day in the lives of middle-class, middle-aged Maggie and Ira Moran. [BKL Jl 88]

Nonfiction

Berton, Pierre. The Arctic Grail: The Quest for the North West Passage and the North Pole, 1818–1909. Viking. [o.p.].

An exciting, engaging, and controversial account of Arctic exploration that vividly details the hardships, hopes, courage, and conflicts of visionary explorers. [BKL O 15 88]

Cagin, Seth and **Dray, Philip.** We Are Not Afraid: The Story of Goodman, Schwerner, and Chaney: The Civil Rights Campaign for Mississippi. Macmillan. [o.p.].

A detailed re-creation of events culminating in the violent deaths of three young men and of the passions that inflamed both sides of the civil rights conflict.

Ellmann, Richard. Oscar Wilde. Knopf, $24.95 (0-394-55484-1); Random, paper, $16 (0-394-75984-2).

Exemplary literary biography by scholar and critic Ellmann, who valued the outrageous Wilde's art as well as his life and examined them as inseparably bound. [BKL Ja 1 88]

Gay, Peter. Freud: A Life for Our Times. Norton, $30 (0-393-02517-9); Doubleday, paper, $14.95 (0-385-26256-6).

An accurate, thoroughly documented biography of the father of psychoanalysis set against the background of his time and the development of his thought. [BKL Ap 1 88]

Goodwin, Richard N. Remembering America: A Voice from the Sixties. Little, Brown, $19.95 (0-316-32024-2); Harper, paper, $13 (0-06-097241-6).

A speechwriter and confidant of President Kennedy re-creates the high hopes and deep disappointments of the rollercoaster 1960s. [BKL S 1 88]

Hansen, Eric. Stranger in the Forest: On Foot across Borneo. Houghton. [Viking, $11.95 (0-14-009586-1); paper, $8.95 (0-14-011726-1)].

An engaging journey into joyously rich hills and forest communities changes the adventurer through the act of leaving familiarity behind. [BKL Ja 15 88]

Lester, Julius. Lovesong: Becoming a Jew. Holt. [Arcade, paper, $12.95 (1-55970-316-4)].

Intrigued by his great-grandfather's Jewish ancestry, novelist and black activist Lester undertakes a surprising and courageous spiritual journey. [BKL D 1 87]

McPherson, James M. Battle Cry of Freedom: The Civil War Era. Oxford, $39.95 (0-19-503863-0); Ballantine, paper, $17.50 (0-345-35942-9).

A masterful and matchless history of the dissolution of the Union and the war itself sheds new light on the meaning of slavery and freedom. [BKL Ja 15 88]

23

Maddox, Brenda. Nora: The Real Life of Molly Bloom. Houghton. [Fawcett, paper, $12.95 (0-449-90410-5)].
A lively, revealing portrait of the earthy woman who shared James Joyce's life and served as inspiration for much of his best work. [BKL Je 1 88]

Pagels, Elaine. Adam, Eve, and the Serpent. Random, $17.95 (0-394-52140-4); paper, $9 (0-679-72232-7).
A provocative study of the Garden of Eden story as it was originally interpreted and then modified by the early Church, transforming in the process the nature of humankind and moral freedom. [BKL Je 1 88]

Sharansky, Natan. Fear No Evil. Random, $19.95 (0-394-55878-2); paper, $10.95 (0-679-72542-3).
A leading Soviet dissident and Jewish activist recounts with warmth, intelligence, and humor his nine harrowing years in KGB custody. [BKL My 15 88]

Notable Books, 1987

Fiction

Barfoot, Joan. Duet for Three. Beaufort. [o.p.].
The subtle bond that links mothers and daughters is explored in this powerful story of conflicting relationships. [BKL D 1 86]

Dorris, Michael. A Yellow Raft in Blue Water. Holt, $16.95 (0-8050-0045-3); Warner, paper, $11.99 (0-446-38787-8).
Three generations of Native American women relate the events of their lives, demonstrating the impact of blood, secrets, and the will to persevere. [BKL Mr 1 87]

Fink, Ida. A Scrap of Time and Other Stories. Pantheon. [Northwestern Univ., paper, $12.95 (0-8101-1259-0)].
A Holocaust survivor writes a devastating collection of stories about Polish Jews who witnessed the horror of annihilation. [BKL Je 1 87]

Gordon, Mary. Temporary Shelter. Random. [o.p.].
Rich stories that reverberate with the flaws of family relationships held in a vise of ethnic and religious heritage. [BKL Ja 15 87]

Hall, Donald. The Ideal Bakery. North Point. [o.p.].
Death, grief, love, and nostalgia are among the prevalent themes of this diverse collection of brilliantly crafted stories. [BKL My 15 87]

Hoffman, Alice. Illumination Night. Putnam. [Fawcett, paper, $5.95 (0-449-21594-6)].
Set on Martha's Vineyard, this enchanting story explores aging, alienation, agoraphobia, maternal love, fidelity, and rejection.

Lopate, Philip. The Rug Merchant. Viking. [o.p.].

A modern parable of a small man of integrity and innocence who refuses to be corrupted by the indifference and cynicism of city life. [BKL Ja 15 87]

McMahon, Thomas. Loving Little Egypt. Viking. [o.p.].
A nearly blind physics prodigy and his disabled friends breach the secrets of the telephone system and comically challenge the powers of Thomas Edison and William Randolph Hearst.

Menaker, Daniel. The Old Left. Knopf, $15.95 (0-394-54678-4).
These stories, rich in humor and charm, relate the loving but often frustrating relationship between David Leonard and his irascible 90-year-old uncle Sol. [BKL Ap 15 87]

Morrison, Toni. Beloved. Knopf, $27.50 (0-394-53597-9); NAL, paper, $10.95 (0-452-26446-4).
Art illuminates history in this powerful story of the black experience and the devastating legacy of slavery after the Civil War. [BKL Jl 87]

Simpson, Mona. Anywhere but Here. Knopf, $18.95 (0-394-55283-0); paper, $12 (0-679-73738-3).
The complex and troubled relationship between a mother and daughter is probed as they move not only from Wisconsin to Beverly Hills but also toward an acceptance of one another. [BKL N 1 86]

Stegner, Wallace. Crossing to Safety. Random. [Penguin, paper, $8.95 (0-14-011249-9)].
A lyrical exploration of an enduring friendship between two couples through good times and bad. [BKL S 1 87]

Thornton, Lawrence. Imagining Argentina. Doubleday. [Bantam, paper, $12.95 (0-553-34579-6)].
During the recent military regime in Argentina, a Buenos Aires playwright discovers he can "see" the fates of the disappeared ones. A chilling portrayal of terror.

Weesner, Theodore. The True Detective. Summit. [Avon, paper, $4.50 (0-380-70499-4)].
A harrowing psychological study of the effects of kidnapping and child molestation on the victim, the abductor, their families, and the investigating detective.

Weldon, Fay. The Shrapnel Academy. Viking. [Penguin, paper, $8.95 (0-14-0097465)].
A curious assortment of visitors and Third World servants assemble for a night of comic mayhem at a military institution named after the inventor of the exploding cannonball. [BKL F 15 87]

Poetry

Lynch, Thomas. Skating with Heather Grace. Knopf. [o.p.].
These elegant, moving poems dwell on death to celebrate life. A remarkable first collection of verse heralding the arrival of an important poetic voice.

Olds, Sharon. The Gold Cell. Knopf, $16.95 (0-394-55699-2); paper, $13 (0-394-74770-4).

Parents, children, courtship, and married love are the themes of these poignant poems that touch the reader on both emotional and intellectual levels.

Nonfiction

Burgess, Anthony. Little Wilson and Big God. Weidenfeld & Nicolson [o.p.].

As playful as any of his novels, the first volume of Burgess' autobiography is a witty and wise evocation of his colorful upbringing, strained marriage, and growing passion for language. [BKL D 15 86]

Donald, David Herbert. Look Homeward: A Life of Thomas Wolfe. Little, Brown. [o.p.].

Sympathetic, well balanced, and meticulously researched, this highly readable biography assumes its place as the definitive life of one of America's most problematic novelists. [BKL O 15 86]

Fjermedal, Grant. The Tomorrow Makers: A Brave New World of Living-Brain Machines. Macmillan. [Microsoft, paper, $8.95 (1-55615-113-6)].

Through in-depth interviews, robotics researchers discuss the fascinating implications of "downloading" the human mind and other advances in artificial intelligence. [BKL Ja 1 87]

Goodwin, Doris Kearns. The Fitzgeralds and the Kennedys. Simon & Schuster. [St. Martin's, paper, $19.95 (0-312-06354-7)].

A sharply focused portrayal, based on exacting research, provides a compassionate family history of one of America's most fascinating political dynasties.

Gornick, Vivian. Fierce Attachments: A Memoir. Farrar. [Simon & Schuster, paper, $8.95 (0-671-65757-7)].

A prominent journalist reveals with candor and wit how her struggle to escape a neurotic childhood has given her an honest, though perverse, new bond with her mother. [BKL Ag 87]

Hayman, Ronald. Sartre: A Life. Simon & Schuster. [Carroll & Graf, paper, $15.95 (0-88184-875-1)].

This biography yields new insights into the private and political lives of Jean-Paul Sartre, chief spokesman for existentialism and a dominant voice in twentieth-century intellectual history. [BKL Je 1 87]

Koonz, Claudia. Mothers in the Fatherland: Women, the Family, and Nazi Politics. St. Martin's. [St. Martin's, paper, $17.95 (0-312-02256-5)].

A ground-breaking exploration of the role of women in the Nazi movement and its ideology. [BKL Ap 15 87]

Miller, Arthur. Timebends. Grove. [Penguin, paper, $16.95 (0-14-086306-0)].

This compelling autobiography covers Miller's Brooklyn childhood, his successes and failures in the theater, his political problems, and his highly publicized marriage to Marilyn Monroe. [BKL S 1 87]

Rhodes, Richard. The Making of the Atomic Bomb. Simon & Schuster. [Simon & Schuster, paper, $16 (0-684-81378-5)].

The history of our most powerful weapon, from its conception in scientific minds to the devastation of Hiroshima and Nagasaki, is recounted with drama, intensity, and wisdom. [BKL Ja 15 87]

Shilts, Randy. And the Band Played On: Politics, People, and the AIDS Epidemic. St. Martin's. [Penguin, paper, $15 (0-14-023221-4)].

A *San Francisco Chronicle* reporter traces the course of this deadly disease, weaving moving human portraits into compelling investigative journalism. [BKL S 15 87]

Notable Books, 1986

Atwood, Margaret. The Handmaid's Tale. Houghton. [Bantam, paper, $8.99 (0-7704-2263-2)].

In the futuristic world of Gilead, a feisty heroine chronicles her rebellion against a repressive, antiwoman society. [BKL D 1 85]

Baker, Will. Mountain Blood. Univ. of Georgia. [o.p.].

Humorous and insightful recollections, yarns, and historical meditations about life in the mountainous mining and lumbering regions of the West in the early twentieth century. [BKL F 15 86]

Beschloss, Michael R. MAYDAY: Eisenhower, Khrushchev, and the U-2 Affair. Harper. [o.p.].

A thoroughly documented account of Gary Powers' U-2 flight on May 1, 1960, and its implications for U.S.-Soviet relations. [BKL F 1 86]

Carillo, Charles. Shepherd Avenue. Atlantic Monthly; dist. by Little, Brown. [o.p.].

A warm, nostalgic novel set in the 1960s relates a child's search for identity in his grandparents' Brooklyn neighborhood after his mother's death. [BKL Mr 15 86]

Carter, Angela. Saints and Strangers. Viking. [Penguin, paper, $10.95 (0-14-008973-X)].

Eight fast-paced fictional explorations with historical and mythic overtones never fail to engage the imagination. [BKL Ag 86]

Charyn, Jerome. Metropolis: New York as Myth, Marketplace, and Magical Land. Putnam. [Avon, paper, $8.95 (0-380-70401-3)].

An urbane tribute by a gifted and knowledgeable writer who brings to life the raw qualities of this exciting city and its special people. [BKL Jl 86]

Critchfield, Richard. Those Days: An American Album. Doubleday/Anchor. [o.p.].

This memoir of the author's midwestern family between 1880 and 1940 paints a resonant portrait of ordinary people who lived during great technological and cultural change. [BKL My 15 86]

Denby, Edwin. The Complete Poems. Random. [o.p.].
Restrained and quietly elegant poems by a noted dance critic express his appreciation of the examined life and of the city solitudes that permit it. [BKL Ag 86]

Dubus, Andre. The Last Worthless Evening. Godine, $15.95 (0-87923-642-6); paper, $12.95 (1-56792-067-5).
An extraordinary collection of short fiction dealing with heroism, social hatred, and the loss of innocence. [BKL D 1 86]

Duras, Marguerite. The War: A Memoir. Pantheon. [New Press, paper, $10 (1-56584-221-9)].
An account of Duras' agonizing wait for her prisoner-of-war husband is the major segment of these narratives set in Nazi-occupied France during World War II. [BKL Je 1 86]

Erdrich, Louise. The Beet Queen. Holt, $16.95 (0-8050-0058-5); Bantam, paper, $12.95 (0-553-34723-3).
A bleak North Dakota landscape is the setting for a provocative novel about gutsy, underclass characters confronting poverty and abandonment. [BKL Jl 86]

Goldberg, Vicki. Margaret Bourke-White: A Biography. Harper. [Addison-Wesley, paper, $14.95 (0-201-09819-9)].
A candid portrayal of a photographer's ground-breaking accomplishments and a sensitive assessment of her eventful life. [BKL My 15 86]

Grooms, Red. Red Grooms: A Retrospective, 1956–1984. Abrams/Pennsylvania Academy of Fine Arts. [o.p.].
A colorful and exciting collection of works by a multimedia artist of enormous talent, originality, and humor.

Henley, Patricia. Friday Night at Silver Star: Stories. Graywolf, paper, $8.50 (0-915308-84-3).
Survivors of the 1960s try to maintain a hippie lifestyle today. [BKL My 15 86]

Hersh, Seymour M. "The Target Is Destroyed": What Really Happened to Flight 007 and What America Knew about It. Random. [o.p.].
A painstaking examination of Russia's destruction of Flight 007 on September 1, 1983, with important lessons to be learned by both the U.S. and the Soviet Union. [BKL O 1 86]

Hochschild, Adam. Half the Way Home: A Memoir of Father and Son. Viking. [o.p.].
An honest exploration of the relationship between a stern, perfectionist father and his insecure young son set against the background of enormous wealth. [BKL Je 1 86]

Hugo, Richard. The Real West Marginal Way: A Poet's Autobiography. Norton, $16.95 (0-393-02326-5); paper, $10.95 (0-393-30860-X).
A posthumous collection of 15 years of essays presenting the intellectual and

emotional life and the sources of creativity of a distinguished American poet. [BKL O 1 86]

Ishiguro, Kazuo. An Artist of the Floating World. Putnam. [Random, paper, $10 (0-679-72266-1)].
   The betrayal of the promise of youth is recalled as a dishonored artist struggles with changing values in war-wrecked Japan.

Jhabvala, Ruth Prawer. Out of India. Morrow. [Simon & Schuster, paper, $9 (0-671-64221-9)].
   Stories selected by the author from previous collections present the panorama of Indian life from a Western perspective. [BKL Ap 15 86]

Lopez, Barry. Arctic Dreams: Imagination and Desire in a Northern Landscape. Simon & Schuster, $22.95 (0-684-18578-4); Bantam, paper, $12.95 (0-553-34664-4).
   An Arctophile evokes a dazzling sense of place as he celebrates the region's landscape, wildlife, and people. [BKL Ja 1 86]

McFadden, Cyra. Rain or Shine: A Family Memoir. Knopf. [o.p.].
   A daughter's bittersweet account of growing up on the rodeo circuit and of her love-hate relationship with a father she could not please. [BKL Mr 15 86]

Malone, Michael. Handling Sin. Little, Brown. [Pocket, paper, $10 (0-671-87526-4)].
   An odyssey that begins as a quest for a missing father and his money develops into a novel of love and reconciliation. A dazzling comedy of epic proportions. [BKL Ap 1 86]

Maslow, Jonathan Evan. Bird of Life, Bird of Death: A Nature's Journey through a Land of Political Turmoil. Simon & Schuster. [o.p.].
   A lighthearted search for Guatemala's legendary quetzal unfolds against a backdrop of poverty, repression, and political instability. [BKL My 1 86]

Matthiessen, Peter. Men's Lives: The Surfmen and Baymen of the South Fork. Random, $29.95 (0-394-55280-6); paper, $10 (0-394-75560-X).
   A striking oral and photographic montage reveals the determination of a fishing community threatened by encroaching society. [BKL My 15 86]

Mehta, Ved. Sound-Shadows of the New World. Norton. [Norton, paper, $8.95 (0-393-30437-X)].
   A sensitive portrayal of growing up in an alien culture as a 15-year-old blind boy leaves India to attend school in Arkansas. [BKL Ja 1 86]

Parfit, Michael. South Light: A Journey to the Last Continent. Macmillan. [o.p.].
   The loneliness and the cold, the magnificence and the beauty—all are vividly captured in this record of a scientific expedition to Antarctica. [BKL Ja 1 86]

Pratt, Charles W. In the Orchard. Tidal. [Pomme, paper, $12.95 (0-9641028-1-1)].
   In this beautifully produced book, the poet creates a highly symbolized world

where, Thoreau-like, he celebrates nature and a return to life's essential facts. [BKL Ap 15 86]

Price, Reynolds. Kate Vaiden. Atheneum. [Simon & Schuster, $16.95 (0-689-11787-6); Ballantine, paper, $5.99 (0-345-34358-1)].
  For almost 40 years, Kate ignored the son she abandoned as a baby; now, in an attempt to win his love, she tells her story. [BKL My 15 86]

Rivabella, Omar. Requiem for a Woman's Soul. Random. [o.p.].
  An Argentine writer's fictionalized account of a priest who pieces together from shreds of paper the harrowing diary of a young woman brutally abducted and tortured by military authorities.

Rosengarten, Theodore. Tombee: Portrait of a Cotton Planter; with the Journal of Thomas B. Chaplin (1822–1890). Morrow. [Morrow, paper, $15 (0-688-11609-4)].
  The life of a typical plantation owner before and after the Civil War, described in his own journal and further reconstructed by an eminent historian. [BKL Jl 86]

Roszak, Theodore. The Cult of Information: The Folklore of Computers and the True Art of Thinking. Pantheon. [Univ. of California, paper, $10 (0-520-08584-1)].
  Roszak warns of dangers that arise in education, politics, and the military when one loses the distinction between machines processing information and minds thinking. [BKL Mr 15 86]

Rush, Norman. Whites. Knopf. [Random, paper, $9 (0-679-73816-9)].
  Witty and ironic stories about whites and blacks caught in a clash of cultures in Botswana. [BKL F 15 86]

Shipler, David K. Arab and Jew: Wounded Spirits in a Promised Land. Times. [Penguin, paper, $11.95 (0-14-010376-7)].
  A history of Jewish-Arab relations in Jerusalem plus an in-depth study of popular misconceptions by both factions and of interacting stereotypes. [BKL S 1 86]

Sperber, A. M. Murrow: His Life and Times. Freundlich, $25 (0-88191-008-2).
  The story of a shy, melancholic man who became the voice of history for many Americans. [BKL Ap 15 86]

Stone, Robert. Children of Light. Knopf, $17.95 (0-394-52573-6); paper, $14 (0-679-73301-9).
  Moviemaking is the frame for an intense novel of a love affair mired in drugs, alcohol, and madness. [BKL Ja 1 86]

Szulc, Tad. Fidel: A Critical Portrait. Morrow. [Avon, paper, $5.95 (0-380-69956-7)].
  Through interviews with Castro, his friends, and colleagues, and with access to revolutionary archives, Szulc produces a politically and historically focused analysis of the Cuban leader. [BKL O 15 86]

Taylor, Peter. A Summons to Memphis. Knopf, $15.95 (0-394-41062-9); Ballantine, paper, $5.99 (0-345-34660-2).

Unresolved conflicts in a genteel southern family are unleashed when the elderly patriarch plans to marry a younger woman. A novel. [BKL Ag 86]

Notable Books, 1985

Adams, Ansel and **Alinder, Mary Street.** Ansel Adams: An Autobiography. Bulfinch, $65 (0-8212-1596-5); paper, $13.95 (0-8212-2241-4).
One of the most well known and admired American photographers recounts a lifelong concern for his art and the preservation of the environment. [BKL Ag 85]

Allende, Isabel. The House of the Spirits. Random, $27.50 (0-394-53907-9); Bantam, paper, $6.50 (0-553-27391-4).
Three magnificent women in successive generations use wisdom and guile to hold together the household of Esteban Trueba in this magical/mystical, larger-than-life epic of a South American family. [BKL Mr 1 85]

Banks, Russell. Continental Drift. Harper. [Harper, paper, $12 (0-06-092574-4)].
The paths of a North American blue-collar worker and a Haitian refugee, each desperately seeking a new life in Florida, converge in the tragic clash of cultures. A novel. [BKL D 15 84]

Caufield, Catherine. In the Rainforest. Random, $24.95 (0-394-52701-1); Univ. of Chicago, paper, $14.95 (0-226-09786-2).
An absorbing examination of the continuing destruction in the name of progress of the world's rain forests, together with the consequences of this action. [BKL D 1 84]

Chute, Carolyn. The Beans of Egypt, Maine. Ticknor & Fields. [Harcourt, paper, $10 (0-15-600188-8)].
A striking and provocative first novel about a host of down-and-out souls trying to survive in rural New England.

Costantini, Humberto. The Long Night of Francisco Sanctis. Harper. [o.p.].
With humor and irony, Costantini portrays an ordinary middle-class man in Argentina who, during a period of political repression, is caught between his need for security and the demands of his conscience. [BKL Ag 85]

DeLillo, Don. White Noise. Viking. [Penguin, paper, $11.95 (0-14-007702-2)].
DeLillo's warmest novel brilliantly examines one extended family's fear of death and the ways in which it copes with the apprehension and indifference of today's nuclear age. [BKL N 1 84]

Doctorow, E. L. World's Fair. Random. [Peter Smith, $21.05 (0-8446-6696-3); Random, paper, $12 (0-679-73628-X)].
A child's vivid description of his boyhood in New York in the 1930s is coupled with his adult reflections on the same time and events. [BKL S 15 85]

Duras, Marguerite. The Lover. Pantheon. [Harper, paper, $10 (0-06-097521-0)].

A finely etched glimpse of a young French woman in 1930s Saigon who escapes her impoverished and unbearable family by entering into a scandalous affair with a mysterious Chinese gentleman. [BKL Je 1 85]

Gordon, Mary. Men and Angels. Random. [Ballantine, paper, $5.99 (0-345-32925-2)].
A contemporary novel about love, especially maternal love, and its limits, told in the alternating voices of a "perfect" mother and an unstable mother's helper. [BKL F 1 85]

Heaney, Seamus. Station Island. Farrar, $20 (0-374-26978-5); paper, $12 (0-374-51935-8).
An Irish setting provides the background for this major poet's best writing, which focuses on the basic themes of self-reproach and moral choice.

Hewat, Alan. Lady's Time. Harper. [o.p.].
Turn-of-the-century ragtime and the blues set the tempo for this sinister story of a mother and son, race and music, mystery and voodoo.

Jones, G. C. Growing Up Hard in Harlan County. Univ. Press of Kentucky. [o.p.].
In this account of life in Kentucky between 1920 and 1950, the colorful, matter-of-fact Jones chronicles the area's changes from farming community to mining center.

Kapuscinski, Ryszard. Shah of Shahs. HBJ/Helen and Kurt Wolff. [Random $10 (0-679-73801-0); paper, $9 (0-394-74074-2)].
A noted Polish journalist gives us impressions of Iran, a nation migrating in time "to a past that seems a lost paradise." [BKL Mr 1 85]

Kidder, Tracy. House. Houghton. [Avon, paper, $12 (0-380-71114-1)].
From idea to moving day, the complexities of building a house and the relationships of those involved. [BKL Ag 85]

Kincaid, Jamaica. Annie John. Farrar, $18.95 (0-374-10521-9); NAL, paper, $9.95 (0-452-26356-5).
A poetic, largely autobiographical novel portrays a young woman's idyllic girlhood in Antigua, her rebellious passage into adolescence, and her search for identity. [BKL Ap 1 85]

Lapierre, Dominique. The City of Joy. Doubleday. [Warner, paper, $6.99 (0-446-35556-9)].
A compelling epic of love, patience, hope, and generosity in a Calcutta slum infested with suffering, sorrow, cruelty, and despair amid India's multilayered society. [BKL O 1 85]

Lelyveld, Joseph. Move Your Shadow: South Africa, Black and White. Times. [Penguin, paper, $11 (0-14-009326-5)].
Exposes the lies and manipulations that have popped up and promoted apartheid, an evil that seems to defy solution. [BKL S 15 85]

Lester, Julius. Do Lord Remember Me: A Novel. Holt. [Arcade, paper, $11.95 (1-55970-322-9)].

The indignities, prejudices, hopes, and promises of a lifetime are recalled as an elderly black preacher writes his own obituary. [BKL D 15 84]

Lucie-Smith, Edward. Art of the 1930's: The Age of Anxiety. Rizzoli. [o.p.].

Beautiful reproductions and brilliant textual analysis show how the art of the 1930s was influenced and molded by the historical and political forces of the period.

Lukas, J. Anthony. Common Ground: A Turbulent Decade in the Lives of Three American Families. Random, $19.95 (0-394-41150-1); paper, $17 (0-394-74616-3).

Centering on Boston's school integration crisis of the 1970s, Lukas presents with sympathy and understanding a comprehensive picture of radical and social conflict. [BKL Je 15 85]

McMurtry, Larry. Lonesome Dove: A Novel. Simon & Schuster, $24.95 (0-671-50420-7); Pocket, paper, $7.99 (0-671-79589-9).

A nineteenth-century cattle drive forms the backdrop for the assemblage of unforgettable characters and mythic traditions that come to symbolize the entire western American experience. [BKL My 15 85]

Maharidge, Dale. Journey to Nowhere: The Sage of the New Underclass. Photos. by Michael Williamson. Doubleday/Dial. [Hyperion, paper, $17.95 (0-7868-8204-2)].

A visual and verbal testament to human suffering in American society offers a compassionate look at people who, having lost jobs and homes, take to the road in final desperation. [BKL Mr 15 85]

Mo, Timothy. Sour Sweet. Random/Vintage. [o.p.].

A tragicomic novel in which a Chinese immigrant family in London, harassed by both government and a secret society, accommodates to a new way of life.

Physician Task Force on Hunger in America. Hunger in America: The Growing Epidemic. Wesleyan Univ. Pr. [Univ. Press of New England, $29.95 (0-8195-5150-3); paper, $14.95 (0-8195-6158-4)].

A study sponsored by the Harvard School of Public Health demonstrates that, as a consequence of federal policy, there are more hungry people in America today than 10 years ago.

Reid, T. R. The Chip: How Two Americans Invented the Microchip and Launched a Revolution. Simon & Schuster. [o.p.].

In an analysis of the development of the semiconductor chip, Reid follows two inventors who, working simultaneously, achieved the same results. [BKL F 15 85]

Robinson, David. Chaplin: His Life and Art. McGraw-Hill. [Da Capo, paper, $21.95 (0-306-80600-2)].

Chaplin's contributions to filmmaking are comprehensively examined in relation to significant events in his personal life in this major biography by the film critic for the *Times* of London. [BKL Ag 85]

Schell, Orville. To Get Rich Is Glorious: China in the Eighties. Pantheon. [NAL, paper, $3.95 (0-451-62437-8)].

Schell's trips to the People's Republic revealed startling Westernization-dismantled communes, private businesses, and the profit system—and led him to raise questions about the future course of China. [BKL F 15 85]

Seagrave, Sterling. The Soong Dynasty. Harper. [Borgo, $39 (0-8095-9087-5); Harper, paper, $16 (0-06-091318-5)].

The lasting contributions and sinister activities of the legendary Soong clan, which included the formidable Mmes. Sun Yat-sen and Chiang Kai-shek, and the family's at-times tortuous struggle for control of modern China. [BKL Mr 1 85]

Theroux, Paul. Sunrise with Seamonsters: Travels and Discoveries, 1964–1984. Houghton. [Houghton, paper, $13.95 (0-395-41501-2)].

Fifty essays fill in autobiographical gaps and document Theroux's development as a masterful travel writer and teacher. [BKL My 15 85]

Tyler, Anne. The Accidental Tourist. Random, $25 (0-394-54698-X); Berkley, paper, $6.99 (0-425-09291-7).

Abandoned by his exasperated wife, a passive, habit-ridden loner turns to his brothers and sister, a new love, and an incorrigible dog and cat to relearn friendship and laughter. [BKL Ag 85]

Warren, Robert Penn. New and Selected Poems, 1923–1985. Random, $19.95 (0-394-54380-7); paper, $20 (0-394-73848-9).

Poems spanning 60 years of efforts to transmute stern American realities into a hard-earned classic lyricism. [BKL Ap 1 85]

Whelan, Richard. Robert Capa: A Biography. Knopf. [Univ. of Nebraska, paper, $14 (0-8032-9760-2)].

A panoramic view of the legendary photographer who captured for all time the grim realities of war. [BKL N 1 85]

Wilson, Roberta and **Wilson, James Q.** Watching Fishes: Life and Behavior on Coral-Reefs. Harper. [Gulf, paper, $15.95 (1-55992-061-0)].

Enhanced by photos and line drawings, a fascinating, vivid account of the mysterious and exotic life/behavior of coral-reef fishes and invertebrates. [BKL D 1 84]

Notable Books, 1984

Avedon, John F. In Exile from the Land of Snows. Knopf. [HarperCollins, paper, $13 (0-06-097574-1)].

The mystery of the Dalai Lama's exile and the Chinese conquest of Tibet unveiled. [BKL Ap 15 84]

Bateson, Mary Catherine. With a Daughter's Eye: A Memoir of Margaret Mead and Gregory Bateson. Morrow. [HarperCollins, paper, $12 (0-06-097573-3)].

A candid and touching portrait of the distinguished anthropologists: an intimate view of their lives and work. [BKL S 15 84]

Bernen, Robert. The Hills: More Tales from the Blue Stacks, Stories of Ireland. Scribner. [o.p.].
Beautifully written pieces that capture the essence of the remote Irish hill country. Quiet appreciation for a people and a way of life scarcely touched by the twentieth century. [BKL Ja 15 84]

Bosworth, Patricia. Diane Arbus: A Biography. Knopf. [Norton, paper, $14 (0-393-31207-0)].
This insightful portrait explores the complex mind and personality of a woman who was obsessed with photographing "people without their masks." [BKL Je 1 84]

Brown, Rosellen. Civil Wars: A Novel. Knopf, $16.45 (0-394-53478-6); Bantam, paper, $5.99 (0-440-21695-8).
A former civil rights leader tries to recapture his activist past, while his wife copes with daily life and continues to grow. [BKL Mr 1 84]

Cheever, Susan. Home before Dark. Houghton. [Bantam, paper, $10 (0-553-35150-8)].
A daughter's effort to set the record straight in a poignant and revealing memoir of her father, John Cheever. [BKL O 1 84]

The Chronicle of the Lodz Ghetto, 1941–1944. Ed. by Lucjan Dobroszycki. Yale, $55 (0-300-03208-0); paper, $27 (0-300-03924-7).
A powerful document of the horrors of daily ghetto life. The physical and psychological tensions of a constrained existence are quietly but persistently recorded.

Coetzee, J. M. Life & Times of Michael K. Viking. [Viking, paper, $10.95 (0-14-007448-1)].
A morality tale that pits the unwavering courage of one simple man against the brutally impersonal forces of his South African homeland. [BKL S 15 83]

Connell, Evan S. Son of the Morning Star. North Point. [Promontory, $14.98 (0-88394-088-4); HarperCollins, paper, $10.95 (0-06-097161-4)].
A meticulously researched re-creation of the Battle of the Little Big Horn, combined with a biography of Custer and a history of the Plains Indians. [BKL Ag 84]

Dalby, Liza Crihfield. Geisha. Univ. of California. [o.p.].
An American university student describes her initiation as the first non-Japanese to enter the geisha's world. [BKL F 15 84]

Doctorow, E. L. Lives of the Poets: Six Stories and a Novella. Random, $14.95 (0-394-52530-2); Avon, paper, $4.95 (0-380-69996-6).
Short narratives followed by a novella that recapitulates and extends the memories, fears, and dreams that shape the stories. [BKL O 1 84]

Donoso, Jose. A House in the Country: A Novel. Knopf. [o.p.].

Using lush imagery to create a surrealistic world, Donoso depicts a wealthy South American dynasty. A novel of powerful psychological, historical, and political implications. [BKL N 15 83]

Erdrich, Louise. Love Medicine: A Novel. Holt, $24 (0-8050-2798-X); Harper-Collins, paper, $13 (0-06-097554-7).
Moving episodes of grief, laughter, and kinship reinforce one another in a strong novel about two contemporary Native American families. [BKL S 1 84]

Foshay, Ella M. Reflections of Nature: Flowers in American Art. Knopf. [o.p.].
A strikingly illustrated history of flower painting in America from William Bartram's botanical drawings to twentieth-century experimentation with decorative and expressive forms.

Gilchrist, Ellen. Victory over Japan: A Book of Stories. Little, Brown. [Little, Brown, paper, $12.95 (0-316-31307-6)].
Southern women portrayed as outrageously funny, moving, tragic, and always appealing. A writer speaks elegantly about her own region.

Greer, Germaine. Sex and Destiny: The Politics of Human Fertility. Harper. [o.p.].
This substantial and lively work questions Western society's attempt to influence attitudes toward human reproduction in developing nations. [BKL F 15 84]

Haruf, Kent. The Tie That Binds: A Novel. Holt. [Holt, paper, $9.95 (0-8050-1869-7)].
A natural style enhances this story of one woman's indomitable spirit and devotion to her tyrannical father and dependent younger brother. [BKL S 1 84]

Hayden, Dolores. Redesigning the American Dream: The Future of Housing, Work, and Family Life. Norton. [Norton, paper, $15.95 (0-393-30317-9)].
A timely and provocative examination of the American dream of single-family housing considered from historical and cross-cultural perspectives. [BKL F 15 84]

Heinrich, Bernd. In a Patch of Fireweed. Harvard, $25 (0-674-44548-1); paper, $8.95 (0-674-44551-1).
A biologist conveys the excitement of field observation and shows how his life experiences influenced his development as a naturalist. [BKL Ap 15 84]

Hughes, Ted. River. Harper. [o.p.].
Marvels of life in and connected with the river are given lyric expression in 43 new poems by Britain's poet laureate. [BKL Je 15 84]

Jacobs, Jane. Cities and the Wealth of Nations: Principles of Economic Life. Random. [Random, paper, $12.50 (0-394-72911-0)].
Vital cities produce strong economies: a study of the urban creation of wealth and prosperity. [BKL My 15 84]

Kenney, Susan. In Another Country: A Novel. Viking. [o.p.].
Six interlocking stories probe the mysteries of family connection, human loss, and emotional survival. [BKL My 15 84]

Lockwood, C. C. The Gulf Coast: Where Land Meets Sea. Louisiana State Univ. $34.95 (0-8071-1170-8).

Beautiful photographs of the ecological system of a unique area accompanied by the photographer-naturalist's perceptive and stimulating commentary. [BKL S 1 84]

Luria, S. E. A Slot Machine, a Broken Test Tube: An Autobiography. Harper. [o.p.].

Thoughtful and engaging recollections on the circumstances that shaped the life of a Nobel Prize–winning biologist. [BKL Ja 1 84]

Lurie, Alison. Foreign Affairs. Random, $15.95 (0-394-54076-X); Avon, paper, $11 (0-380-70990-2).

The tale of two American scholars on sabbatical in London, both from the same university, both entangled with romantic interests, and both reacting to the unexpected. [BKL Ag 84]

Mehta, Ved. The Ledge between the Streams. Norton, $17.50 (0-393-01828-8)].

The childhood and adolescence of the writer; his efforts to lead a normal life despite his blindness and a chaotic India coming to independence. [BKL Mr 15 84]

Morris, Jan. Journeys. Oxford, $25 (0-19-503452-X); paper, $8.95 (0-19-503606-9).

Thirteen witty and elegant essays about a succession of journeys to locales in the U.S., Europe, and Asia by an accomplished travel writer. [BKL Ap 15 84]

Olds, Sharon. The Dead and the Living: Poems. Knopf. [Random, paper, $13 (0-394-71563-2)].

A painful but passionate cycle of poems that honors relationships, both living and dead. [BKL D 15 83]

Pawel, Ernst. The Nightmare of Reason: A Life of Franz Kafka. Farrar. [Farrar, paper, $15 (0-374-52335-5)].

This definitive and moving study of a significant writer exposes the human anguish that is central to his work. [BKL My 15 84]

Phillips, Jayne Anne. Machine Dreams. Dutton/Seymour Lawrence. [Pocket, paper, $10 (0-671-74235-3)].

The machines that symbolize America in peace and war form the backdrop for the successive voices of a loving but disintegrating family. [BKL Je 15 84]

Powell, Padgett. Edisto. Farrar, $11.95 (0-374-14651-9); Holt, paper, $9.95 (0-8050-1370-9).

A precocious 12-year-old boy learns about life from an assortment of eccentric characters in a South Carolina coastal town. A hilarious yet poignant first novel.

Sakurai, Atsushi. Salmon. Knopf. [o.p.].

Magnificent photographs and informative text give a breathtaking glimpse into the mysterious migration of salmon and their extraordinary last rite. [BKL Jl 84]

Shirer, William L. The Nightmare Years, 1930–1940. Little, Brown. [o.p.].
A vibrant eyewitness account of the harrowing events of the Hitler years. [BKL Mr 1 84]

Spence, Jonathan D. The Memory Palace of Matteo Ricci. Viking. [Penguin, paper, $13.95 (0-14-008098-8)].
Meditations on a sixteenth-century Jesuit in China imaginatively link contemporary social themes to symbols and pictures Ricci used in early missionary works. [BKL O 15 84]

Swift, Graham. Waterland. Poseidon. [Random, paper, $11 (0-679-73979-3)].
The enchantment of the English fens saturates this novel of brewmasters and lockkeepers haunted by repercussions of violence, incest, and murder in their family history.

Talbott, Strobe. Deadly Gambits: The Reagan Administration and the Stalemate in Nuclear Arms Control. Knopf. [o.p.].
A diplomatic correspondent critically analyzes in nontechnical terms U.S. arms control politics and policies since 1980. [BKL S 1 84]

Terkel, Studs. "The Good War": An Oral History of World War Two. Pantheon. [Ballantine, paper, $7.99 (0-345-32568-0)].
A masterful portrait of a national experience as described by the men and women who lived it. [BKL Ag 84]

Terry, Wallace. Bloods: An Oral History of the Vietnam War by Black Veterans. Random. [Ballantine, paper, $5.95 (0-345-31197-3)].
Candid, eloquent, bitter, unique testimonies.

Unger, Douglas. Leaving the Land: A Novel. Harper. [Univ. of Nebraska, paper, $12 (0-8032-9560-X)].
A resilient woman struggles to hold on to her Dakota farm in the face of encroaching agribusiness and her son's indifference to the land. [BKL D 15 83]

Welty, Eudora. One Writer's Beginnings. Harvard, $15.95 (0-674-63925-1); Warner, paper, $7.99 (0-446-39328-2).
The well-known author's Mississippi childhood recounted not only as a loving tribute to her parents and grandparents but also as an evocative introduction to her creative roots. [BKL F 15 84]

Wideman, John Edgar. Brothers and Keepers. Holt. [Penguin, paper, $11 (0-14-008267-0)].
In a sensitive look at family strength in times of trouble, a noted novelist offers a testimony of love for his convict brother. [BKL O 1 84]

Yehoshua, A. B. A Late Divorce. Doubleday. [Harcourt, paper, $12.95 (0-15-649447-7)].
The many voices of an Israeli family reverberate in a searing tale of crises and clashing values.

Zweig, Paul. Walt Whitman: The Making of the Poet. Basic Books. [o.p.].
Personal experiences and cultural growth are combined in this fresh approach to the development of the Good Gray Poet. [BKL Ap 1 84]

Notable Books, 1983

Bradford, Sarah. Disraeli. Stein & Day. [o.p.].
A neatly sculptured portrait of the nineteenth-century British statesman, achieving an admirable balance between the personal and the political life of a remarkable man. [BKL Je 15 83]

Bricktop and **Haskins, James.** Bricktop. Atheneum. [o.p.].
Spunky memoirs of a black jazz singer who scrabbled her way up from Chicago saloons to her own nightclub in Paris and insouciant hobnobbing with celebrities. [BKL Jl 83]

Carver, Raymond. Cathedral: Stories. Knopf. [Random, paper, $10 (0-679-72369-2)].
Surface simplicity belies the inner complexity of these stories, which reveal the vague menace and moral collapse of ordinary lives. [BKL S 1 83]

Chase, Joan. During the Reign of the Queen of Persia: A Novel. Harper. [Ballantine, paper, $5.99 (0-345-31525-1)].
Three generations of midwestern women survive and continue to grow through sheer feminine endurance and determination.

Chatwin, Bruce. On the Black Hill. Viking. [Penguin, paper, $11.95 (0-14-006896-1)].
Twin brothers living on a Welsh farm share everything in an 80-year coexistence. A novel rich in the oddities, wonders, and tragedies of the human experience. [BKL O 1 83 Upfront]

Clampitt, Amy. The Kingfisher: Poems. Knopf. [Knopf, paper, $18 (0-394-71251-X)].
"The design might be thought of as an illuminated manuscript in which all the handwork happens to be verbal." [BKL Ja 15 83]

Didion, Joan. Salvador. Simon & Schuster. [Random, paper, $9 (0-679-75183-1)].
Report from a country where terror, fear, and repression have become the way of everyday life. [BKL F 1 83 Upfront]

Down & Out in the Great Depression: Letters from the "Forgotten Man." Ed. by Robert S. McElvaine. Univ. of North Carolina. [Univ. of North Carolina, paper, $10.95 (0-8078-4099-8)].
Authentic, heartbreaking voices of the poor evoke the mood of the 1930s, when desperation mingled with hope and trust in FDR and Mrs. Roosevelt.

Drew, Elizabeth. Politics and Money: The New Road to Corruption. Macmillan. [o.p.].
How the methods used to raise the vast sums of money needed to win political office are perverting the American political process. [BKL Je 15 83 Upfront]

Dubus, Andre. The Times Are Never So Bad: A Novella & Eight Short Stories. Godine, $14.95 (0-87923-459-8); paper, $11.95 (0-87923-641-8).
Unblinking realism characterizes a collection that examines unexpected disturbances of domestic life. [BKL Jl 83]

Egerton, John. Generations: An American Family. Univ. Press of Kentucky, $15 (0-8131-1482-9).
An extraordinary picture of 250 years of American history revealed through the lives and words of an ordinary family: a Kentucky couple married 74 years and their ancestors and descendants.

Fossey, Dian. Gorillas in the Mist. Houghton. [Houghton, paper, $10.95 (0-685-06802-1)].
Thirteen years of gorilla research in a remote, mountainous area of Africa recounted by a sensitive woman primatologist. [BKL Je 1 83 Upfront]

Gage, Nicholas. Eleni. Random, $19.95 (0-394-52093-9); Ballantine, paper, $5.95 (0-345-32494-3).
Haunted by memories of his mother, executed during the Greek civil war of the 1940s, the author, seeking vengeance, returns to his village and reconstructs her last days. [BKL Mr 15 83 Upfront]

García Márquez, Gabriel. Chronicle of a Death Foretold. Knopf, $22 (0-394-53074-8); Ballantine, paper, $5.95 (0-345-31002-0).
The tyranny of traditional moral codes is revealed in the testimony of witnesses to the murder of a small-town dandy. A metaphysical detective novel by the Nobel Prize winner. [BKL Mr 1 83 Upfront]

Heat Moon, William Least. Blue Highways: A Journey into America. Atlantic Monthly; dist. by Little, Brown. [Houghton, paper, $12.95 (0-395-58568-6)].
Traveling the back roads in search of inner peace and his Native American roots, the author discovers much about himself and the people of the "unsung side of America." [BKL Ja 15 83]

Helprin, Mark. Winter's Tale. Harcourt, $26.95 (0-15-197203-6); paper, $15 (0-15-600194-2).
A magical novel set in the future and the past dealing with the eternal quest for a truly just city. [BKL Ag 83 Upfront]

Hersh, Seymour M. The Price of Power: Kissinger in the Nixon White House. Summit. [o.p.].
A masterful diplomat and the president he served revealed as a Machiavellian force in American foreign policy between 1968 and 1973.

Hilts, Philip J. Scientific Temperaments: Three Lives in Contemporary Science. Simon & Schuster. [o.p.].
An arresting account of the dazzling achievements of the trailbreakers: particle-physicist Robert Wilson, geneticist Mark Ptashne, and computer-language specialist John McCarthy. [BKL F 1 83]

Isaacs, Arnold R. Without Honor: Defeat in Vietnam and Cambodia. Johns Hopkins Univ. [o.p.].
Firsthand account of the fall of South Vietnam told with great emotional impact by a journalist using previously classified materials.

Jensen, Robert and **Conway, Patricia.** Ornamentalism: The New Decorativeness in Architecture & Design. Clarkson N. Potter. [o.p.].
New ways of shaping and seeing our postmodern man-made environments, set forth in sumptuous photographs and lucid text. [BKL F 1 83]

Kennedy, William. Ironweed: A Novel. Viking. [Penguin, paper, $10.95 (0-14-007020-6)].
A touching portrayal of the wanderings of Francis Phelan, an ex-con and drifter, in Albany, New York, during the Depression. [BKL N I 83]

Lamb, David. The Africans. Random, $17.95 (0-394-51887-X); paper, $12 (0-394-75308-9).
A litany of the weaknesses and strengths, the failures and successes of the nations of Africa, together with prescriptions for the future. [BKL Ja 15 83]

LeVot, Andre. F. Scott Fitzgerald: A Biography. Doubleday. [o.p.].
A French critic takes a fresh and penetrating look at the troubled life of the quintessential American novelist of the 1920s. [BKL Ap 15 83]

Liang Heng and **Shapiro, Judith.** Son of the Revolution. Knopf. [Random, paper, $12 (0-394-72274-4)].
Autobiography of a young man who grew up in China during and after the Cultural Revolution and survived the turmoil and tragedies by strength of will, intelligence, and accident.

Loewinsohn, Ron. Magnetic Field(s): A Novel. Knopf. [o.p.].
In this unusual debut, a robber, a composer, and a fantasy are intricately linked through emotions, spaces, and physical sensations. [BKL Je 1 83]

MacLaverty, Bernard. Cal. Braziller. [Norton, paper, $11 (0-393-31332-8)].
The consequences of violence intensify for Cal McCrystal when he becomes involved with the widow of an IRA victim. A novel that takes a hard look at the life of the urban poor in Northern Ireland.

Malamud, Bernard. The Stories of Bernard Malamud. Farrar, $17.95 (0-374-27037-6); NAL, paper, $12.95 (0-452-26354-9).
Twenty-five stories celebrate seemingly ordinary lives with compassion and humor. [BKL S 15 83 Upfront]

Murdoch, Iris. The Philosopher's Pupil. Viking. [Viking, paper, $11.95 (0-14-006695-0)].
A simple story about the relationship between teacher and pupil is developed into a richly layered extravaganza as an unlikely cast of characters percolate in the hot springs of an English spa. [BKL Ap 1 83 Upfront]

Page, Joseph A. Peron: A Biography. Random. [o.p.].
The first full-length English-language study of the charismatic Argentinean dictator who changed his native land for good and ill. [BKL Jl 83]

Pancake, Breece D'J. The Stories of Breece D'J Pancake. Atlantic Monthly; dist. by Little, Brown. [Holt, paper, $9.95 (0-8050-0720-2)].
A hauntingly powerful and perceptive collection depicting the lives of desperate people struggling for identity and survival in the mountain hollows of West Virginia. [BKL D 1 82]

Parry, Linda. William Morris Textiles. Viking/Studio. [o.p.].
Exquisitely illustrated survey of Morris' contributions to textile design and manufacture. [BKL My 15 83]

Petrosky, Anthony. Jurgis Petraskas: Poems. Louisiana State Univ. [Books on Demand, paper, $25 (0-608-00869-9)].
Strong and passionate poems memorializing four generations of the poet's Lithuanian American family and their blue-collar world. [BKL Mr 1 83]

Porter, Eliot. All Under Heaven: The Chinese World. Text by Jonathan Porter. Pantheon. [o.p.].
Master photographs of the natural and human landscape of China combine with an informed text to reveal unity in the diversity of the Chinese world. [BKL D 15 83]

Radosh, Ronald and **Milton, Joyce.** The Rosenberg File: A Search for the Truth. Holt. [o.p.].
Were Julius and Ethel Rosenberg guilty of treason? An exhaustive analysis of interviews and newly available government material provides thought-provoking answers. [BKL Jl 83]

Rockwell, John. All American Music: Composition in the Late Twentieth Century. Knopf. [o.p.].
Musical forms, from classical through salsa, are analyzed in 20 essays focusing on representative American composers. [BKL Mr 1 83]

Rushdie, Salman. Shame. Knopf. [o.p.].
A chimerical tale set in a country that may or may not be modern Pakistan, where everything is seen at a slight angle to reality. [BKL S 15 83 Upfront]

Silverman, Jonathan. For the World to See: The Life of Margaret Bourke-White. Viking/Studio. [o.p.].
A photo-biography of the photojournalist who recorded important social and historical events of the recent past in her magnificent pictures and poignant prose. [BKL My 15 83]

Song, Cathy. Picture Bride. Yale. [Yale, paper, $10 (0-300-02969-1)].
Colorful and luminous poems gracefully and quietly etch memories of childhood and the lives of people journeying into the world.

Theroux, Paul. The London Embassy. Houghton. [o.p.].
In 18 short stories, the narrator, an American diplomat, observes the humorous eccentricities of both American and British colleagues at his new post. [BKL F 1 83 Upfront]

Updike, John. Hugging the Shore: Essays and Criticism. Knopf, $30 (0-394-53179-5); Ecco, paper, $18 (0-88001-398-2).
A collection of brilliantly conceived reviews and essays from the noted American writer. [BKL S 1 83]

Warner, William W. Distant Water: The Fate of the North Atlantic Fisherman. Atlantic Monthly; dist. by Little, Brown. [o.p.].
The plight of the beleaguered fishermen of five nations, who toil heroically under adverse conditions, and an indictment of the factory-ship system. [BKL Mr 15 83]

Wideman, John Edgar. Sent for You Yesterday. Avon/Bard. [Random, paper, $11 (0-679-72029-4)].
A richly allusive novel of conflict between individualism and family connectedness as experienced growing up black in Pittsburgh. [BKL Je 1 83]

Wilcox, Fred A. Waiting for an Army to Die: The Tragedy of Agent Orange. Random. [Seven Locks, paper, $10.95 (0-932020-68-2)].
Against the indifference of government bureaucrats and chemical manufacturers, Vietnam veterans battle for recompense for the physical and emotional damage to them and their children. [BKL Jl 83]

Wright, Stephen. Meditations in Green. Scribner. [Dell, paper, $11.95 (0-385-31521-X)].
A gut-wrenching, drug-drenched Vietnam War novel, juxtaposing the horror and banality of military life with the unique pain of adjustment back in the "world." [BKL O 1 83]

Notable Books, 1982

Anderson, Jervis. This Was Harlem: A Cultural Portrait, 1900–1950. Farrar. [Farrar, paper, $17 (0-374-51757-6)].
Harlem during its heyday: the development of its unique literature, music, drama, and social clubs and the effects of war, the Depression, and oppression on the lives of its people. [BKL F 15 82]

The Auschwitz Album: A Book Based upon an Album Discovered by a Concentration Camp Survivor, Lili Meier. Text by Peter Heilman. Random. [o.p.].
The only existing photographic record of a "selection" for extermination. [BKL N 15 82]

Baker, Russell. Growing Up. Congdon & Weed. [Penguin, paper, $10 (0-452-25550-3)].
Warm and honest memories of a Depression childhood that shaped the character and perception of the witty *New York Times* columnist. [BKL S 15 82]

Ballantyne, Sheila. Imaginary Crimes. Viking. [Penguin, paper, $9.95 (0-14-006540-7)].
With a mother who drinks and a father who wanders, Sonya needs to be a survivor and she is, without self-pity and with much humor. A novel. [BKL F 15 82]

Berriault, Gina. The Infinite Passion of Expectation: Twenty-five Stories. North Point. [o.p.].
Clear depiction of varieties of human relationships and feelings, of emotions made nearly tangible, and of life expectations momentarily faced and traded away. [BKL N 1 82]

Braudel, Fernand. The Structures of Everyday Life: The Limits of the Possible. Harper. [Univ. of California, paper, $22.50 (0-520-08114-5)].
A cornucopia of detail on the economy and varied aspects of living in the world, from the Middle Ages to the Industrial Revolution. [BKL Ja 1 82]

Brown, Bruce. Mountain in the Clouds: A Search for the Wild Salmon. Simon & Schuster. [Knopf, $29.95 (0-394-49973-5); Simon & Schuster, paper, $12.95 (0-02-013095-3)].
A moving plea for the preservation of a courageous species caught in the environmental crisis. [BKL My 15 82]

Campbell, Jeremy. Grammatical Man: Information, Entropy, Language, and Life. Simon & Schuster. [o.p.].
The history and implication of information theory provide a convincing argument for seeing life as "grammatical" in its tendency toward order and complexity. [BKL S 1 82]

Caro, Robert A. The Path to Power. (The Years of Lyndon Johnson, v.1) Knopf. [Random, paper, $18 (0-679-72945-3)].
A revealing account of the development of LBJ's political genius from his youth in the Texas Hill Country to his defeat for the Senate in 1941. [BKL D 1 82]

DeLillo, Don. The Names. Knopf. [Random, paper, $12 (0-679-72295-5)].
An ambitious, literary novel that explores the alienation of expatriate Americans. A complex vision of lives filled with boredom and menace. [BKL S 1 82]

Del Vecchio, John M. The 13th Valley: A Novel. Bantam. [Bantam, paper, $5.95 (0-553-26020-0)].
A realistic treatment of the Vietnam War portraying the conflicts, anxieties, and heroism of soldiers for whom time and purpose are measured in terms of survival.

Eckholm, Erik P. Down to Earth: Environment and Human Needs. Norton. [o.p.].
A powerful account of the disastrous effects of pollution on the "global under-

class," and a realistic proposal for cooperation between environmentalists and industrialists.

Fisher, M. F. K. As They Were. Knopf. [Random, paper, $12 (0-394-71348-6)].
Twenty entrancing memories of the places, images, feelings, flavors, and encounters that have shaped an extraordinary writer. [BKL Ap 15 82]

Forche, Carolyn. The Country between Us. Harper. [Harper, paper, $10 (0-06-090926-9)].
The terrors of oppression in El Salvador and Czechoslovakia, and a piercing dread of emptiness in life in the States, projected in poems of uncanny power.

Gernes, Sonia. The Way to St. Ives. Scribner. [o.p.].
A compassionate novel about loss of innocence and the search for trust and understanding in the life of a middle-aged, midwestern Catholic woman. [BKL Je 15 82]

Hoffman, Alice. White Horses. Putnam. [Berkley, paper, $6.50 (0-425-13980-8)].
Myth and fantasy interwoven in a dreamlike novel of a young woman's struggle to find freedom and release from the past. [BKL Ap 1 82]

Hoffman, Ethan. Concrete Mama: Prison Profiles from Walla Walla. Text by John McCoy. Univ. of Missouri. [o.p.].
Arresting, often shocking photographs complement interviews with convicts and others involved with survival behind the walls. [BKL Ap 15 82]

Holliday, J. S. The World Rushed In: The California Gold Rush Experience. Simon & Schuster. [Simon & Schuster, paper, $15.95 (0-671-25538-X)].
A skillful re-creation of the 1848 gold-rush journey based on diaries and letters of William Swain. [BKL D 15 81]

Ishiguro, Kazuo. A Pale View of Hills. Putnam. [Random, paper, $10 (0-679-72267-X)].
In this subtle and graceful novel, a troubled Japanese mother remembers postwar Nagasaki and unsettling changes in personal and cultural values. [BKL Ap 15 82]

Keegan, John. Six Armies in Normandy: From D-Day to the Liberation of Paris, June 6th–August 25th, 1944. Viking. [Penguin, paper, $12.95 (0-14-023542-6)].
Fresh insights on the history, performance, and national characteristics of American, British, Canadian, Polish, Free French, and German military units. [BKL Ap 1 82]

Kogawa, Joy. Obasan. Godine. [Doubleday, paper, $9.95 (0-385-46886-5)].
Seeking the truth behind a harsh, motherless childhood, a Canadian Nisei learns how silent love protected her from the destructive awareness of war and internment. A novel.

Lacey, Robert. The Kingdom. Harcourt. [Avon, paper, $5.95 (0-380-61762-5)].

A superb account of the rise of Ibn Sa'ud and his family—how they rule Saudi Arabia and dominate the Arab world. [BKL Ja 15 82]

Madson, John. Where the Sky Began: Land of the Tallgrass Prairie. Houghton. [Iowa State Univ., $24.95 (0-8138-2513-X); paper, $19.95 (0-8138-2515-6)].
A detailed natural history conveying the beauty and fierceness of this unique American region, with an appeal for its preservation. [BKL Ap 15 82]

Mason, Bobbie Ann. Shiloh and Other Stories. Harper. [Univ. Press of Kentucky, $18 (0-8131-1948-0); HarperCollins, paper, $12 (0-06-091330-4)].
K-Mart clerks, truck drivers, Rook-playing widows, and flea-market traders populate these stories set in Kentucky. [BKL O 15 82]

Millgate, Michael. Thomas Hardy: A Biography. Random. [St. Martin's, paper, $17.95 (0-312-12233-0)].
A complex, balanced, and sympathetic view of the writer as a man in relation to his life and work. [BKL Mr 15 82]

Murray, William. Italy: The Fatal Gift. Dodd, Mead. [o.p.].
In this chronicle of a love affair with Italy, the spirit of her people and the moods of her cities are captured by an American reporter of Italian descent. [BKL Ag 82]

Noel Hume, Ivor. Martin's Hundred. Knopf, $25 (0-394-50728-2).
An archaeological detective story in which a lost settlement near Williamsburg, Virginia, comes back to vivid life. [BKL Mr 1 82]

Nye, Naomi Shihab. Hugging the Jukebox. Dutton. [o.p.].
The wonder and magic of the smallest things, and the largest, captured in poems set in the American Southwest, Mexico, and Central and South America.

Ondaatje, Michael. Running in the Family. Norton. [Random, paper, $10 (0-679-74669-2)].
A sensitive and amusing search for self. This Canadian author returns to Ceylon and pieces together family history from recollection, legend, and scandal. [BKL O 1 82]

Pais, Abraham. "Subtle is the Lord . . . " The Science and the Life of Albert Einstein. Oxford, $35 (0-19-85390-7); paper, $16.95 (0-19-520438-7).
The scientific and intellectual context and impact of Einstein's work, and his own attitudes toward it, documented and elucidated by a physicist.

Piercy, Marge. Circles on the Water: Selected Poems of Marge Piercy. Knopf. [Random, paper, $16 (0-394-70779-6)].
Feminist poems that dance with anger and lusty humor, yet are touched with tenderness. [BKL My 15 82]

Plowden, David. An American Chronology: The Photographs of David Plowden. Viking. [o.p.].
Beautifully printed photographs documenting changing and changeless Amer-

ica, enhanced by David McCullough's introductory text describing Plowden's method of work and commitment to his craft. [BKL O 15 82]

Rodriguez, Richard. Hunger of Memory: The Education of Richard Rodriguez, An Autobiography. Godine. [Bantam, paper, $5.99 (0-553-27293-4)].
    A Mexican American's provocative essays on the conflict created by his family's traditional values and his own search for identity and acceptance. [BKL Ja 15 82]

Schell, Jonathan. The Fate of the Earth. Knopf. [Avon, paper, $4.95 (0-380-61325-5)].
    A relentless statement of the case against nuclear weapons and the present generation's duty to banish them from the earth. [BKL Ap 15 82]

Simpson, Eileen. Poets in Their Youth: A Memoir. Random. [Farrar, paper, $10.95 (0-374-52261-8)].
    Analytical and generous recollections by John Berryman's ex-wife of the young years of the poet and his tragic literary generation. [BKL Jl 82]

Singer, Isaac Bashevis. The Collected Stories of Isaac Bashevis Singer. Farrar. [Farrar, paper, $18 (0-374-51788-6)].
    Forty-seven mystical and realistic tales reveal the power of a master storyteller. [BKL Ja 1 82]

Soyinka, Wole. Ake: The Years of Childhood. Random, $14.95 (0-394-52807-7); paper, $12 (0-679-72540-7).
    The son of a Yoruba Christian clergyman describes his early childhood discoveries, delights, and accommodations to tradition and change in his West African village. [BKL S 15 82]

Thurman, Judith. Isak Dinesen: The Life of a Storyteller. St. Martin's. [St. Martin's, paper, $16 (0-312-13525-4)].
    A life that reads like a tale she told. [BKL N 1 82]

Tyler, Anne. Dinner at the Homesick Restaurant. Random, $25 (0-394-52381-4); Ivy, paper, $5.99 (0-8041-0882-X).
    Eccentric members of a Baltimore family struggle and survive because of, and in spite of, a fierce and energetic mother. A novel. [BKL D 15 81]

Updike, John. Bech Is Back. Knopf, $25 (0-394-52806-9); Fawcett, paper, $5.99 (0-449-20277-1).
    More rollicking misadventures in the literary life of blocked writer Henry Bech, including the publication of his long-awaited second novel. [BKL S 1 82]

Vargas Llosa, Mario. Aunt Julia and the Scriptwriter. Farrar. [Avon, paper, $9.95 (0-380-70046-8)].
    A wonderfully inventive comic novel by the Peruvian writer in which the main plot intermingles with episodes from increasingly zany radio serials. [BKL Je 15 82]

Wongar, B. Barbaru: Stories. Univ. of Illinois. [o.p.].

Twelve tales of magic and transformation create the world of the Australian Aboriginals. [BKL N 1 82]

Notable Books, 1981

Allen, Gay Wilson. Waldo Emerson. Viking. [o.p.].
Material from thousands of unpublished Emerson papers included in this authoritative literary biography reveals the transcendental leader's personal and intellectual struggles. [BKL S 1 81]

Ashbery, John. Shadow Train. Viking. [o.p.].
This collection of 50 16-line poems is mysteriously seductive, puzzlingly evocative. [BKL My 1 81]

Atwood, Margaret. Two-headed Poems. Simon & Schuster. [o.p.].
Poems of life stripped to the essentials, of grim humor confronting terror, violence, and death, of severe tenderness and inextinguishable hope. [BKL Mr 15 81]

Berke, Roberta. Bounds Out of Bounds: A Compass for Recent American and British Poetry. Oxford. [o.p.].
An inviting introduction to the major schools of poetry, the poets who shaped them, and the works they created. [BKL My 1 81]

Bowen, Elizabeth. The Collected Stories of Elizabeth Bowen. Random, $25 (0-394-51666-4); Ecco, paper, $13.95 (0-88001-224-2).
Bowen's civilized prose controls themes of passion, the occult, and the imaginative life of children in these 79 stories. [BKL Ja 15 81]

Brent, Peter. Charles Darwin: A Man of Enlarged Curiosity. Harper. [o.p.].
The development of Darwin's curiosity about and reverence for nature throughout his life, unfolded in the setting, pace, and texture of his Victorian world. [BKL O 1 81]

Carpenter, Humphrey. W. H. Auden: A Biography. Houghton. [Houghton, paper, $10.95 (0-395-32439-4)].
Enriched by Auden's previously unpublished letters and manuscripts, this biography delineates the passions and eccentricities of a leading poet of our century. [BKL S 15 81]

Carver, Raymond. What We Talk about When We Talk about Love. Knopf. [Random, paper, $9.95 (0-679-72305-6)].
Seventeen stark, haunting stories of ordinary individuals encountering horrific aspects of human nature and suffering the dislocations of an unpredictable existence. [BKL Ap 1 81]

Fallows, James. National Defense. Random, $12.95 (0-394-51824-1).
Advocating realistic, cost-effective defense options for the U.S. in the 1980s,

Fallows provocatively critiques current military policies and planning. [BKL Je 15 81]

From the Country of Eight Islands: An Anthology of Japanese Poetry. Ed. and tr. by Hiroaki Sato and Burton Watson. Univ. of Washington. [Columbia, paper, $16.50 (0-231-06395-4)].
Japanese poetry spanning 15 centuries as it evolved from pure, classic simplicity and the highest idealization of emotion to an individualized voice under Western influence.

Garside, Roger. Coming Alive: China after Mao. McGraw-Hill. [o.p.].
A summary of the political upheavals after the death of Mao, in which the conservative thrust of Deng Xiaoping prevailed.

Goodfield, June. An Imagined World: A Story of Scientific Discovery. Harper. [Univ. of Michigan, $39.50 (0-472-09462-9); paper, $16.95 (0-472-06462-2)].
This account of the struggle, insight, and creativity of a young scientist, researching the nature of Hodgkin's disease, enhances our understanding of scientific discovery.

Gordimer, Nadine. July's People. Viking. [Penguin, paper, $10.95 (0-14-006140-1)].
Fleeing the black revolution, a liberal South African white family becomes totally dependent on their former servant. An eloquent, prophetic novel that exposes the distorting heritage of colonialism. [BKL F 15 81]

Gould, Stephen Jay. The Mismeasure of Man. Norton. [Norton, paper, $11.95 (0-393-31067-1)].
Can human intelligence be determined without the influence of the social and political environment on the scientist's theory and practice? [BKL S 1 81]

Halberstam, David. The Breaks of the Game. Knopf. [Ballantine, paper, $5.99 (0-345-29625-7)].
An expansive investigation of the making and breaking of a professional basketball team—the Portland Trail Blazers. [BKL O 1 81]

Hampl, Patricia. A Romantic Education. Houghton. [Houghton, paper, $14.95 (0-395-60200-9)].
A young Minnesota poet and writer of the sixties generation seeks her roots in golden Prague, the dream city of her spirited grandmother. [BKL Ja 15 81]

Hughes, Robert. The Shock of the New. Knopf. [Knopf, paper, $40 (0-679-72876-7)].
A lively text, coupled with plentiful illustrations, provides a fascinating account of modern art from 1889 through the early seventies. [BKL Ja 15 81]

Johanson, Donald C. and **Edey, Maitland A.** Lucy: The Beginnings of Humankind. Simon & Schuster. [Simon & Schuster, paper, $14 (0-671-72499-1)].

An animated presentation of modern theory about man's ancestors, with emphasis on the early fossil skeletal remains unearthed by Johanson at Hadar, Ethiopia. [BKL Ja 1 81]

McCullough, David. Mornings on Horseback. Simon & Schuster. [Peter Smith, $24.05 (0-8446-6732-3); Simon & Schuster, paper, $14.95 (0-671-44754-8)].
Theodore Roosevelt's early years, when his personality and character were molded and tempered by his devoted father, "Greatheart," and an uncommon array of uncanny and nurturing women. [BKL Ap 15 81]

Malone, Dumas. The Sage of Monticello. (Jefferson and His Time, v.6) Little, Brown. [Little, Brown, paper, $15.95 (0-316-54478-7)].
Thomas Jefferson living his retirement years in fruition as an educational entrepreneur, gardener, architect, reader, letter writer, and family man. [BKL Je 15 81]

Mariani, Paul. William Carlos Williams: A New World Naked. McGraw-Hill. [Norton, paper, $14.95 (0-393-30672-0)].
The grandly human story of how a pediatrician from a small town in New Jersey became a major voice in twentieth-century poetry. [BKL 0 1 81]

Mooney, Ted. Easy Travel to Other Planets. Farrar. [Random, paper, $10 (0-679-73883-5)].
A marvelous first novel in which the author weaves his tale effortlessly through time and space with glimpses of the many shapes of love along the way. [BKL Jl 15 81]

Neely, Richard. How Courts Govern America. Yale. [Yale, paper, $14 (0-300-02980-2)].
With humor and clarity, a Virginia Supreme Court judge discusses the structure of the judicial system in America and the role of the courts and legislative bodies in effecting change in American life.

Nijinska, Bronislava. Bronislava Nijinska: Early Memoirs. Holt. [Duke Univ., paper, $18.95 (0-8223-1295-6)].
A leading dancer, choreographer, and teacher for five decades, Nijinska recalls a dazzling era in dance history and provides unique insight into her brother Vaslav Nijinsky's development and artistic achievement. [BKL 0 15 81]

O'Connor, Frank. Collected Stories. Knopf, $20 (0-394-51602-8); paper, $18 (0-394-71048-7).
The loneliness of the human condition threads through these vivid, humorous tales of Irish life by a master of the modern short story. [BKL Je 1 81]

Peters, F. E. Ours: The Making and Unmaking of a Jesuit. Marek. [o.p.].
The author's growth during nine years as a seminarian, from entry at 18 to his decision to leave, reveals the shaping of a person by a community. [BKL Je 1 81]

Plante, David. The Country. Atheneum. [o.p.].
This elegant and precisely written novel explores the anguish of seven sons as their aged parents become more withdrawn and their father dies. [BKL 0 1 81]

Plath, Sylvia. The Collected Poems. Ed. by Ted Hughes. Harper. [Harper, paper, $17 (0-06-090900-5)].
This volume allows the reader to follow a major poet's development, from schoolgirl experimentation to meticulous poetic expression and anguished authority. [BKL S 15 81]

Pond, Elizabeth. From the Yaroslavsky Station: Russia Perceived. Universe, $16.50 (0-87663-450-1); paper, $8.95 (0-87663-853-1).
Russian history is contrasted with contemporary Soviet life and attitudes, as revealed by Pond's traveling companions on a transSiberian railroad.

Robinson, Marilynne. Housekeeping. Farrar. [Bantam, paper, $5.99 (0-553-27872-X)].
Images of a river haunt this novel of recollection about unbearable choices between permanence and transience. [BKL N 15 80]

Santoli, Al. Everything We Had: An Oral History of the Vietnam War by Thirty-three American Soldiers Who Fought It. Random. [Ballantine, paper, $5.95 (0-345-32279-7)].
Candid and gripping reminiscences by officers and enlisted men and women—platoon leaders, nurses, rear-echelon organizers, and POWs.

Schwartz-Nobel, Loretta. Starving in the Shadow of Plenty. Putnam. [Smithmark, $11.98 (0-399-12522-1)].
Facts combined with personal experiences document the problems related to hunger in the U.S. today: energy misuse, vanishing natural resources, depreciating farmlands, inflation, and sources of funding.

Smith, Adam. Paper Money. Summit. [o.p.].
Our loss of the financial power game and its long-range effect on our fiscal stability, told with a taunting, vibrant wit. [BKL F 1 81]

Spence, Jonathan D. The Gate of Heavenly Peace: The Chinese and Their Revolution, 1895–1980. Viking. [Penguin, paper, $13.95 (0-14-006436-0)].
The violence and vitality of modern China made comprehensible through biographical vignettes of intellectuals and artists who commented revealingly on this turbulent era. [BKL JI 15 81]

Spencer, Elizabeth. The Stories of Elizabeth Spencer. Doubleday. [Penguin, paper, $9.95 (0-14-006436-0)].
Superb evocation of people and places characterizes these 33 stories written over five decades. [BKL F 15 81]

Stratton, Joanna L. Pioneer Women: Voices from the Kansas Frontier. Simon & Schuster. [Simon & Schuster, paper, $12.95 (0-671-44748-3)].
The rigorous challenges of life on the prairie are revealed in personal recollections and wonderful photographs. [BKL Mr 15 81]

Timerman, Jacobo. Prisoner without a Name, Cell without a Number. Knopf, $12.50 (0-394-51448-3); paper, $10 (0-679-72048-0).

An Argentine newspaper publisher's harrowing account of his imprisonment and torture as an advocate of social justice and of the inner strength that enabled him to survive. [BKL My 15 81]

Totman, Conrad. Japan before Perry: A Short History. Univ. of California. [Univ. of California, paper, $14 (0-520-04134-8)].
How Japan, its social institutions, and its increasing population developed in cycles of fragmentation and reconsolidation from prehistoric through early modern times.

Tuchman, Barbara. Practicing History: Selected Essays. Knopf, $16.50 (0-394-52086-6); Ballantine, paper, $12 (0-345-30363-6).
A splendid potpourri of essays and addresses that includes the craft of historical writing as as an effective discourse on what our nation can learn from history. [BKL Je 15 81]

Updike, John. Rabbit Is Rich. Random, $30 (0-394-52087-4); Fawcett, paper, $5.99 (0-449-24548-9).
Middle-aged and middle-class Harry ("Rabbit") Angstrom is beset by his troublesome son and by images of mortality in Updike's poetic, acutely observed novel of contemporary American life. [BKL Je 1 81]

Wilford, John Noble. The Mapmakers. Knopf. [Random, paper, $19 (0-394-75303-8)].
A survey of the development of cartography: its metamorphosis from guesswork to science, from antiquity to the modern era.

Woods, Donald. Asking for Trouble: Autobiography of a Banned Journalist. Atheneum. [Peter Smith, $25.05 (0-8446-6324-7)].
This recounting of Woods' lifelong struggle for journalistic integrity, a tenet which resulted in his exile from South Africa, culminates with an exciting escape. [BKL Je 15 81]

Notable Books, 1980

American Folk Painters of Three Centuries. Ed. by Jean Lipman and Tom Armstrong. Hudson Hills. [o.p.].
Vivid color reproductions of the masterpieces of 37 primitive artists and essays on their lives and work illustrate the achievements and creativity of the American folk tradition.

Arnold, Eve. In China. Knopf. [o.p.].
The rich complexity of this enormous land is illuminated in magnificent color photographs of landscape and people. Picture journalism at its best.

Atwood, Margaret. Life before Man. Simon & Schuster. [Bantam, paper, $10.95 (0-553-37782-5)].

Fantasies of prehistoric times offer the only solace from the turmoil and dissatisfaction of a modern marriage. A novel.

Bogan, Louise. Journey around My Room: The Autobiography of Louise Bogan. Viking. [o.p.].
Passages from her private papers and public writings disclose the life and craft of the late Louise Bogan, a leading poet of our age.

Calvino, Italo. Italian Folktales. Harcourt, $27.95 (0-15-145770-0); paper, $19.95 (0-15-645489-0).
A treasury that captures the earthly, pragmatic, indomitable spirit of a rich body of folk literature.

Desai, Anita. Clear Light of Day. Harper. [Penguin, paper, $10 (0-14-010859-9)].
The changing relationships and perceptions among the four children of a Hindi family evoke the growing tension and violence in prepartition India. A novel.

Drabble, Margaret. The Middle Ground. Knopf. [Ivy, paper, $4.95 (0-8041-0362-3)].
A successful journalist caught up in the complexities of her personal life struggles to define her future.

Flaubert, Gustave. The Letters of Gustave Flaubert, 1830–1857. Selected, ed., and tr. by Francis Steegmuller. Harvard/Belknap. [Harvard, paper, $9.95 (0-674-52637-6)].
The spontaneity of personal letters reveals the development and range of Flaubert's art and passions from early boyhood through the writing of and public reaction to *Madame Bovary*.

Gibson, Margaret. The Butterfly Ward. Vanguard. [o.p.].
In these short stories, tortured souls flutter between transient phases of insanity and normality.

Gould, Stephen Jay. The Panda's Thumb: More Reflections in Natural History. Norton. [Norton, paper, $10.95 (0-393-30819-7)].
The excitement and challenge of "doing" science are captured in disarming, literate essays that entertain and instruct by focusing on the curiosities and vagaries of evolutionary theory.

Kaplan, Justin. Walt Whitman: A Life. Simon & Schuster. [o.p.].
The Good Gray Poet comes alive in all his majesty and frailty, triumphs and failures, in this gripping biography by a Pulitzer Prize–winning author.

Keneally, Thomas. Confederates. Harper. [Harper, paper, $12 (0-06-091446-7)].
A novel about the Civil War in Virginia in 1862, when the South seemed to be winning, that follows the lives of fictional and and historical characters in gritty, scarring scenes of battle.

Kiely, Benedict. The State of Ireland: A Novella and Seventeen Stories. Godine. [o.p.].

A gifted storyteller captures the piety and irreverence, wit and wickedness of his compatriots in this uniquely unparochial collection.

Kingston, Maxine Hong. China Men. Knopf. [Knopf, paper, $10 (0-679-72328-5)].
Voices of Chinese emigrants echo in a dreamlike blend of oral tradition, memoir, and history of their exile in the New World.

Kramer, Jane. Unsettling Europe. Random. [o.p.].
Telling profiles of four groups of migrant workers typical of millions who fled their impoverished homelands. This flight, a contemporary phenomenon, has altered the complexion of industrialized Europe and resulted in mutually painful cultural shock.

Lanes, Selma G. The Art of Maurice Sendak. Abrams, $34.98 (0-8109-8063-0).
A delightfully illustrated study of how a leading artist has responded to the challenge of creating books for today's children.

Lash, Joseph P. Helen and Teacher: The Story of Helen Keller and Anne Sullivan Macy. Delacorte/Seymour Lawrence. [American Foundation for the Blind, paper, $19.95 (0-89128-234-3)].
This biography plunges you into Keller's sensibility—radically intelligent, cut off from sight and sound. It gives a new view of a powerful, interlocking relationship.

Manchester, William. Goodbye, Darkness: A Memoir of the Pacific War. Little, Brown. [Dell, paper, $6.99 (0-440-32907-8)].
A noted author revisits the scenes of battle he and fellow WWII Marines endured almost four decades earlier, recalling the savagery and waste of war with conflicting emotions of pride and revulsion.

Massie, Robert K. Peter the Great: His Life and World. Random, $14.99 (0-517-06483-9); Ballantine, paper, $14 (0-345-29806-3).
A man of curiosity and ingenuity, Peter the Great forced a nation out of medievalism, built a navy when he had no ships and a powerful army from illiterate peasants, created a city from a swamp, and, in spite of his cruelties and absurdities, changed the course of Russian history.

Meredith, William. The Cheer. Knopf. [o.p.].
The cheer that can give heart against an evil world is "hidden in right words" in these cleanly crafted poems.

Morris, Wright. Plains Song: For Female Voices. Harper. [David Godine, paper, $10.95 (0-87923-835-6)].
Tough independence and the ability to survive isolation, loneliness, and change are demonstrated in the fictional lives of three generations of women who attempt to fulfill their personal dreams on the plains of Nebraska.

Pablo Picasso: A Retrospective. Ed. by William Rubin. Museum of Modern Art. [o.p.].

This magnificent book provides a permanent record of the life work of a master artist.

Percy, Walker. The Second Coming. Farrar. [Ivy, paper, $5.99 (0-8041-0542-1)].
Assaulted by memories, prosperous Will Barrett flees the banality of his materialistic existence with a mentally unbalanced but essentially wise young girl. A novel.

Pym, Barbara. A Glass of Blessings. Dutton. [NAL, paper, $8.95 (0-525-48512-0)].
Everything is understated in this resonant comic novel of a young wife whose social existence centers on the Church of England.

Silk, Leonard and **Silk, Mark.** The American Establishment. Basic. [o.p.].
As lively as it is thoughtful, this study traces the evolution of a "third force" in the American polity and attempts to discover how well such institutions as Harvard, the *New York Times*, and the Ford Foundation have observed the disinterested pursuit of the public good.

Steel, Ronald. Walter Lippmann and the American Century. Atlantic/Little, Brown. [Random, paper, $15.95 (0-394-74731-3)].
A brilliant portrayal of a distinguished American journalist who analyzed rather than sought power yet wielded tremendous influence in this century.

Strand, Mark. Selected Poems. Atheneum. [Random, paper, $14 (0-679-73301-9)].
Absence, emptiness, and nothingness take on a vibrant fullness of meaning as the poet encounters the sharp reality of everyday things.

Strouse, Jean. Alice James: A Biography. Houghton. [Houghton, paper, $10.95 (0-395-59773-0)].
The younger sister of William and Henry James, Alice James lived the life of an invalid, constrained by nineteenth-century and family conventions but remarkable for her intelligence and tenacity.

Toole, John Kennedy. A Confederacy of Dunces. Louisiana State Univ., $22.95 (0-8071-0657-7); Grove, paper, $11.95 (0-8021-3020-8).
This farcical, satiric novel follows an antic misfit's quest for transcendence in New Orleans.

Troyat, Henri. Catherine the Great. Elsevier-Dutton. [NAL, $13.95 (0-452-01120-5); Berkley, paper, $5.99 (0-452-07981-3)].
Enthralling biography of the passionately ambitious German-born ruler of Russia during the turbulent 1700s.

Vendler, Helen. Part of Nature, Part of Us: Modern American Poets. Harvard, $32 (0-674-65475-7); paper, $16.95 (0-674-65476-5)].
These critical essays explore every dimension a poem could be thought to take and open the techniques of poetry to all readers.

Watt, Ian. Conrad in the Nineteenth Century. Univ. of California. [Univ. of California, paper, $13 (0-520-04405-3)].
   A distinguished biography closely analyzing the sources, historical context, and philosophical foundations of Conrad's fiction through *Heart of Darkness* and *Lord Jim*.

Welty, Eudora. The Collected Stories of Eudora Welty. Harcourt. [Harcourt, paper, $14 (0-15-618921-6)].
   In 41 stories—comic, sensual, lyrical—Welty shows how ordinary lives can blaze into myth.

Notable Books of the 1970s

Notable Books, 1979

Adams, Alice. Beautiful Girl: Stories. Knopf. [o.p.].
Gracefully written stories of lives revealed in acts of love, denial, and infidelity.

Blythe, Ronald. The View in Winter: Reflections on Old Age. Harcourt. [o.p.].
A painful, eloquent look into the empty lives of the elderly residents of an English village as they remember the past and wait out their final days.

Conot, Robert. A Streak of Luck. Seaview. [Da Capo, paper, $16.95 (0-306-80261-9)].
Engrossing biography of Thomas Alva Edison, the genius who helped fashion the modern age and who took advantage of every possibility to further his inventive designs.

Drucker, Peter F. Adventures of a Bystander. Harper. [Transaction, paper, $21.95 (1-56000-738-9)].
Beginning with his privileged Viennese childhood, the founder of modern management theory recalls a rich and varied life that has brought him in contact with some of the most creative figures of the twentieth century.

Edel, Leon. Bloomsbury: A House of Lions. Lippincott & Crowell. [o.p.].
Shapely, astute biographical essays on nine Bloomsbury figures who influenced the course of English and world art, literature, and politics.

Energy Future: Report of the Energy Project at the Harvard Business School. Ed. by Robert Stobaugh and Daniel Yergin. Random. [Random, paper, $6.95 (0-394-71063-0)].
A well-reasoned argument opting for conservation and solar technology as answers to America's growing energy crisis.

Epstein, Helen. Children of the Holocaust: Conversations with Sons and Daughters of Survivors. Putnam. [Penguin, paper, $12.95 (0-14-011284-7)].
Painful efforts of children to understand how their parents survived Hitler's final solution.

Epstein, Leslie. King of the Jews. Coward, McCann. [Norton, paper, $9.95 (0-393-30959-2)].
A comic, heroic depiction of the horror of life in a World War II Polish ghetto and of the fictional Jewish leader, shrewd, theatrical Trumpelman.

Ferlinghetti, Lawrence. Landscapes of Living & Dying. New Directions. [o.p.].

These poems survey the sad rites and flashy absurdities of America with exuberant wit and issue a manifesto of oneness with nature.

Fraser, Antonia. Royal Charles: Charles II and the Restoration. Knopf. [o.p.].
A vivid, sympathetic biography of a multifaceted monarch whose resilience and courage enabled him to survive one of the most turbulent periods of English and European history.

Harvard Guide to Contemporary American Writing. Ed. by Daniel Hoffman. Harvard. [Harvard, paper, $19.95 (0-674-37537-8)].
Incisive and approachable essays that both dispel confusion and generate curiosity about significant groups of writers.

Haviaras, Stratis. When the Tree Sings. Simon & Schuster. [o.p.].
A lyrical first novel about the survival of the human spirit in Greece during World War II.

Hendricks, Gordon. The Life and Work of Winslow Homer. Abrams. [o.p.].
Splendid illustrations and design enhance this critical biography of an American artist who was acclaimed in his lifetime and has remained a popular favorite.

Hoagland, Edward. African Calliope: A Journey to the Sudan. Random. [Lyons & Burford, paper, $14.95 (1-55821-370-8)].
Hoagland proves the ideal guide to the exotic landscape and gallery of people that make up the largest of African nations.

Hoffman, Alice. The Drowning Season. Dutton. [Penguin, paper, $9.95 (0-452-26302-6)].
A novel about two women named Esther—grandmother and granddaughter—who attempt to break away from the hatred and clannishness of their family and find peace.

Kendall, Elizabeth. Where She Danced: American Dancing, 1880–1930. Knopf. [Univ. of California, paper, $13 (0-520-05173-4)].
This account of Ruth St. Denis' career and its roots in nineteenth-century feminism also focuses on other influential dancers and shows how modern American dance affected many facets of our culture.

Keneally, Thomas. Passenger. Harcourt. [o.p.].
An unborn son narrates the odyssey of his indomitable mother in this fresh and exciting Australian novel.

Kunitz, Stanley. The Poems of Stanley Kunitz, 1928–1978. Atlantic/Little, Brown. [o.p.].
Twenty provocative new poems and selections from the past 50 years by this most readable of major American poets.

Lasch, Christopher. The Culture of Narcissism: American Life in an Age of Diminishing Expectations. Norton. [Norton, paper, $11.95 (0-393-30738-7)].

This devastating critique of American society uses narcissism as a metaphor for our culture, examining the erosion of personal fulfillment and the absence of a solution.

Le Roy Ladurie, Emmanuel. Carnival in Romans. Braziller. [Braziller, paper, $8.95 (0-8076-0991-9)].
Civil war, religious fanaticism, and revolutionary insurrection in sixteenth-century provincial France are made relevant for today.

Levine, Philip. 7 Years from Somewhere: Poems. Atheneum. [o.p.].
These poems celebrate lost souls beaten down by forces they cannot understand or control.

Lewis, Norman. Naples '44. Pantheon. [Holt, paper, $14.95 (0-8050-3373-4)].
A Goyaesque portrait of life in war-ravaged Naples as depicted by a British novelist and correspondent who was there.

Litwack, Leon. Been in the Storm So Long: The Aftermath of Slavery. Knopf. [Knopf, paper, $17 (0-394-74398-9)].
Although the Civil War was over, the letters, interviews, and diaries used as the basis for this book reveal that the former slaves' struggle for freedom had just begun.

Lorenz, Konrad. The Year of the Greying Goose. Harcourt. [o.p.].
A scientist's complete accord with the natural world is captured through the stunning interrelation of words and photographs to document Lorenz's research in animal behavior.

Lottman, Herbert. Albert Camus: A Biography. Doubleday. [o.p.].
Portrait of the French intellectual who has had continuing moral impact yet was estranged from his own time.

Mailer, Norman. The Executioner's Song. Little, Brown. [Random, $20 (0-679-42471-7); Warner, paper, $7.99 (0-446-34521-0)].
From the life, crimes, imprisonment, and death of Gary Gilmore, Mailer has written an American tragedy that's also a reflection of the American West.

Malamud, Bernard. Dubin's Lives. Farrar. [Penguin, paper, $10.95 (0-14-01876-0)].
A resonant, seemingly spontaneous, mysterious novel about a biographer's breakdown and partial regeneration.

Morgan, Dan. Merchants of Grain. Viking. [o.p.].
In this first global look at the shadowy grain trade, Morgan reveals the five giant companies and their profound effect on the politics of food.

Morowitz, Harold J. The Wine of Life and Other Essays on Societies, Energy, and Living Things. St. Martin's. [Ox Bow, $18.95 (0-312-88227-0)].
Literate, sprightly, instructive essays in the biological sciences by a noted biochemist and humanist.

Morris, Edmund. The Rise of Theodore Roosevelt. Coward, McCann. [Ballantine, paper, $16 (0-345-33902-9)].
A surprisingly fresh and intimate retelling of the courage, flair, determination, and sense of destiny that resulted in the making of a president.

Munro, Alice. The Beggar Maid: Stories of Flo and Rose. Random. [Random, $10 (0-679-73271-3); Penguin, paper, $6.95 (0-14-006011-1)].
Short, interconnected stories of an attractive girl growing up in the "poor part" of Toronto and her stepmother, who battles and manipulates but still fascinates her.

Oates, Joyce Carol. Unholy Loves: A Novel. Vanguard. [o.p.].
A distinguished guest poet with declining creative powers becomes the focus of academic jealousies and intrigues.

O'Connor, Flannery. The Habit of Being: Letters. Ed. by Sally Fitzgerald. Farrar, $35 (0-374-16769-9); paper, $18 (0-374-52104-2).
Warmth, sharp wit, and reflections on theological, moral, and artistic values distinguish the letters of this complex writer whose fiction was the deeply felt expression of her Catholicism.

Pearson, John. The Sitwells: A Family's Biography. Harcourt. [Harcourt, paper, $7.95 (0-15-682676-3)].
A vivid biography of Edith, Osbert, and Scheverell, that trio of eccentrics and self-promoters who were at the center of twentieth-century English cultural life.

Pritchett, V.S. The Myth Makers: Literary Essays. Random. [Random, $11.95 (0-394-50472-0)].
A master stylist reexamines the contributions to the art and magic of storytelling by great European and Latin American writers from Tolstoy to Garcia Marquez.

Puig, Manuel. Kiss of the Spider Woman. Knopf. [Amereon, $21.95 (0-8488-0614-X); Random, paper, $11 (0-679-72449-4)].
In tracing the growth of love between two men in an Argentine prison cell, this novel of perfectly crafted dialogue explores the theme of dominance and submission that underlies political oppression.

Roth, Philip. The Ghost Writer. Farrar. [Random, $10 (0-679-74898-9)].
A young writer's encounter with his expectations and creative fantasies while visiting his literary idol.

Ryan, Cornelius and **Ryan, Kathryn Morgan.** A Private Battle. Simon & Schuster. [o.p.].
Compelling account of the historian's struggle with cancer, prepared from hidden journals and tapes by his widow, who adds her own important insights.

Shawcross, William. Sideshow: Kissinger, Nixon and the Destruction of Cambodia. Simon & Schuster. [o.p.].
A step-by-step narrative of Cambodia's experience with the U.S. and of Henry Kissinger's role within that drama.

Spencer, Scott. Endless Love. Knopf. [Ballantine, paper, $4.95 (0-345-35624-1)].
A boy's obsessive love for a girl and her family and the tragic interaction of their lives until he learns to accept reality. A novel.

Steinfels, Peter. The Neoconservatives: The Men Who Are Changing America's Politics. Simon & Schuster. [o.p.].
A sober analysis of a body of thought that increasingly influences public policymaking and may pose a threat to democratic values.

Tafel, Edgar. Apprentice to Genius: Years with Frank Lloyd Wright. McGraw-Hill. [Dover, paper, $10.95 (0-486-24801-1)].
Photographs and drawings illuminate this re-creation of Wright's methods, successes, and failures, by an early disciple who remains devoted to Wright's work while recognizing his personal weaknesses/foibles.

Thomas, Gordon and **Morgan-Witts, Max.** The Day the Bubble Burst: A Social History of the Wall Street Crash of 1929. Doubleday. [o.p.].
Focusing on the lives of varied participants, the authors re-create the frenzied race to Black Friday.

Updike, John. The Coup. Random, $27.50 (0-394-50268-X); Fawcett, paper, $5.99 (0-449-24259-5).
Narrated by the egomaniacal ruler of an imaginary African nation, this mordant, funny novel is, among other things, a satire of America's impact on other cultures.

Updike, John. Problems and Other Stories. Random, $19.95 (0-394-50705-3); Fawcett, paper, $4.95 (0-449-21103-7).
The disturbances and stress of contemporary society are brilliantly encapsulated in Updike's tragicomic observations of human lives and experiences.

Vonnegut, Kurt. Jailbird: A Novel. Delacorte. [Bantam, paper, $6.50 (0-440-15473-1)].
Big business, Watergate, and other controversial phenomena are spoofed with sentimental pessimism. And so on.

Walcott, Derek. The Star-Apple Kingdom. Farrar. [o.p.].
These poems reveal a precise and inventive imagery used to explore the poet's Caribbean heritage.

Wolfe, Tom. The Right Stuff. Farrar, $30 (0-374-25033-2); Bantam, paper, $6.99 (0-55-327556-9).
An intimate look at the first U.S. astronauts and other pioneers of the space age and the mystique that bound them into a unique fraternity.

Notable Books, 1978

Berg, A Scott. Max Perkins: Editor of Genius. Dutton. [Pocket, paper, $6.95 (0-671-68174-5)].
The rich biography of the legendary editor who nurtured such literary figures as Hemingway, Fitzgerald, and Wolfe.

Bernstein, Jeremy. Experiencing Science. Basic. [o.p.].
Intriguing glimpses into the delights and difficulties of the world of science by a physicist who has been the *New Yorker* "science watcher" for almost 20 years.

Brown, Rosellen. Tender Mercies. Knopf. [Bantam, paper, $5.99 (0-440-021696-6)].
Dan and Laura's solid but not invulnerable marriage is tested to the utmost when his act of careless bravado leaves her a quadriplegic. A moving, disquieting novel.

Chatwin, Bruce. In Patagonia. Summit. [Penguin, paper, $10.95 (0-14-011291-X)].
Mysterious South American land revealed in a splendid, witty travel narrative.

Cheever, John. The Stories of John Cheever. Random, $29.95 (0-394-50087-3); Ballantine, paper, $6.95 (0-345-33567-8).
This chronological collection of Cheever's best spans three decades of magnificent storytelling.

Chen Jo-hsi. The Execution of Mayor Yin and Other Stories from the Great Proletarian Cultural Revolution. Indiana Univ. [Indiana Univ., paper, $12.95 (0-253-20231-0)].
Memories of ordinary life in China transformed into subtle, subversive fiction.

Clark, Kenneth. An Introduction to Rembrandt. Harper. [o.p.].
Highly informed and expertly executed biographical essays and critical analyses on the work, themes, and career of the master.

Cowley, Malcolm. And I Worked at the Writer's Trade: Chapters of Literary History, 1918–1978. Viking. [o.p.].
Distinguished critic, editor, and historian analyzes with affection trends and trendmakers of the American literary scene.

Davis, John H. The Guggenheims: An American Epic. Morrow. [Sure Sellers, $19.95 (0-944007-07-4); paper, $12.95 (1-56171-072-5)].
A candid and engrossing look at how the Guggenheim mining fortune was built and spent and its impact on economic and cultural history.

Epstein, Samuel. The Politics of Cancer. Sierra Club; dist. by Scribner. [o.p.].

A well-documented account of the increase in environmentally caused cancers and the failure of both government and business to act.

Erickson, Carolly. Bloody Mary. Doubleday. [Morrow, paper, $15 (0-688-11641-8)].
An absorbing, sympathetic, and readable biography of the remarkable Mary Tudor and her tumultuous era.

Fairlie, Henry. The Parties: Republicans and Democrats in this Century. St. Martin's. [o.p.].
A witty analysis of the fumblings and failures of leadership in both parties by a veteran British observer.

Furbank, P. N. E. M. Forster: A Life. Harcourt. [Harcourt, paper, $16.95 (0-15-628651-3)].
A compassionate account of the hidden life of this important twentieth-century novelist.

Gaines, Ernest J. In My Father's House. Knopf. [Random, paper, $10 (0-679-72791-4)].
The past cannot be denied in this dramatic confrontation between a wronged son and a successful civil rights leader. A novel.

García Márquez, Gabriel. Innocent Erendira and Other Stories. Harper. [Borgo, $29 (0-8095-9052-2)].
Our half-conscious emotions are explored through luscious and fantastic imagery in this collection of intriguingly bizarre tales.

Gifford, Barry and **Lee, Lawrence.** Jack's Book: An Oral Biography of Jack Kerouac. St. Martin's. [St. Martin's, paper, $12.95 (0-313-11338-2)].
The voices of those who shared Kerouac's spiritual odyssey provide a vivid portrait of the Beat Generation and one of its heroes.

Gordon, Mary. Final Payments. Random. [Ballantine, paper, $6.99 (0-345-32973-2)].
The death of her father forces a young Irish Catholic woman to define her own life and deal with her newfound freedom. A novel.

Gornick, Vivian. The Romance of American Communism. Basic. [o.p.].
Probing interviews of 47 American men and women explaining their initial infatuation with the Communist Party and their ultimate disillusionment.

Greene, Graham. The Human Factor. Simon & Schuster. [Simon & Schuster, paper, $5.99 (0-671-64850-0)].
Spellbinding storytelling about the ambiguous world of espionage. A novel.

Hall, Donald. Remembering Poets: Reminiscences and Opinions: Dylan Thomas, Robert Frost, T. S. Eliot, Ezra Pound. Harper. [o.p.].
Personal encounters with the forces of creativity and self-destruction in the lives of four giants of twentieth-century poetry.

Hendin, Josephine. Vulnerable People: A View of American Fiction since 1945. Oxford. [Oxford, paper, $7.95 (0-19-502620-9)].
Provocative interpretations of Updike, Mailer, Vonnegut, Oates, and Didion offer many plausible explanations of today's perplexing novels.

Irving, John. The World according to Garp. Dutton. [Ballantine, paper, $5.95 (0-345-36676-X)].
A comic-tragic, realistic-fantastic, hilarious-horrific romp through the life of T. S. Garp.

Jacobsen, Josephine. A Walk with Raschid, and Other Stories. Jackpine. [o.p.].
Elegantly written, tension-edged portrayals of moments of personal revelation.

Johnson, Diane. Lying Low. Knopf. [o.p.].
Perceptive characterization and graceful writing in a novel about people hiding out in an old boardinghouse.

Jones, James. Whistle. Delacorte. [Bruccoli Clark Layman, $35 (0-89723-017-5); Dell, paper, $5.99 (0-440-39262-4)].
This posthumous novel completes the author's World War II trilogy and depicts the deleterious effects of army life on American GIs in peace and war.

Kazin, Alfred. New York Jew. Knopf. [o.p.].
New York City ambience and the peccadilloes of many significant U.S. writers are spliced within this critic's memoir.

Le Roy Ladurie, Emmanuel. Montaillou: The Promised Land of Error. Braziller. [Random, paper, $16.95 (0-394-72964-1)].
Based on Inquisitorial records, this is a uniquely fascinating account of the daily life, manners, and mores of a heretical village in fourteenth-century France.

Madden, David. The Suicide's Wife. Bobbs-Merrill. [o.p.].
A startling psychological portrait of a woman who must cope with her husband's bewildering death and her sudden independence from the past. A novel.

Manchester, William. American Caesar, Douglas MacArthur, 1880–1964. Little, Brown, $40 (0-316-54498-1); Bantam, paper, $7.99 (0-440-30424-5).
A reappraisal of the paradoxical character and career of the controversial American general.

Matthiessen, Peter. The Snow Leopard. Viking. [Penguin, paper, $12.95 (0-14-010266-3)].
A physically arduous trek through the Himalayas proves a revealing counterpoint to the author's own spiritual pilgrimage.

Meyer, Susan E. America's Great Illustrators. Abrams. [Galahad, $24.98 (0-88365-645-0)].
Lucid commentary on popular American illustrators whose art mirrors our past and present. Handsomely illustrated.

Murdoch, Iris. The Sea, the Sea. Viking. [Viking, paper, $11.95 (0-14-005199-6)].
Women, both incidental and central to his past, intrude upon a meddlesome egotist writing his memoirs in a secluded house by the sea.

O'Brien, Tim. Going after Cacciato. Delacorte. [Bantam, paper, $11.95 (0-385-28349-0)].
Reality blurs into fantasy in this surrealistic novel about a young Vietnam War deserter and his pursuers.

Porter, Andrew. Music of Three Seasons: 1974–1977. Farrar. [o.p.].
A collection of distinguished and illuminating opinion and commentary from the music critic of the *New Yorker*.

Rich, Adrienne. The Dream of a Common Language: Poems, 1974–1977. Norton. [Norton, paper, $8.95 (0-393-31033-7)].
In succinct, powerful language, Rich explores a variety of relationships among women.

Salisbury, Harrison. Black Night, White Snow: Russia's Revolution, 1905–1917. Doubleday. [Da Capo, paper, $16.95 (0-306-80154-X)].
A fast-moving narrative describing the series of events that toppled the tsarist regime and ultimately brought the Bolsheviks to power.

Sarton, May. A Reckoning. Norton $11.95 (0-393-08828-6); paper, $5.95 (0-393-30075-3).
Laura Spelman makes her dying a positive experience and finds her greatest support in a lifelong friend rather than in her family. A novel.

Schlesinger, Arthur M. Robert Kennedy and His Times. Houghton. [Ballantine, paper, $6.95 (0-345-32547-8)].
Written by a longtime friend and associate, this is an extensive, partisan account of the man, his background, and his accomplishments.

Shapiro, Karl. Collected Poems: 1940–1977. Random. [o.p.].
The writer's choice from a lifetime of self-revelatory achievement.

Shaw, Irwin. Short Stories: Five Decades. Delacorte. [o.p.].
The collected tales of a popular storyteller reflect changes in our lives and outlooks over the past 50 years.

Silberman, Charles E. Criminal Violence, Criminal Justice. Random, $15 (0-394-48306-5); paper, $12 (0-394-74147-1).
Demolishes myths long held about crime, criminals, and the American legal system.

Sontag, Susan. Illness as Metaphor. Farrar. [Peter Smith, $20.80 (0-8446-6827-3); Doubleday, paper, $9.95 (0-385-26705-3)].
A brilliant essay on how we wrongly conceptualize illness and the resultant harrowing effects on both patient and society.

Swenson, May. New and Selected Things Taking Place: Poems. Atlantic/Little, Brown. [o.p.].
A unique, humorous, and thoughtful collection that is accessible on many levels.

Theroux, Paul. Picture Palace. Houghton. [Penguin, paper, $10.95 (0-14-005072-8)].
Unrequited, incestuous passion compels photographer Maude Pratt to question her artistic success and personal failure in this novel of wit and invention.

Tuchman, Barbara W. A Distant Mirror: The Calamitous 14th Century. Random, $50 (0-394-40026-7); Ballantine, paper, $16 (0-345-34957-1).
A picture of society in the Middle Ages, which makes clear the gulf that separates the modern and medieval world and those striking similarities which make that age a mirror of our own.

Warren, Robert Penn. Now and Then: Poems, 1976–1978. Random. [Random, paper, $5.95 (0-394-73515-3)].
These poems reveal the many varieties of talent in a poet still growing and developing.

White, Theodore H. In Search of History: A Personal Expedition. Harper. [Warner, paper, $7.95 (0-446-34657-8)].
Recollections of a life spent on the journalistic front lines reveal an intense search for traditional American values.

Wilhelm, Kate. Somerset Dreams and Other Fictions. Harper. [o.p.].
Those uncomfortable areas that hover between the real and unreal are explored in this finely crafted collection of speculative fiction.

Will, George F. The Pursuit of Happiness, and Other Sobering Thoughts. Harper. [o.p.].
Writing about everything from *Playboy* magazine to raising children, Will, an articulate conservative, always makes us think.

Wills, Garry. Inventing America: Jefferson's Declaration of Independence. Doubleday. [Buccaneer, $29.95 (1-56849-536-6); Random, paper, $11 (0-394-72735-5)].
An informative reinterpretation of philosophies and foundations of the Jefferson Declaration.

Notable Books, 1977

Ashbery, John. Houseboat Days. Viking. [o.p.].
The poet's dreamlike pursuit of time and memory—recording the haunting and hallucinatory shifts of thought from recognizable landscapes to regions both transparent and mysterious.

Baryshnikov, Mikhail. Baryshnikov at Work. Knopf. [Knopf, paper, $22.95 (0-394-73587-0)].
A perceptive, technically brilliant dancer describes with candor the 26 roles he learned or re-created during his first three years in the West.

Bate, Walter Jackson. Samuel Johnson. Harcourt. [Harcourt, paper, $10.95 (0-15-679259-1)].
Reveals the complexities of the eternally fascinating literary giant, perhaps even better than Boswell.

Berlant, Anthony and **Kahlenberg, Mary Hunt.** Walk in Beauty: The Navajo and Their Blankets. Little, Brown/New York Graphic Society. [o.p.].
Dramatically illustrated history of the Navajo's spirit and culture, expressed in the colors and patterns of their weaving.

Berryman, John. Henry's Fate & Other Poems, 1967–1972. Farrar. [o.p.].
A posthumous collection that includes 45 previously unpublished *Dream Songs*, further evidence of the poet's stunning mastery.

Bishop, Elizabeth. Geography III. Farrar. [Farrar, paper, $9 (0-374-51440-2)].
With the exactitude of a mapmaker, the poet uses an austere, meditative style to etch the rich landscape of her private world.

Brain, Robert. Kolonialagent. Harper. [o.p.].
A novel as fin de siècle diary reveals the arrogance and righteousness of the colonials who "civilized" Africa.

Caputo, Philip. A Rumor of War. Holt. [Ballantine, paper, $12 (0-345-38656-6)].
Caputo's transformation from an idealistic marine to an accused murderer of civilians during the no-win war in Vietnam.

Cooper, Patricia and **Buferd, Norma Bradley.** The Quilters: Women and Domestic Art. Doubleday. [Doubleday, paper, $15.95 (0-385-12039-7)].
Photographs of the quilts, the women, and their land enhance moving interviews with southwestern folk artists.

Djilas, Milovan. Wartime. Harcourt. [Harcourt, paper, $7.95 (0-15-694712-9)].
The rise of communism and partisan fighting in Yugoslavia during World War II, told by one of the major participants.

Drew, Elizabeth. American Journal: The Events of 1976. Random. [o.p.].
Behind the headlines and on the sidelines of the Carter-Ford presidential race, by a cool, capable journalist.

Emerson, Gloria. Winners and Losers: Battles, Retreats, Gains, Losses and Ruins from a Long War. Random. [Norton, paper, $12.95 (0-393-30925-8)].
Interviews reinforce a reporter's perception of the Vietnam War's destructive effects.

Espy, Willard R. Oysterville: Roads to Grandpa's Village. Clarkson N. Potter. [o.p.].

Outstanding book design enriches this affectionate family history of the author's hometown on the Washington coast.

French, Marilyn. The Women's Room. Simon & Schuster. [Ballantine, paper, $12 (0-345-38181-5)].
How marriage, American suburban style, turned the wives of the 1950s into the women of the 1970s. A novel.

Gardner, John Champlin. The Life and Times of Chaucer. Knopf. [o.p.].
A lively reconstruction of the poet and his age.

Gavin, Thomas. Kingkill. Random. [o.p.].
A rich and raw re-creation of the nineteenth-century medicine show and the hunchbacked genius who nightly manipulated the Celebrated Automated Chess Player. A novel.

Gibbons, Boyd. Wye Island: Outsiders, Insiders and Resistance to Change. Johns Hopkins Univ., $20.95 (0-8018-1936-9); Resources for the Future, paper, $12.95 (0-915707-23-9).
Microcosmic view of the universal dilemma of the conflict between developers and traditional landowners.

Hanley, James. A Dream Journey. Horizon. [o.p.].
The dedication and despair, silences and sufferings of an artist and his wife. A novel of human need and dependence.

Harris, Marvin. Cannibals and Kings: The Origins of Cultures. Random. [Random, paper, $12 (0-679-72849-X)].
Stone age to energy crisis—stimulating reconsideration of many common theories.

Hennig, Margaret and **Jardim, Anne.** Managerial Woman. Anchor/Doubleday. [Pocket, paper, $5.99 (0-671-67431-5)].
A well-documented study of women in the corporate structure.

Herr, Michael. Dispatches. Knopf. [Random, paper, $11 (0-679-73525-9)].
Catches and conveys the devastating differences of the Vietnam conflict.

Joyes, Claire. Monet at Giverny. Two Continents. [o.p.].
A warm and intelligent study of a painter whose genius at capturing the beauty of changing light transformed the world of art.

Leakey, Richard E. and **Lewin, Roger.** Origins. Dutton. [Penguin, paper, $11.95 (0-14-015336-5)].
"What new discoveries reveal about the emergence of our species and its possible future."

Lowell, Robert. Day by Day. Farrar. [Farrar, $12.95 (0-374-13525-8); paper, $9 (0-374-51471-2)].

In this verse autobiography, the poet's anguish and exhilaration illuminate his struggles with age and death.

McCullough, David. The Path between the Seas: The Creation of the Panama Canal, 1870–1914. Simon & Schuster. [American Society of Civil Engineers, $14.95 (0-685-75146-5); Simon & Schuster, paper, $14.95 (0-671-24409-4)].
The conquest of tropical disease and tons of earth told as urgent social history.

McPhee, John. Coming into the Country. Farrar, $22.95 (0-374-12645-3); paper, $9.95 (0-374-52287-1).
Alaska: its natural grandeur and unusual people observed by a thoughtful, stylish journalist who makes us see, hear, and think.

Mitford, Jessica. A Fine Old Conflict. Knopf. [o.p.].
A truly funny book about life with the Communist Party by a former member who remains proud of the party's goals and influence.

Morante, Elsa. History: A Novel. Knopf. [o.p.].
A neo-realist portrayal of war-ravaged Rome and its effect on one small family.

Morrison, Toni. Song of Solomon. Knopf, $24 (0-394-49784-8); NAL, paper, $10.95 (0-45-226011-6).
The son of a prosperous black midwestern family solves some old mysteries concerning his origins in a journey through the South. A novel.

Naipaul, Vidiadhar Suraiprasad. India: A Wounded Civilization. Knopf. [Random, paper, $10 (0-394-72463-1)].
Exploratory surgery on the mind of India, revealing the intellectual malaise resulting from centuries of foreign domination and inertia.

Packard, Vance Oakley. The People Shapers. Little, Brown. [o.p.].
An alarming portrayal of behavioral engineers and their aim for surer control of the human race.

Percy, Walker. Lancelot. Farrar. [Ivy, paper, $5.99 (0-8041-0380-1)].
Surrealistic fiction that vividly depicts the decay of a southern aristocrat.

Sagan, Carl. The Dragons of Eden: Speculations on the Evolution of Human Intelligence. Random, $10.95 (0-394-41045-9); Ballantine, paper, $6.99 (0-345-34629-7).
Freewheeling and fascinating theories.

Sampson, Anthony. The Arms Bazaar: From Lebanon to Lockheed. Viking. [o.p.].
A critical assessment of international munitions peddlers.

Savage, Thomas. I Heard My Sister Speak My Name. Little, Brown. [o.p.].
Adopted Amy McKinney's decision to search out her true parents is the keystone of this timeless, beautifully written novel of clan traditions.

Scott, Paul. Staying On. Morrow. [Avon, paper, $3.50 (0-380-46045-9)].
An elderly British couple vainly attempts to maintain the Empire's traditions in India in this ironic novel of quiet failure.

Selzer, Richard. Mortal Lessons: Notes on the Art of Surgery. Simon & Schuster. [Harcourt, paper, $12 (0-15-600400-3)].
Essays in a baroque style elevate the body's parts and the surgeon's arts to poetic ritual.

Shreve, Susan Richards. A Woman like That. Atheneum. [o.p.].
The psychological effect of a family murder warps the emotional life of a young woman. A novel.

Taylor, Peter. In the Miro District and Other Stories. Knopf. [Ballantine, paper, $4.95 (0-345-90170-3)].
A varied, graceful offering of short stories by a contemporary master of the genre.

Theroux, Paul. The Consul's File. Houghton. [o.p.].
Twenty short stories, closely connected by place, character, and theme, reveal the clash of cultures in absurd comic and poignant scenes.

Vidal, Gore. Matters of Fact and Fiction: Essays, 1973–1976. Random. [o.p.].
Sparkling literary and political pieces laced with wit and venom.

White, Elwyn Brooks. The Essays of E. B. White. Harper. [Harper, paper, $13 (0-06-090662-6)].
Vintage collection of the warmth and wisdom of one of the most loved American writers.

Winn, Marie. The Plug-in Drug. Grossman/Viking. [Penguin, paper, $10.95 (0-14-007698-0)].
Argues persuasively that young children exposed to excessive television watching become passive observers removed from genuine feeling.

Wright, Richard. American Hunger. Harper. [Borgo, $27 (0-8095-9067-1); Harper, paper, $11 (0-06-090991-9)].
A segment of autobiography illuminating those years (1927–36) when the author of *Black Boy* reacted to Chicago and the Communist Party.

Notable Books, 1976

Alther, Lisa. Kinflicks; A Novel. Knopf. [NAL, paper, $12.95 (0-452-27677-2)].
Flashbacks reveal Ginny Babcock's sad, funny progress from cheerleader to lesbian to farmer to housewife. First fiction.

Arlen, Michael J. The View from Highway #1: Essays on Television. Farrar. [o.p.].
A thought-provoking study of the shortcomings of television programming and its impact.

Auden, Wystan Hugh. Collected Poems of W. H. Auden. Ed. by Edward Mendelson. Random. [o.p.].
Selected poems Auden himself wanted preserved.

Baskin, John. New Burlington: The Life and Death of an American Village. Norton. [New Amsterdam, paper, $11.95 (1-5613-1044-1)].
An elegiac encounter with the lives and memories of Ohio villagers whose rural past is doomed by the twentieth century.

Bass, Jack and **De Vries, Walter.** The Transformation of Southern Politics: Social Change and Political Consequence since 1945. Basic. [Univ. of Georgia, paper, $24.95 (0-8203-1728-4)].

Bettelheim, Bruno. The Uses of Enchantment: The Meaning and Importance of Fairy Tales. Knopf. [Random, $27.50 (0-394-49771-6); paper, $12 (0-679-72393-5)].
A Freudian defense of fairy tales as a traditional means of universal communication.

Borgese, Elisabeth Mann. The Drama of the Oceans. Abrams. [o.p.].
Beautifully illustrated study of nature's most majestic and mysterious realm, now on the brink of cataclysm.

Brown, Rosellen. The Autobiography of My Mother. Doubleday. [Bantam, paper, $5.99 (0-440-21694-X)].
A novel of a successful lawyer, her directionless, sensual daughter, and the child who is the focus of their final struggle.

Bryan, C. D. B. Friendly Fire. Putnam. [o.p.].
One family's persistent, painful search for the true circumstances of their son's death in Vietnam.

Caudill, Henry M. The Watches of the Night. Atlantic/Little, Brown. [o.p.].
Thirteen years after *Night Comes to the Cumberlands*, Caudill returns to find that federal programs have turned the mountain people into welfare clients and failed to stop the destruction of the land.

Cornelisen, Ann. Women of the Shadows. Atlantic/Little, Brown. [Penguin, paper, $9.95 (0-14-014785-3)].
A graphic presentation of the harsh lives and the courage of five women in a poor Italian village.

Dangerfield, George. The Damnable Question: A Study in Anglo-Irish Relations. Atlantic/Little, Brown. [o.p.].

A powerful book that brings together the tragic facts about Anglo-Irish relations between 1800 and the Easter Uprising.

Davies, William Robertson. World of Wonders. Viking. [Viking, paper, $11.95 (0-14-016796-X)].
A master illusionist recounts his rise to fame and in so doing gives the final answer to "Who killed Boy Staunton?" The third novel in the illustrious trilogy that began with *The Fifth Business.*

Des Pres, Terrence. The Survivor: The Anatomy of Life in the Death Camps. Oxford. [Oxford, paper, $11.95 (0-19-502703-5)].
A convincing argument, based upon personal accounts, that survival in concentration camps required strong feelings of community and responsibility.

Fallaci, Oriana. Interview with History. Liveright. [Houghton, paper, $14.95 (0-395-25223-7)].
Through 14 interviews, a talented journalist reveals the strengths and weaknesses of the powerful.

Fincher, Jack. Human Intelligence. Putnam. [o.p.].
Compendium of recent research with special attention to the shortcomings of traditional measurement.

Fuentes, Carlos. Terra Nostra; A Novel. Farrar. [Farrar, paper, $25 (0-374-51750-9)].
A fictional fusion of history and fantasy in graceful translation. This quixotic, erotic epic is as complex and breathtaking as the Spanish culture at its core.

García Márquez, Gabriel. Autumn of the Patriarch. Harper. [Borgo, $33 (0-8095-9137-5); Harper, paper, $12 (0-06-091963-9)].
An extravagant novel of the last days of a mythic dictator who ruled 200 years, sired 5,000 children, and died in squalor.

Gardner, John Champlin. October Light. Knopf. [Random, paper, $15 (0-679-72133-9)].
Fictional evocation of the value of endurance, dramatized through human conflicts of a Vermont farm and interlocked with exerpts from a melodramatic novel.

Glasser, Ronald J. The Body Is the Hero. Random. [o.p.].
A readable explanation of the ways in which defense mechanisms of the body can organize either to protect or to work against our well-being.

Gramont, Sanche de. The Strong Brown God: The Story of the Niger River. Houghton. [o.p.].
Cultures clash and blend along the river Niger in a vivid narrative of exploration, exploitation, and survival.

Green, Martin Burgess. Children of the Sun: A Narrative of "Decadence" in England after 1918. Basic. [o.p.].

An examination of the generation who refused to follow their fathers' patterns of living and so created a brilliant new era in British life and art.

Guest, Judith. Ordinary People. Viking. [Viking, paper, $6.95 (0-14-006517-2)].
The return of a young son from a mental hospital triggers reexaminations and new awareness of family relationships. A first novel.

Gutman, Herbert George. The Black Family in Slavery and Freedom, 1750–1925. Pantheon. [Random, paper, $20 (0-374-72451-8)].
A landmark book that will bring about a reevaluation of the slave experience.

Haley, Alex. Roots: The Saga of an American Family. Doubleday, $25 (0-385-03787-2); Bantam, paper, $6.99 (0-44-017464-3).
Epic story of Haley's heritage, traced back over seven generations to a small village in West Africa.

Hall, Edward Twitchell. Beyond Culture: Into the Cultural Unconscious. Anchor. [Peter Smith, $21.50 (0-8446-6551-7); Doubleday, paper, $11 (0-385-12474-0)].
Demonstrates the dangers of applying one's own processes of thought to civilizations with other customs and languages.

Harris, Richard. Freedom Spent. Little, Brown. [o.p.].
Three case studies which show that, even in America, the legal and judicial systems will protect individual rights only if citizens remain determined and vigilant.

Howe, Irving. World of Our Fathers. Harcourt, $34.95 (0-15-146353-0); Schocken, paper, $19 (0-8052-0928-X).
A rich and varied evocation of Jewish immigrant experience at the turn of the century.

Jhabvala, Ruth Prawer. Heat and Dust. Harper. [Peter Smith, $21 (0-8446-6335-2); Simon & Schuster, paper, $11 (0-671-64657-5)].
The love affair of a contemporary English woman in India echoes a romance that occurred a half-century earlier. A novel.

Jury, Mark and **Jury, Daniel.** Gramp. Grossman/Viking. [o.p.].
One family's decision to keep a dying grandfather at home results in this unflinchingly honest photographic essay.

Keegan, John. Face of Battle. Viking. [Penguin, paper, $12.95 (0-14-004897-9)].
Three British victories over a period of 500 years are thoroughly examined in this original and brilliant work.

Kingston, Maxine Hong. The Woman Warrior: Memoirs of a Girlhood Among Ghosts. Random, $24.95 (0-394-40067-4); paper, $11 (0-679-72188-6).
A young American woman recounts memories and myths from her Chinese heritage in an effort to reconcile past and present cultures.

Kovic, Ron. Born on the Fourth of July. McGraw-Hill. [Pocket, paper, $5.50 (0-671-73914-X)].

An angry cry from the heart of a young man who went to Vietnam with youthful idealism and returned broken in body and spirit.

Lukas, J. Anthony. Nightmare: The Underside of the Nixon Years. Viking. [o.p.].
Comprehensive, documented chronology of White House machinations from 1969 through 1974.

McNeill, William Hardy. Plagues and Peoples. Anchor. [Peter Smith, $21.75 (0-8446-6492-8)].
Stimulating theories based on the interaction between civilizations and disease organisms in world history.

Price, Richard. Bloodbrothers. Houghton. [Avon, paper, $9 (0-380-77476-3)].
The summer of choice for an 18-year-old Italian American is the focus of a vivid novel that embellishes the familiar family theme with dramatic intensity.

Rukeyser, Muriel. The Gates: Poems. McGraw-Hill. [o.p.].
Select and varied poems, from political through sensual.

Sheehy, Gail. Passages: Predictable Crises of Adult Life. Dutton. [Bantam, paper, $7.50 (0-55-327106-7)].
Patterns of development common to many adult Americans.

Smedley, Agnes. Portraits of Chinese Women in Revolution. Feminist, $35 (1-55861-075-8); paper, $14.95 (0-912670-44-4).
Powerful descriptions of suffering and turmoil in the struggle for liberation. Written between 1928 and 1941.

Smith, Hedrick. The Russians. Quadrangle. [Random, $30 (0-8129-1086-9); Ballantine, paper, $6.99 (0-345-31746-7)].
Astute, eminently readable observations of Soviet lifestyles and attitudes in the early 1970s.

Spark, Muriel. The Takeover. Viking. [o.p.].
The upper classes get their comeuppance in this sparkling, witty novel.

Toland, John. Adolf Hitler. Doubleday. [Doubleday, paper, $19.95 (0-385-42053-6)].
Drawn from more than 250 interviews and available facts, including some previously unpublished. A basic work.

Trevor, William. Angels at the Ritz and Other Stories. Viking. [o.p.].
Incidents and individuals spotlighted and explored with grace, accuracy, and humanity.

Tyler, Anne. Searching for Caleb. Knopf. [Ivy, paper, $5.99 (0-8041-0883-8)].
A beautifully crafted novel in which grandfather Peck and his grandson's wife break the traditions of four stultifying generations.

Updike, John. Marry Me: A Romance. Knopf, $22.95 (0-394-40856-X); Fawcett, paper, $5.99 (0-44-920361-1).
Four married suburbanites stumble into the pitfalls of conscience and inconvenience on the rocky roads of love.

Vidal, Gore. 1876; A Novel. Random, $19.95 (0-394-49750-3); Ballantine, paper, $5.99 (0-345-34626-2).
Wickedly wise telescoping of the scandals and intrigues that marked America's presidential election in its centennial year.

Warner, William W. Beautiful Swimmers: Watermen, Crabs and the Chesapeake Bay. Little, Brown, $24.95 (0-316-92326-5); Penguin, paper, $6.95 (0-14-004405-1).
A vivid and affectionately wrought description of the Chesapeake Bay area.

White, Elwyn Brooks. Letters of E. B. White. Harper. [Harper, paper, $20 (0-06-091517-X)].
Clarity, candor, intelligence, and wit glow from the pages of what may prove to be White's autobiography.

Yates, Richard. Easter Parade: A Novel. Delacorte/Seymour Lawrence. [Random, paper, $8.95 (0-679-72230-0)].
Tragic tale of two sisters who spend a lifetime seeking the love and security they were denied in childhood.

Ygiesias, Helen. Family Feeling. Dial. [o.p.].
A strong-willed woman struggles through the tangles of Jewish family relationships in a superbly written novel.

Notable Books, 1975

Barnet, Richard J. Global Reach; The Power of the Multi-National Corporations. Simon & Schuster. [o.p.].
Illustrates the ways in which giant corporations affect both international politics and everyday lives.

Barreno, Maria Isabel; Horta, Maria Teresa; and **Da Costa, Maria Veino.**
The Three Marias: New Portuguese Letters. Doubleday. [o.p.].
Passionately personal convictions orchestrated to reveal women reaching for all aspects of humanity.

Bellow, Saul. Humboldt's Gift. Viking. [Penguin, $12.95 (0-14-007271-3)].
An exuberant picaresque novel detailing the influence of an erratic poet on the life of a middle-aged biographer questing after truth.

Berlin, Ira. Slaves without Masters: The Free Negro in the Antebellum South. Pantheon. [Norton, paper, $14.95 (1-56-584028-3)].
A wide-ranging study of the precarious world of the free black in the South.

Bickel, Alexander M. The Morality of Consent. Yale. [Yale, paper, $11 (0-300-02119-4)].
The late proponent of constitutional restraint argues that the test of a legal order is in its moral authority.

Brink, André P. Looking on Darkness. Morrow. [o.p.].
An Afrikaaner's intensely moving novel portraying one "coloured" man's unshakable will to be human in South Africa's racist society.

Brody, Alan. Coming To. Berkley. [o.p.].
A novel about contemporary marriage reveals the agony of two people who love each other but want to retain their own individuality.

Brownmiller, Susan. Against Our Will. Simon & Schuster. [Fawcett, paper, $12.50 (0-44-990820-8)].
A documentation of how rape has been used to keep women in a subordinate state, with a plea for the eradication of this exploitation.

Davidowicz, Lucy S. The War against the Jews: 1933–1945. Holt. [Bantam, paper, $15.95 (0-55-334532-X)].
Comprehensive country-by-country examination of the Nazis' planned extermination of the Jews and the response of the victims.

Doctorow, E. L. Ragtime. Random, $14.50 (0-679-60088-4); paper, $12 (0-679-73626-3).
A stylish blend of fiction and reality in which Freud, Ford, and Emma Goldman improbably trip through the America of pre–World War I.

Drabble, Margaret. The Realms of Gold. Knopf. [Ivy, paper, $5.99 (0-8041-0363-1)].
Ironic novel of an archaeologist who finds the cure for her restlessness, not in the "digs" of Africa, but in the English Midlands of her birth.

Drew, Elizabeth. Washington Journal: The Events of 1973–1974. Random. [o.p.].
Uniquely perceptive view of Watergate and what it was like to live in Washington during the crisis.

Eiseley, Loren. All the Strange Hours: Excavations of a Life. Scribner. [Peter Smith, $24.25 (0-8446-5978-9); Simon & Schuster, paper, $11 (0-684-18907-0)].
Memories of an unhappy childhood, of a vagrant youth, of animals and men—interpreted "to bespeak the autumn years."

Fleming, Thomas. 1776: Year of Illusions. Norton. [o.p.].
A lively history that renders in human terms the people, the events, and the mistakes of the American Revolution.

Frassanito, William A. Gettysburg: A Journey in Time. Scribner. [Simon & Schuster, paper, $19 (0-684-14696-7)].
A haunting photographic re-creation of the famous battleground—then and now.

Fuchs, Victor. Who Shall Live? Health, Economics and Social Choice. Basic. [o.p.].
An important statement on how limited resources will affect our future choices.

Galbraith, John Kenneth. Money: Whence It Came, Where It Went. Houghton. [Houghton, paper, $13.95 (0-395-71085-5)].
An enjoyable history of banking that debunks the myths of finance.

Gardner, Howard. The Shattered Mind: The Person after Brain Damage. Knopf. [Random, paper, $11.55 (0-394-71946-8)].
Lucid description, with case studies, of what happens to the brain and the person before, during, and after a stroke.

Gill, Brendan. Here at the New Yorker. Random. [o.p.].
A malicious, sparkling account of this unique magazine spiced with anecdotes about its famous and not-so-famous staff.

Greer, Ben. Slammer. Atheneum. [o.p.].
A powerful, shocking novel depicting the violence and tensions among men in a southern prison.

Grönoset, Dagfinn. Anna. Knopf. [o.p.].
A Norwegian farm woman emerges from harsh and brutal surroundings in a triumph of survival and dignity.

Handke, Peter. A Sorrow Beyond Dreams: A Life Story. Farrar. [o.p.].
A son's tribute to an ordinary woman whose lifelong struggle against poverty and loneliness ended in madness and suicide.

Harington, Donald. The Architecture of the Arkansas Ozarks. Little, Brown. [Harcourt, paper, $7.95 (0-15-607880-5)].
The bawdy, epic novel of a region charting the cumulative effects that dwellings, the land, and the people have on each other.

Hibbert, Christopher. The House of Medici: Its Rise and Fall. Morrow. [Morrow, paper, $13 (0-68-805339-4)].
A highly readable biography of the Florentine banking family and its impact on history.

Horgan, Paul. Lamy of Santa Fe: His Life and Times. Farrar. [Farrar, paper, $18 (0-374-51588-3)].
A leisurely, informative treatment of the remarkable and engaging first archbishop of Santa Fe.

James, D. Clayton. The Years of MacArthur: v.11, 1941–1945. Houghton. [o.p.].
A well-rounded appraisal that acknowledges the general's military genius but also vividly depicts his character flaws.

Jones, James. WWII: A Chronicle of Soldiering. Grosset. [o.p.].

Contemporary drawings and paintings of World War II enhanced by a lusty text written from the combat soldier's point of view.

Kerr, Walter. The Silent Clowns. Knopf, $20 (0-394-46907-0); Da Capo, paper, $18.95 (0-306-80387-9).
Chaplin, Keaton, Langdon, Laurel & Hardy, Lloyd—their art and genius lovingly revealed in words and pictures by a penetrating critic.

Knightley, Phillip. The First Casualty; From the Crimea to Vietnam: The War Correspondent as Hero, Propangandist, and Myth Maker. Harcourt. [Harcourt, paper, $16.95 (0-15-631130-5)].
In every war, the first victim is truth.

Lewis, R. W. B. Edith Wharton: A Biography. Harper. [Fromm, paper, $15.95 (0-8806-4020-0)].
Absorbing delineation of the character and world of the socially prominent author based on exclusive access to her manuscripts and papers.

Matthiessen, Peter. Far Tortuga: A Novel. Random. [Random, paper, $14 (0-394-75667-3)].
In rhythmic dialect, the crew of a schooner plays out a universal drama.

Mee, Charles L. Meeting at Potsdam. Evans. [Franklin Square, $14.95 (1-879957-50-7)].
A thought-provoking speculation on the personalities and motivations of the chief protagonists in the 1945 conference that set the cold war in motion.

Nance, John. The Gentle Tasaday: A Stone Age People in the Philippine Rain Forest. Harcourt. [o.p.].
An illuminating account of their introduction to a different culture.

Nash, Ogden. I Wouldn't Have Missed It: Selected Poems of Ogden Nash. Little, Brown, $29.95 (0-31-6598305).
A meticulous selection by the poet's daughters of the amazing verse of one of the wittiest commentators on the twentieth century. Introduction by Archibald MacLeish.

Owens, Bill. Our Kind of People. Straight Arrow. [o.p.].
A wry photographic look at Americans' propensities to join, organize, and socialize in prescribed patterns.

Pope-Hennessy, James. Robert Louis Stevenson. Simon & Schuster. [o.p.].
A vibrant account of the personal and literary life of a master storyteller.

Porter, Sylvia. Sylvia Porter's Money Book. Doubleday. [o.p.].
"How to earn it, spend it, save it, invest it, borrow it, and use it to better your life."

Rossner, Judith. Looking for Mr. Goodbar. Simon & Schuster. [Pocket, paper, $5.95 (0-671-73575-6)].

A young woman's frantic search for love without commitment ends in violent death. A novel.

Scott, Paul. A Division of the Spoils. Morrow. [Avon, paper, $11 (0-380-71811-1)].
The last days of British rule in India are captured in the actions and interactions of the people involved. The final volume in Scott's *Raj Quartet*.

Scully, Vincent. Pueblo/Mountain, Village, Dance. Viking. [Univ. of Chicago, $72 (0-2267-4392-6)].
A handsomely produced synthesis of architecture and cultural anthropology outlined with a profound respect for American Indian tradition.

Sewall, Richard B. The Life of Emily Dickinson. 2v. Farrar. [Harvard, paper, $22.95 (0-674-53080-2)].
The times, the people, the places, and the poetry are intricately examined in this readable scholarly biography.

Sexton, Anne. The Awful Rowing toward God. Houghton. [o.p.].
A final, compelling cry from the heart by an intensely personal poet.

Smith, Page and **Daniel, Charles.** The Chicken Book. Little, Brown. [o.p.].
Serious but highly entertaining history of mankind's backyard friend, in fact and fiction, from ancient to present times.

Smith, W. Eugene and **Smith, Aileen M.** Minamata. Holt. [Center for Creative Photography, paper, $3 (0-938262-05-X)].
Chilling words and unforgettable photographs tell of a Japanese village's fight to protect its people from chemical pollution and the horrible disease produced by it.

Theroux, Paul. The Great Railway Bazaar: By Train through Asia. Houghton. [Viking, $11.95 (0-14-024980-X); Pocket, paper, $12 (0-671-72648-X)].
More than a travel diary of geographic description—an exploding kaleidoscope of people and places.

Vonnegut, Mark. The Eden Express. Praeger. [o.p.].
A young man's account of his terifying descent into madness and his subsequent recovery.

Wain, John. Samuel Johnson. Viking. [Trans-Atlantic, paper, $27.50 (0-333-61881-5)].
Fresh, wise, and witty life of the stupendous eighteenth-century intellectual.

W. H. Auden: A Tribute. Ed. by Stephen Spender. Macmillan. [o.p.].
Thirty-six memoirs in prose and poetry from an unofficial biography in which the personality of the poet and man is vividly revealed.

Woiwode, Larry. Beyond the Bedroom Wall; A Family Album. Farrar. [Penguin, paper, $8.95 (0-14-012186-2)].

A fine sense of place and character distinguishes this novel about four generations of a North Dakota family.

Notable Books, 1974

Fiction

Adams, Richard. Watership Down. Macmillan, $40 (0-380-00293-0); Avon, paper, $12 (0380-00428-3).
Bravery, treachery, tradition, and vivid personalities enliven this tale of a group of rabbits escaping from danger.

Berry, Wendell. The Memory of Old Jack. Harcourt. [Harcourt, paper, $8.95 (0-15-658670-3)].
The testament of a simple man whose love of the land nourishes and sustains him for 92 years.

Calvino, Italo. Invisible Cities. Harcourt. [Harcourt, paper, $7.95 (0-15-645390-0)].
Fantasy and philosophy merge in a prophetic work about an empire whose cities grow from heroic dreams to gargantuan nightmares.

Godwin, Gail. The Old Women. Knopf. [Ballantine, paper, $12 (0-345-38991-3)].
A "liberated" woman breaks away from the love of a perfectionist grandmother, a domineering lover, and a demanding friend to find freedom alone.

Heller, Joseph. Something Happened. Knopf. [Bantam, paper, $6.99 (0-44-020441-0)].
The cruelty and ineffectiveness of modern personal and business relationships are mercilessly exposed in a novel of humor and despair.

Konrád, George. The Case Worker. Harcourt. [o.p.].
A social worker in Budapest tells how the unbearable and shocking lives of his clients affect his own life.

Stone, Robert. Dog Soldiers. Houghton. [Penguin, paper, $11 (0-14-009835-6)].
The moral decay resulting from U.S. involvement in Vietnam is the theme of this novel whose action follows the route of a heroin shipment.

Nonfiction

Bailyn, Bernard. The Ordeal of Thomas Hutchinson. Harvard. [Harvard, paper, $16.50 (0-674-64161-2)].
A sympathetic picture of the much villified Loyalist governor of Massachusetts at the time of the American Revolution.

Bedford, Sybille. Aldous Huxley: A Biography. Knopf. [Trans-Atlantic, paper, $44 (0-333-58509-7)].
The English novelist and intimate friend of the Huxley family brilliantly brings alive the life and times of a "wholly civilized man."

Berger, Raoul. Executive Privilege: A Constitutional Myth. Harvard, $38 (0-674-27425-3).
The existence of executive privilege as invoked by the U.S. presidents is strongly denied in this perceptive and thoroughly researched analysis.

Bernstein, Carl and **Woodward, Bob.** All the President's Men. Simon & Schuster. [Buccaneer, $29.95 (1-56849-568-4); Simon & Schuster, paper, $12 (0-671-89441-2)].
Two young *Washington Post* reporters' suspenseful account of their investigation of the Watergate scandal.

Bronowski, Jacob. The Ascent of Man. Little, Brown. [Little, Brown, paper, $29.95 (0-316-10933-9)].
A stunningly illustrated study of man's biological uniqueness, his mysterious origins, and his imaginative steps toward understanding what he is.

Caro, Robert A. The Power Broker: Robert Moses and the Fall of New York. Random, $45.50 (0-394-48076-7); paper, $24 (0-394-72024-5).
A strong indictment of a nonelected official who controlled New York's public works for almost 40 years.

Dillard, Annie. Pilgrim at Tinker Creek. Harper's Magazine. [Harper, paper, $13 (0-06-091545-5)].
Sensitive journal of a year's observations of the beauty and violence of nature.

Genovese, Eugene D. Roll, Jordan, Roll: The World the Slaves Made. Pantheon. [Random, paper, $17 (0-394-71652-3)].
Penetrating reassessment of the paternalistic culture in the antebellum South.

Hawke, David Freeman. Paine. Harper. [Norton, paper, $14.95 (0-393-30919-3)].
Candid, knowledgeable biography of the incredibly diverse, brilliant propagandist and revolutionary idealist.

Heyen, William. Noise in the Trees: Poems and a Memoir. Vanguard. [o.p.].
Lyrics in precise language and a memoir in crisp prose by a young, original talent who has a deep reverence for the natural world.

Lacey, Robert. Sir Walter Raleigh. Atheneum. [o.p.].
An authentic Elizabethan—poet, adventurer, failed politician—is portrayed in this smoothly paced biography.

Miller, Merle. Plain Speaking: An Oral Biography of Harry S. Truman. Berkley. [Berkley, paper, $6.99 (0-425-09499-5)].
Conversations with HST that expertly re-create his impudent, refreshing personality and character.

Moorhouse, Geoffrey. The Fearful Void. Lippincott. [o.p.].
A journey through the desert reveals as much of the writer's inner landscape as it does of the Sahara.

Morison, Samuel Eliot. The European Discovery of America: The Southern Voyages, A. D. 1492–1616. Oxford, $39.95 (0-19-501832-0); paper, $19.95 (0-19-508272-9).
This sweeping narrative recaptures in sparkling prose the adventures of Columbus, Magellan, Drake, and other explorers of their time.

Nilsson, Lennart. Behold Man: A Photographic Journey of Discovery Inside the Body. Little, Brown, $29.95 (0-316-60751-7).
Human physiology enhanced with extraordinary photographs that show minute portions of the body magnified up to 20,000 times.

Pirsig, Robert M. Zen and the Art of Motorcycle Maintenance: An Inquiry into Valves. Morrow, $22.95 (0-68-800230-7); paper, $12.95 (0-68-805230-4).
The twilight world of mental illness is explored in this real-life odyssey of the author and his son.

Rather, Dan and **Gates, Gary Paul.** The Palace Guard. Harper. [o.p.].
Two television newsmen study Nixon's White House staff from early dedication, through growth of power, to Watergate.

Rosengarten, Theodore. All God's Dangers: The Life of Nate Shaw. Knopf. [Random, paper, $14 (0-679-72761-2)].
A remarkable oral history of a black sharecropper whose spirit remained unbroken through a long and difficult life.

Scott, Rachel. Muscle and Blood. Dutton. [o.p.].
A devastating documentary of the hidden horror of industrial slaughter in America caused by new technologies extracting dollars at the expense of the worker.

Secrest, Meryle. Between Me and Life: A Biography of Romaine Brooks. Doubleday. [o.p.].
The triumphant story of an American woman who overcame a dark Victorian childhood and the social restrictions of her time to become an artist of distinction.

Terkel, Studs. Working: People Talk about What They Do All Day and How They Feel about What They Do. Pantheon. [Ballantine, paper, $6.95 (0-345-32569-9)].
Alive with humor and honesty, these interviews reveal much of the psychology behind the American work ethic.

Thomas, Lewis. The Lives of a Cell; Notes of a Biology Watcher. Viking. [Penguin, paper, $10.95 (0-14-004743-3)].
Humanistic essays that speculate on the implications of modern microbiology.

Weintraub, Stanley. Whistler: A Biography. Weybright & Talley. [o.p.].

A revealing portrait of an outrageous Victorian whose contributions to art were ironically overshadowed by his contentious character.

Notable Books, 1973

Bell, Daniel. The Coming of Post-Industrial Society. Basic. [Basic, paper, $18 (0-465-09713-8)].
A provocative description of the social structure's transformation to postindustrial society, with a forecast for the future.

Bly, Robert. Sleepers Joining Hands. Harper. [Harper, paper, $10 (0-06-090785-1)].
Strong, visionary poems exploring the contemporary American consciousness.

Bohlen, Charles E. Witness to History, 1929–1969. Norton. [o.p.].
A penetrating and personal appraisal of an epic period in American history, by the late U.S. career diplomat.

Böll, Heinrich. Group Portrait with Lady. McGraw-Hill. [Avon, paper, $4.95 (0-380-00020-2)].
In this novel, the fate of a young woman living in Nazi Germany is seen through sardonic vignettes of people around her.

Boorstin, Daniel J. The Americans: The Democratic Experience. Random, $39.95 (0-394-48724-9); paper, $16 (0-394-71011-8).
Mosaic of events and personalities that shaped people's lives from the Civil War to now.

Botting, Douglas. Humboldt and the Cosmos. Harper. [o.p.].
The life and work of the nineteenth-century German scientist and explorer in a format that is a credit to fine bookmaking.

Bracegirdle, Brian. The Archaeology of the Industrial Revolution. Dickinson Univ. [o.p.].
A full-color pictorial survey, with appropriate text, of the remains of Britain's Industrial Revolution.

Bruce, Robert V. Bell: Alexander Graham Bell and the Conquest of Solitude. Little, Brown. [Cornell Univ., $47.50 (0-8014-2419-4); paper, $17.95 (0-8104-9691-8)].
The remarkable life of a giant of American technology—his inventions and work with teaching the deaf.

Carlson, Joel. No Neutral Ground. Crowell. [o.p.].
After 20 years defending black clients against an unjust legal system, a white South African lawyer realizes his efforts helped maintain the status quo.

Carrighar, Sally. Home to the Wilderness. Houghton. [o.p.].

A memoir of the tortured childhood of the esteemed naturalist and her struggle to heal its scars in later life.

Clive, John. Macaulay: The Shaping of the Historian. Knopf. [Harvard, paper, $18.50 (0-6745-4005-0)].
A meticulous biography providing insight into pre-Victorian social and political thought and action.

Cowley, Malcolm. A Second Flowering: Works and Days of the Lost Generation. Viking. [o.p.].
Perceptive recollections and evaluations of American literary greats the author has personally known.

Curtain, Sharon R. Nobody Ever Died of Old Age. Atlantic/Little, Brown. [o.p.].
A young writer's brash and angry report on the problems of aging in a youth-oriented society.

Davis, Kenneth S. FDR: The Beckoning of Destiny, 1882–1928. Putnam. [Random, paper, $15 (0-679-74879-2)].
Intertwining strands of patrician tradition and twentieth-century political, economic, and social forces that formed President Roosevelt's complex, mercurial character.

Fraser, Antonia. Cromwell, the Lord Protector. Knopf. [Donald Fine, paper, $17.95 (0-9176-5790-X)].
A biography of epic scope that sheds new light on the personality of the English soldier-statesman.

Goldman, Peter. The Death and Life of Malcolm X. Harper. [Univ. of Illinois, paper, $12.95 (0-2520-0774-3)].
The black revolutionary's last years—the impact of his life and the evolution of his ideology.

Hass, Robert. Field Guide. Yale. [Yale, paper, $10 (0-3000-1651-4)].
Anecdotal, earthy lyrics by a sensitive and informed young poet.

Hellman, Lillian. Pentimento: A Book of Portraits. Little, Brown. [NAL, paper, $3.95 (0-451-14089-3)].
The past shows through in these sketches of people and events that illuminate the author's character.

Hodgins, Eric. Trolley to the Moon. Simon & Schuster. [o.p.].
Vitality and sorrow surge through the memories of a writer's early years.

Hughes, Emmet John. The Living Presidency. Coward. [o.p.].
Keen scholarship and deft style characterize this timely analysis of leadership and of the ways in which the U.S. presidency has been defined by the men who have filled the office.

Jhabvala, Ruth Prawer. Travelers. Harper. [o.p.].
A sensitive novel in which the characters weave a tapestry of life in modern India.

Johannsen, Robert W. Stephen A. Douglas. Oxford. [o.p.].
A full-scale biography of the nineteenth-century paradoxical politician.

Kazin, Alfred. Bright Book of Life. Atlantic/Little, Brown. [o.p.].
A vibrant critique of American novels and novelists since World War II.

La Grange, Henri-Louis. Mahler. Doubleday. [o.p.].
The monumental first volume of the life and world of the composer-conductor up to his marriage with Alma Schindler.

Lynes, Russell. Good Old Modern: An Intimate Portrait of the Museum of Modern Art. Atheneum. [o.p.].
How a tradition-shattering idea to give contemporary art a showplace affected the tastes of a generation and changed museums everywhere.

MacKenzie, Norman and **MacKenzie, Jeanne.** H. G. Wells. Simon & Schuster. [o.p.].
The life and times of the great early-twentieth-century novelist, science-fiction writer, and science popularizer.

McGuane, Thomas. Ninety-two in the Shade. Farrar. [Penguin, paper, $10 (0-14-009907-7)].
A novel, set in today's Key West, of the fierce competition between two men in a violent world.

Mitford, Jessica. Kind and Usual Punishment: The Prison Business. Knopf. [o.p.].
A sweeping indictment of the American prison system, analyzing its brutality and failure to rehabilitate.

Moore, Brian. Catholics. Holt. [o.p.].
A novel of conflict between faith and tradition within the church.

Murdoch, Iris. The Black Prince. Viking. [Penguin, paper, $15 (0-14-003934-1)].
A complex, multilevel novel of the varieties of love that hound the narrator, an unsuccessful novelist in his sixties.

Nicholson, Nigel. Portrait of a Marriage. Atheneum. [Simon & Schuster, paper, $12.95 (0-689-70597-2)].
A son's narrative of his famous parents' unusual yet successful marriage provides a framework for his mother's diary.

Patai, Raphael. The Arab Mind. Scribner. [Simon & Schuster, paper, $16.95 (0-684-17810-9)].
Dispassionate explication of a culture, a people, and a way of life.

Perrett, Geoffrey. Days of Sadness, Years of Triumph: The American People, 1939–1945. Coward. [Univ. of Wisconsin, paper, $17.50 (0-2991-0394-3)].
Changes wrought in the U.S. during World War II are characterized as a social revolution.

The Poetry of Black America: An Anthology of the 20th Century. Ed. by Arnold Adoff. Harper, $25 (0-06-020089-8).
A comprehensive collection of black poetry, strong on rhythm and rhetoric, that includes critical essays.

Pogue, Forrest C. George C. Marshall: Organizer of Victory, 1943–45. Viking. [o.p.].
Two eventful years of momentous actions and decisions are recorded in this third volume of Marshall's biography.

Puig, Manuel. Heartbreak Tango; A Serial. Dutton. [Penguin, paper, $8.95 (0-14-100661-8)].
The oppressive realities of Argentine small-town life revealed in a novelistic montage of film images and parodies of popular romantic writing.

Pynchon, Thomas. Gravity's Rainbow. Viking. [Penguin, paper, $15 (0-14-010661-8)].
A wildly inventive novel, continually exploding and scattering brilliant observations on the absurdities of our times.

Rabe, David. The Basic Training of Pavlo Hummel and Sticks and Bones. Viking. [o.p.].
Two powerful plays that examine the effects of the Vietnam War on the soldier in the field and and on the returned veteran.

Ruesch, Hans. Back to the Top of the World. Scribner. [o.p.].
The simple and stylized lives of polar Eskimos are effectively depicted in this novel of survival.

Russell, Ross. Bird Lives! The High Life and Hard Times of Charlie (Yardbird) Parker. Charterhouse. [Da Capo, paper, $15.95 (0-306-80679-7)].
A vivid re-creation of the notable jazz alto-saxophonist who led a major movement in American music.

Schaller, George B. Golden Shadows, Flying Hooves. Knopf. [Univ. of Chicago, paper, $20.50 (0-2267-3650-4)].
The facinating report of three years of observing Tanzania's great predators in their individual and group behavior.

Schlesinger, Arthur M. Jr. The Imperial Presidency. Houghton. [Houghton, paper, $12.95 (0-395-51561-0)].
A history of the gradual take-over by the presidency of the constitutional powers originally reserved for Congress.

Schwarz-Bart, Andre. A Woman Named Solitude. Atheneum. [o.p.].

A novel about the strange and melancholy mulatto slave who became the catalyst for the black insurrection on eighteenth-century Guadeloupe.

Sheaffer, Louis. O'Neill, Son and Artist. Little, Brown. [AMS, $75 (0-4042-0322-1)].
This second panel in a brilliant biographical study shows how the playwright transmuted private history and secret anguish into art.

Truman, Margaret. Harry S. Truman. Morrow. [Avon, paper, $12.50 (0-3807-2112-0)].
A daughter's intimate, affectionate biography of her famous father.

Van Der Zee, Henri and **Van Der Zee, Barbara.** William and Mary. Knopf. [o.p.].
The lives and colorful background of the rulers who influenced both English and Dutch history.

Van Duyn, Mona. Merciful Disguises, Published and Unpublished Poems. Atheneum. [Simon $ Schuster, paper, $9.95 (0-689-11294-7)].
Skillfully fashioned poems about the implications of loving people, places, and things, written with a lively sense of humor.

Vidal, Gore. Burr. Random. [Ballantine, paper, $5.95 (0-345-33921-5)].
A witty, urbane novel that gives a fresh interpretation of the enigmatic Aaron Burr and his contemporaries.

Wilson, Lanford. The Hot L Baltimore. Hill & Wang. [Farrar, paper, $9.95 (0-374-52165-4)].
A play of nostalgia and humor in which a hotel facing the bulldozer and its inhabitants facing eviction symbolize the lost values and disappearing hopes and dreams of American civilization.

Notable Books, 1972

Alvarez, Alfred. The Savage God; A Study of Suicide. Random. [Norton, paper, $8.95 (0-393-30657-7)].
A lucid interpretation of self-destruction, focusing on the creative personality.

Ammons, A. R. Collected Poems: 1951–1971. Norton. [o.p.].
Intensely personal poems by a meticulous craftsman.

Barry, Joseph Amber. Passions and Politics: A Biography of Versailles. Doubleday. [o.p.].
The royal palace serves as the framework for this study of prerevolutionary France.

Barthelme, Donald. Sadness (Novel). Farrar. [o.p.].

Short stories examining life at middle age with great wit and tenderness.

Beauvoir, Simone de. The Coming of Age. Putnam. [Norton, paper, $14 (0-393-31443-X)].
An indictment on society's indifference toward the aged.

Bell, Quentin. Virigina Woolf; A Biography. Harcourt. [Harcourt, paper, $18 (0-15-693580-5)].
The forces that shaped a complex woman form the core of her nephew's incisive interpretation.

Berteaut, Simone. Piaf: A Biography. Harper. [o.p.].
The famous French singer's life frankly told by her half-sister.

Brecher, Edward M and the editors of Consumer Reports. Licit and Illicit Drugs. Little, Brown. [Little, Brown, paper, $14.95 (0-316-10717-4)].
The Consumers Union report on narcotics, stimulants, depressants, inhalants, hallucinogens, and marijuana—including caffeine, nicotine, and alcohol.

Broder, David S. The Party's Over: The Failure of Politics in America. Harper. [o.p.].
The political parties: what killed them as effective forces and how they can be reborn.

Brooks, Paul. The House of Life: Rachel Carson at Work. Houghton. [Houghton, paper, $9.95 (0-39-551742-7)].
Achievements of a pioneer conservationist, illustrated with selections from her published and unpublished writings.

Brower, Brock. The Late Great Creature (Novel). Atheneum. [o.p.].
The world of horror movies is the background for this hilarious but chilling novel.

Calder, Nigel. The Restless Earth: A Report on the New Geology. Viking. [o.p.].
A revolutionary theory explaining earthquakes and volcanic activity, with vivid illustrations.

Caudill, Harry M. My Land Is Dying. Dutton. [o.p.].
A powerful condemnation of strip mining and its effects on people and their environment.

The Children of Pride: A True Story of Georgia and the Civil War. Ed. by Robert Manson Myers. Yale. [Yale, paper, $20 (0-300-04053-9)].
Letters of a plantation family are creatively edited to provide a vivid picture of a time, a place, and a people.

Coke, Van Deren. The Painter and the Photograph: From Delacroix to Warhol. Univ. of New Mexico. [o.p.].
An eye-opening demonstration of the reliance of many artists on the photograph as a source of information.

Coles, Robert. Children of Crisis: v.2, Migrants, Sharecroppers, Mountaineers; v.3, The South Goes North. Atlantic/Little, Brown. [Little, Brown, paper, v.2, $24.95 (0-31-615176-9); v.3, $19.95 (0-31-615177-7)].
A monumental study of the many voices of America's poor.

Douglas, Paul H. In the Fullness of Time: The Memoirs of Paul H. Douglas. Harcourt. [o.p.].
The full life and times of the former senator whose career was devoted to public service.

Edel, Leon. Henry James, The Master: 1901–1916. Lippincott. [o.p.].
Concludes the masterful study of James, the artist, and James, the man.

FitzGerald, Frances. Fire in the Lake: The Vietnamese and the Americans in Vietnam. Atlantic/Little, Brown. [Random, paper, $14 (0-679-72394-3)].
A young correspondent's fresh explanation of war rising out of cultures of conflict.

Friedman, Bernard Harper. Jackson Pollock: Energy Made Visible. McGraw-Hill. [o.p.].
The tragic life and wide-ranging influence of the foremost abstract expressionist.

Gaines, Charles. Stay Hungry. Doubleday. [o.p.].
Strong fictional treatment of the exaggerated male ego.

Gardner, John Champlin. The Sunlight Dialogues (Novel). Knopf. [Random, paper, $12 (0-394-74394-6)].
A novel that is a world-sized view of the complexities of small-town American life.

Halberstam, David. The Best and the Brightest. Random. [Random, $30 (0-679-41062-7); Fawcett, paper, $15 (0-449-90870-4)].
A reassessment of the men who shaped the events leading to the involvement of the U.S. in Southeast Asia.

Holmes, Charles Shiveley. The Clocks of Columbus: The Literary Career of James Thurber. Atheneum. [o.p.].
The wild and wonderful world of the man with a "warm heart and an angry mind."

Jackson, Barbara Ward and **Dubos, Rene Jules.** Only One Earth: The Care and Maintenance of a Small Planet. Norton. [o.p.].
The social, economic, and political dimensions of the world ecology crisis.

Jencks, Christopher. Inequality: A Reassessment of the Effect of Family and Schooling in America. Basic. [o.p.].
Claims improved education brings frustration, not success, to America's poor.

Kennan, George Frost. Memoirs, v.2., 1950–1963. Atlantic/Little, Brown. [Pantheon, paper, $15.95 (0-394-71626-4)].

The cold war period when Kennan's career shifted between scholar-historian and ambassador.

Lash, Joseph P. Eleanor: The Years Alone. Norton. [Norton, $14.95 (0-393-07361-0)].
The emergence of an exceptional woman as a world citizen.

Lenz, Siegfried. The German Lesson (Novel). Hill & Wang. [Norton, paper, $15.95 (0-8112-0982-2)].
A novel of confrontation between the creative artist's need for freedom and Nazi Germany's insistence on blind obedience.

McCullough, David G. The Great Bridge. Simon & Schuster. [Simon & Schuster, paper, $16 (0-671-45711-X)].
The Brooklyn Bridge—an engineering feat that symbolized the aspirations of its age.

Miller, Jason. That Championship Season. Atheneum. [Dramatists Play Service, paper, $5.25 (0-8222-1126-2)].
An explosive reunion of four former teammates and their coach dramatizes American values and personal failures.

Moorhouse, Geoffrey. Calcutta. Harcourt. [o.p.].
Extremes of Indian life in the world's fourth largest city.

Peirce, Neal R. The Megastates of America; People, Politics, and Power in the Ten Great States. Norton. [o.p.].
The impact of the areas where more than half the population live.

Rogers, Thomas. The Confession of a Child of the Century by Samuel Heather (Novel). Simon & Schuster. [Ultramarine, $25 (0-671-21266-4)].
Rogers' anti-hero struggles with the generation gap, war, and defection in a funny novel about the 1950s.

Singer, Isaac Bashevis. Enemies, A Love Story (Novel). Farrar. [Farrar, paper, $11 (0-374-51522-0)].
Tragicomic novel about a man's entanglement with three wives.

Solzhenitsyn, Alexander Isaevich. August 1914 (Novel). Farrar. [Farrar, paper, $19.95 (0-374-51999-4)].
The opening days of World War I provide the setting for this epic novel on the breakdown of the old order of Russia.

Stansky, Peter and **Abrahams, William Miller.** The Unknown Orwell. Knopf. [Stanford Univ., paper, $17.95 (0-8047-2342-7)].
A study of the elusive Eric Blair, who at age 30 transformed himself into George Orwell.

Storm, Hyemeyohsts. Seven Arrows (Novel). Harper. [Ballantine, paper, $18 (0-345-32901-5)].

A Plains Indian evokes the spirit of his people in this beautifully illustrated work.

Terrill, Ross. 800,000,000: The Real China. Atlantic/Little, Brown. [o.p.].
An informed reporter's impressions and interviews provide insight into a reopening country.

Turnbull, Colin M. The Mountain People. Simon & Schuster. [Simon & Schuster, paper, $12 (0-671-64098-4)].
Social disintegration of an African tribe, with appalling implications for modern civilization.

Welty, Eudora. The Optimist's Daughter (Novel). Random, $16 (0-394-55587-2); paper, $9 (0-679-72883-X).
A gentle novel that delves into the past to produce acceptance and understanding of the present.

Wills, Garry. Bare Ruined Choirs: Doubt, Prophecy, and Radical Religion. Doubleday. [o.p.].
Provocative personal insights into the roots, confusion, and strengths of contemporary American Catholicism.

Woodham-Smith, Cecil Blanche FitzGerald. Queen Victoria: From her Birth to the Death of the Prince Consort. Knopf. [Donald Fine, paper, $9.95 (0-917657-95-1)].
New material illuminates the life of the girl and the young queen.

Notable Books, 1971

Amado, Jorge. Tent of Miracles (Novel). Knopf. [Avon, paper, $10 (0-38-075472-X)].
An exuberant, vital novel of Brazilian life.

Blunt, Wilfrid. The Compleat Naturalist: A Life of Linnaeus. Viking. [o.p.].
Lavishly illustrated biography of the great eighteenth-century Swedish botanist.

Brown, Charles H. William Cullen Bryant. Scribner. [o.p.].
Authoritative biography of the poet-politician and his America.

Brown, Dee Alexander. Bury My Heart at Wounded Knee; An Indian History of the American West. Holt, $27.50 (0-8050-1045-9); paper, $14.95 (0-8050-1730-5).

Clark, Ronald William. Einstein: The Life and Times. World. [Random, $19.99 (0-517-14718-1); Avon, paper, $15 (0-38-072148-1)].
A warm and human portrait of the man and his contemporaries.

Cornelisen, Ann. Vendetta of Silence (Novel). Atlantic/Little, Brown. [o.p.].

A novel of an American woman's life within the subtle stratifications of a southern Italian town.

Doctorow, E. L. The Book of Daniel: A Novel. Random, $8.95 (0-394-60501-2); paper, $11 (0-679-73657-3).
Re-creates the atmosphere of hysteria of the Rosenberg era.

Elon, Amos. The Israelis: Founders and Sons. Holt. [Penguin, paper, $11.95 (0-14-0169695)].
Contrasts the founders of Israel and their far less idealistic offspring.

Flanner (Genet), Janet. Paris Journal, v.2, 1965–1971. Atheneum. [o.p.].
An expatriate's elegant recording of culture and politics in de Gaulle's Paris.

Gaines, Ernest J. The Autobiography of Miss Jane Pittman. Dial. [Bantam, paper, $4.99 (0-55-326357-9)].
A novel of a hundred-year-old black woman's life, told with dignity and pride.

Gardner, John Champlin. Grendel (Novel). Knopf, $15.95 (0-394-47143-1); paper, $8 (0-679-72311-0).
A taut, gripping novel retells the Beowulf legend from the monster's viewpoint.

Garrett, George. Death of the Fox (Novel). Doubleday. [Harcourt, paper, $14.95 (0-15-625233-3)].
A fictional life of Walter Raleigh, abundant in historical detail and speculation.

Glasser, Ronald J. 365 Days. Braziller. [o.p.].
A unique and compassionate view of medics in Vietnam.

Greer, Germaine. The Female Eunuch. McGraw-Hill. [o.p.].
A witty, well-balanced view of women's liberation.

Grunberger, Richard. The 12-Year Reich. Holt. [Da Capo, paper, $17.95 (0-306-80660-6)].
A devastating picture of Hitler worship in all aspects of German social life.

Hart, Sir Basil Henry Liddell. History of the Second World War. Putnam. [o.p.].
Succinct history of a war the author thought was "unnecessary."

Houston, James A. The White Dawn; An Eskimo Saga (Novel). Harcourt. [Harcourt, paper, $8 (0-15-696256-X)].
A stark novel of the white man's corrosive effects on the Eskimo's primitive life.

Hughes, Ted. Crow: From the Life and Songs of the Crow. Harper. [o.p.].
Evocations of fear and suffering expressed in elemental rhythms.

Illich, Ivan D. Deschooling Society. Harper. [o.p.].
A revolutionary thesis proposed the education of youth outside formal schooling.

Landolfi, Tommaso. Cancerqueen and Other Stories. Dial. [o.p.].
Tales of the unusual and fantastic by a unique talent.

Lartigue, Jacques-Henri. Diary of a Century. Studio-Viking. [o.p.].
A hilarious look at life through the diary and lens of a French photographer.

Lash, Joseph P. Eleanor and Franklin. Norton. [NAL, paper, $5.95 (0-451-14076-1)].
The childhood, marriage, and growth of a remarkable woman.

Lawick-Goodall, Baroness Jane van. In the Shadow of Man. Houghton.
[Houghton, paper, $14.94 (0-395-33145-5)].
Study of the startlingly manlike social relationships among wild chimpanzees.

Maxwell, Neville George Anthony. India's China War. Pantheon. [o.p.].
A timely interpretation of the much-misunderstood border war of 1962.

McHale, Tom. Farragan's Retreat (Novel). Viking. [o.p.].
A jarringly funny novel of Irish Catholics in Philadelphia.

McPhee, John A. Encounters with the Archdruid. Farrar, $19.95 (0-374-14822-8); paper, $9 (0-374-51431-3).
One man's battle to save the country's remaining natural areas.

Meyer, Michael Leverson. Ibsen; A Biography. Doubleday. [o.p.].
Definitive examination of the towering dramatist and his plays.

Morison, Samuel Eliot. The European Discovery of America; The Northern Voyages; A. D. 500–1600. Oxford, $39.95 (0-19-501377-8); paper, v.1, $19.95 (0-19-508271-0); v.2, $19.95 (0-19-508272-9).
Accounts of the early adventurer-explorers recorded with zest, humor, and scholarship.

Morris, Wright. Fire Sermon (Novel). Harper. [Univ. of Nebraska, paper, $9.95 (0-8032-8104-8)].
Story of the transfer and conflict of generations told with simplicity and artistry.

Navasky, Victor S. Kennedy Justice. Atheneum. [o.p.].
The inner workings of Robert Kennedy's Justice Department in its settings of personalities and politics.

New York Times. The Pentagon Papers. Bantam. [McGraw-Hill, paper, $10.90 (0-07-028380-X)].
Previously secret documents on our involvement in Vietnam with far-reaching political and social effects.

Ouologuem, Yambo. Bound to Violence (Novel). Harcourt. [Heineman, paper, $9.95 (0-435-90099-4)].
Imaginative history of Black Africa in poetic prose.

Panter-Downes, Mollie. London War Notes, 1939–1945. Farrar. [o.p.].
Acute observations of the English homefront.

Percy, Walker. Love in the Ruins (Novel). Farrar, $27.95 (0-374-19302-9); Ivy, paper, $5.99 (0-8041-0378-X).
A disturbing, satirical novel of America in the 1980s.

Piro, Richard. Black Fiddler. Morrow. [o.p.].
A black school's production of *Fiddler on the Roof* encourages racial understanding.

Piven, Frances Fox and **Cloward, Richard A.** Regulating the Poor: The Functions of Public Welfare. Pantheon. [Random, $12 (0-679-74516-5)].
A harrowing account of of public assistance as a tool for political gain.

Plath, Sylvia. Crossing the Waters; Transitional Poems. Harper. [Borgo, $25 (0-8095-9058-1); Harper, paper, $9 (0-06-090789-4)].
Dark visions of the human condition in sharp, incisive poems.

Puig, Manuel. Betrayed by Rita Hayworth (Novel). Dutton. [Norton, paper, $11 (0-393-31384-0)].
A comic novel of Argentine family life complicated by the Hollywood idiom.

Sajer, Guy. The Forgotten Soldier. Harper. [Buccaneer, $34.95 (0-89966-843-7); Brassey's, paper, $16.95 (0-0803-7437-9)].
Acid-etched prose on the hell of carnage, noise, and insanity of war.

Skinner, Burrhus Frederic. Beyond Freedom and Dignity. Knopf. [o.p.].
Controversial approach to the place of individual freedom in society.

Thomas, Hugh. Cuba: The Pursuit of Freedom. Harper. [o.p.].
An assessment of Cuban history culminating with Castro and the revolution.

Tuchman, Barbara (Wertheim). Stilwell and the American Experience in China, 1911–1945. Macmillan, $60 (0-02-620290-5); Buccaneer, $34.95 (1-56849-604-4).
Perceptive analysis of the times and the man.

Wilson, Edmund. Upstate: Records and Recollections of Northern New York. Farrar. [Syracuse Univ., paper, $15.95 (0-8156-2499-9)].
An old family house evokes bittersweet memories of a literary life.

Wright, James. Collected Poems. Wesleyan. [Univ. Press of New England, $30 (0-8195-4031-5); paper, $16.95 (0-8195-6022-7)].
Superb translations and compassionate original verse.

Zindel, Paul. The Effect of Gamma Rays on Man-in-the-Moon Marigolds. Harper, $18 (0-06-026829-8); Bantam, paper, $5.50 (0-55-328028-7).
A funny, tough-minded play about a young girl's struggle for identity.

Notable Books, 1970

Angelou, Maya. I Know Why the Caged Bird Sings. Random, $23 (0-394-42986-9); Bantam, paper, $4.99 (0-55-327937-8).
A courageous young black woman's candid memoir of a life of love and anguish.

Arlen, Michael J. Exiles. Farrar. [o.p.].
A son's loving memoir of his mother and his author-father evokes the fabled era of the 1920s.

Barthelme, Donald. City Life (Novel). Farrar. [o.p.].
A striking collection of short stories in which the nature of art, literature, and modern life is considered with stylistic virtuosity.

Bellow, Saul. Mr. Sammler's Planet (Novel). Viking. [Penguin, paper, $11.95 (0-14-018936-X)].
Aging Arthur Sammler, having survived the Nazis' efforts to exterminate him, drifts through New York's West Side, scrutinizing the rotten fabric of modern society.

Bowen, Catherine Drinker. Family Portrait. Little, Brown. [o.p.].
An unusually candid view of a great biographer's own large and talented family, absorbing in the richness of its personalities.

Buechner, Thomas S. Norman Rockwell, Artist and Illustrator. Abrams. [o.p.].
A comprehensive and lavish collection of the artist's work and a critical exposition of his developing style and portrayal of his view of American life.

Burns, James MacGregor. Roosevelt: The Soldier of Freedom. Harcourt. [o.p.].
An awesome body of political and military knowledge is marshaled into a provocative analysis of Roosevelt in World War II.

Clark, Ramsey. Crime in America: Observations on Its Nature, Causes, Prevention and Control. Simon & Schuster. [o.p.].
A former attorney general gives his personal view of one of America's most pressing problems and explores the conflict inherent in the current program of crime prevention and control.

Daniels, Jonathan. Ordeal of Ambition; Jefferson, Hamilton, Burr. Doubleday. [o.p.].
The clash of three towering personalities shapes the destiny of a new nation.

Dickey, James. Deliverance (Novel). Houghton. [Dell, paper, $10.95 (0-385-31387-X)].
The character and endurance of four men are put to the test in a harrowing adventure; the first novel of a distinguished poet.

Didion, Joan. Play It as It Lays (Novel). Farrar. [Farrar, paper, $9 (0-374-52171-9)].

This dispassionate novel leanly etches the quiet desperation of a woman of our times.

García Márquez, Gabriel. One Hundred Years of Solitude (Novel). HarperCollins, $30 (0-06-11418-5); paper, $13 (0-06-091965-5).
A novel about a prolific family living in isolated splendor in a remote Colombian village, told in language as lush as its setting.

Gaylin, Willard. In the Service of Their Country: War Resisters in Prison. Viking. [o.p.].
A disturbing and revealing study of the effect of imprisonment on selective service violators who chose jail rather than deferment or exile.

Hersh, Seymour M. My Lai 4: A Report on the Massacre and Its Aftermath. Random. [o.p.].
Agonizing questions about responsibility and the brutalizing effects of war are raised by a Pulitzer Prize–winning reporter in this shocking account of an alleged massacre by American troops in Vietnam.

Huxtable, Ada Louise. Will They Ever Finish Bruckner Boulevard? Macmillan. [Univ. of California, paper, $14 (0-5200-6205-1)].
A witty, often devastating look at urban blight and architectural change in our cities.

Jackson, Jonathan George. Soledad Brother: The Prison Letters of George Jackson. Coward-McCann. [Lawrence Hill, paper, $14.95 (1-5565-2230-4)].
Impassioned and embittered letters testify to the condition of being black and in prison.

Mandel'shtam, Nadezhda. Hope against Hope: A Memoir. Atheneum. [Macmillan, paper, $13.95 (0-689-70530-1)].
An authentic and moving account of Stalin's purge of Russian intellectuals, one of whom was the author's husband, the poet Osip Mandelstam.

Martin, Malachi. The Encounter. Farrar. [o.p.].
Christianity, Judaism, and Islam: the forces that made these religions great and their changing roles in the world today.

Mehta, Ved Parkash. Portrait of India. Farrar. [Yale, paper, $20 (0-300-05538-2)].
The complexity of present-day India is interpreted against the background of the country's turbulent past.

Meriwether, Louise. Daddy Was a Numbers Runner (Novel). Prentice-Hall. [Feminist, paper, $10.95 (0-935312-57-9)].
A talented black novelist portrays the vitality, poverty, and tenderness of a young girl's life in the mean streets of Harlem during the 1930s.

Mitford, Nancy. Zelda: A Biography. Harper. [HarperCollins, paper, $15 (0-06-091069-0)].

A romantic, painful study of Zelda and F. Scott Fitzgerald and their mad pursuit of the elusive American dream.

Millett, Kate. Sexual Politics. Doubleday. [Simon & Schuster, paper, $12 (0-67-170740-X)].
A spirited dissection of the male-dominated literature of the classic and intellectual history of the power struggle between man and woman.

Ostrow, Joanna. In the Highlands since Time Immemorial (Novel). Knopf. [o.p.].
A memorable first novel that captures the mood and landscape of a harsh way of life soon to disappear.

Silberman, Charles E. Crisis in the Classroom: The Remaking of American Education. Random. [o.p.].
An exhaustive survey and condemnation of the state of American education, with concrete suggestions for reform.

Speer, Albert. Inside the Third Reich: Memoirs. Macmillan. [Buccaneer, $45.95 (1-56849-337-1); Macmillan, paper, $16 (0-02-037500-X]
This assessment of unlimited power allied with modern technology, written by Hitler's minister of war, has frightening implications for our society.

Steegmuller, Francis. Cocteau: A Biography. Little, Brown. [David Godine, paper, $17.95 (0-8792-3606-X)].
A genius of the arts and a unique personality is brilliantly portrayed against a rich canvas of creative activity.

Terkel, Studs. Hard Times: An Oral History of the Great Depression. Pantheon. [Random, paper, $13 (0-394-74691-0)].
A mosaic of reactions to the wounding experience of the grim 1930s.

Welty, Eudora. Losing Battles (Novel). Random. [Random, paper, $12 (0-679-72882-1)].
The human foibles of three generations of a rural southern family are revealed in a rich and loving story of a birthday reunion.

West, Paul. Words for a Deaf Daughter. Harper. [Dalkey Archive, paper, $12.95 (1-56478-036-8)].
A poet attempts to enter his daughter's silent world. A compassionate and joyful book.

Wiesel, Eliezer. A Beggar in Jerusalem (Novel). Random. [Schocken, paper, $14 (0-8052-0897-6)].
Israel's Six-Day War provides the framework for a probing philosophical novel about the Jewish experience.

Notable Books of the 1960s

Notable Books, 1969

Acheson, Dean Gooderham. Present at the Creation: My Years in the State Department. Norton, $29.95 (0-393-07448-X); paper, $16.95 (0-393-30412-4).

Adamson, J. H. and **Folland, H. F.** The Shepherd of the Ocean: An Account of Sir Walter Raleigh and His Times. Gambit. [o.p.].

Bettelheim, Bruno. The Children of the Dream. Macmillan. [o.p.].

Blythe, Ronald. Akenfield: Portrait of an English Village. Pantheon. [Random, paper, $10 (0-394-73847-0)].

Dubos, René Jules. So Human an Animal. Scribner. [o.p.].

Duncan, David Douglas. Self-Portrait: U.S.A. Abrams. [o.p.].

Eide, Ingvard. American Odyssey: The Journey of Lewis and Clark. Rand McNally. [o.p.].

Eiseley, Loren C. The Unexpected Universe. Harcourt. [Harcourt, paper, $9.95 (0-15-692850-7)].

Erikson, Erik Homburger. Gandhi's Truth: On the Origins of Militant Nonviolence. Norton. [Peter Smith, $21.30 (0-8446-6743-9); Norton, paper, $11.95 (0-393-31034-5)].

Fowles, John. The French Lieutenant's Woman (Novel). Little, Brown, $29.95 (0-316-29099-8); NAL, paper, $5.99 (0-451-16375-3).

Fraser, Antonia. Mary, Queen of Scots. Delacorte. [Bantam, paper, $16.95 (0-385-31129-X)].

Gerzon, Mark. The Whole World Is Watching: A Young Man Looks at Youth's Dissent. Viking. [o.p.].

Hannum, Alberta Pierson. Look Back with Love: A Recollection of the Blue Ridge. Vanguard. [o.p.].

Hellman, Lillian. An Unfinished Woman: A Memoir. [In *Three: An Unfinished Woman, Pentimento, Scoundrel Time*]. Little, Brown, $19.95 (0-316-35514-3).

Hoopes, Donelson F. Winslow Homer Watercolors. Watson-Guptill. [Watson-Guptill, paper, $16.95 (0-8230-2326-5)].

Howarth, David Armine. Trafalgar: The Nelson Touch. Atheneum. [o.p.].

Hurlbut, Cornelius Searle. Minerals and Man. Random. [o.p.].

Ibuse, Masuji. Black Rain (Novel). Kodansha. [Kodansha, paper, $9.95 (0-3741-2716-6)].

Jarrell, Randall. The Complete Poems. Farrar, $45 (0-374-12716-6); paper, $14.95 (0374-51305-8).

Kendrick, Alexander. Prime Time: The Life of Edward R. Murrow. Little, Brown [o.p.].

Luke, Peter. Hadrian VII. Knopf. [o.p.].

Matthiessen, Peter. Sal Si Puedes: Cesar Chavez and the New American Revolution. Random. [o.p.].

McHarg, Ian L. Design with Nature. Natural History. [Wiley, $45 (0-471-55797-8); Natural History, paper, $15.95 (0-385-05509-9)].

Moorehead, Alan. Darwin and the Beagle. Harper [o.p.].

Murdoch, Iris. Bruno's Dream (Novel). Viking. [Penguin, paper, $10.95 (0-14-003176 6)]

Nabokov, Vladimir Vladimirovich. Ada; or, Ardor: A Family Chronicle (Novel). McGraw-Hill. [Random, paper, $16 (0-679-72522-9)].

Oates, Joyce Carol. Them (Novel). Vanguard. [Fawcett, paper, $5.95 (0-44-920692-0)].

Roth, Philip. Portnoy's Complaint (Novel). Random. [Random, paper, $11 (0-679-75645-0)].

Rudofsky, Bernard. Streets for People: A Primer for Americans. Doubleday. [o.p.].

Salisbury, Harrison Evans. The 900 Days; The Siege of Leningrad. Harper. [Da Capo, paper, $16.95 (0-3068-0253-8)].

Scheffer, Victor B. The Year of the Whale. Scribner. [Lyons & Burford, paper, $16.95 (1-55821-448-8)].

Sexton, Anne. Love Poems. Houghton. [Houghton, paper, $11.95 (0-39-551760-5)].

Talese, Gay. The Kingdom and the Power. World. [Ivy, paper, $5.99 (0-8041-1057-3)].

Vesaas, Tarjei. The Birds (Novel). Morrow. [Dufour, paper, $24 (0-7206-0701-9)].

Vonnegut, Kurt. Slaughterhouse Five; or, The Children's Crusade (Novel). Delacorte, $22.50 (0-385-31208-3).

Woiwode, L. What I'm Going to Do, I Think (Novel). Farrar. [o.p.].

Notable Books, 1968

Barzun, Jacques. The American University: How It Runs, Where It is Going. Harper. [Univ. of Chicago, paper, $15.95 (0-22-603845-9)].

Beagle, Peter S. The Last Unicorn (Novel). Viking. [NAL, paper, $9.95 (0-451-45052-3)].

Berryman, John. His Toy, His Dream, His Rest: 308 Dream Songs. Farrar. [o.p.].

Bowen, Elizabeth. Eva Trout; or, Changing Scenes (Novel). Knopf. [Peter Smith, $19 (0-8446-6709-9); Penguin, paper, $10.95 (0-14-018298-5)].

Brooks, Gwendolyn. In the Mecca; Poems. Harper. [o.p.].

Cartier-Bresson, Henri. The World of Henri Cartier Bresson. Viking. [o.p.].

Cleaver, Eldridge. Soul on Ice. McGraw-Hill. [Bantam, paper, $6.50 (0-44-021128-X)].

Collins, Larry and **Lapierre, Dominique.** Or I'll Dress You in Mourning. Simon & Schuster. [o.p.].

Flexner, James Thomas. George Washington in the American Revolution, 1775–1783. Little, Brown, $35 (0-31-628595-1).

Gary, Romain. The Dance of Genghis Cohn (Novel). World. [o.p.].

Gibson, William. A Mass for the Dead. Atheneum. [Akadine, $29.95 (1-888173-01-7)].

Greenberg, Daniel S. The Politics of Pure Science. New American Library. [o.p.].

Grier, William H. and **Cobbs, Price M.** Black Rage. Basic. [HarperCollins, paper, $13 (0-46-500701-5)].

Holroyd, Michael. Lytton Strachey; A Critical Biography. Holt. [Farrar, $35 (0-374-19439-4); paper, $19 (0-374-52465-3)].

Holt, John Caldwell. How Children Learn. Pitman. [Addison-Wesley, paper, $11 (0-201-48404-8)].

Jensen, Oliver Ormerod and others. American Album. American Heritage; dist. by Simon & Schuster. [Houghton Mifflin, paper, $19.95 (0-685-42995-4)].

Kohl, Herbert R. 36 Children. New American Library. [NAL, paper, $10.95 (0-452-26463-4)].

Krock, Arthur. Memoirs: Sixty Years on the Firing Line. Funk & Wagnalls. [o.p.].

Lacouture, Jean. Ho Chi Minh: A Political Biography. Random. [o.p.].

Lifton, Robert Jay. Death in Life: Survivors of Hiroshima. Random. [Univ. of North Carolina, paper, $19.95 (0-8078-4344-X)].

McAlmon, Robert and **Boyle, Kay.** Being Geniuses Together, 1920–1930. Doubleday. [Farrar, paper, $13.50 (0-865-47149-5)].

Mailer, Norman. The Armies of the Night: History as a Novel, the Novel as History. New American Library. [NAL, paper, $11.95 (0-452-27279-3)].

Malraux, André. Anti-Memoirs. Holt. [o.p.].

Menninger, Karl Augustus. The Crime of Punishment. Viking. [o.p.].

Meryman, Richard. Andrew Wyeth. Houghton. [Abrams, $19.95 (0-8109-3956-8)].

Michener, James Albert. Iberia: Spanish Travels and Reflections. Random, $29.95 (0-394-42982-6); Fawcett, paper, $6.95 (044-920733-1).

Mydans, Carl and **Mydans, Shelley Smith.** The Violent Peace. Atheneum. [o.p.].

Nourissier, Francois. The French. Knopf. [o.p.].

Orwell, George. Collected Essays, Journalism and Letters. 4v. Harcourt. [o.p.].

Pepper, Curtis Bill. An Artist and the Pope: Based upon the Personal Recollections of Giacomo Manzu. Grossett. [o.p.].

Pritchett, V. S. A Cab at the Door. Random, $16 (0-679-60103-1).

Report by the U.S. National Advisory Commission on Civil Disorders. U.S. Govt. Print. Office. [o.p.].

Rosten, Leo Calvin. The Joys of Yiddish; A Relaxed Lexicon. McGraw-Hill. [Pocket, paper, $5.99 (0-671-72813-X)].

Sarton, May. Plant Dreaming Deep. Norton. [Peter Smith, $19.30 (0-8446-6094-9)]; Norton, paper, $5.95 (0-393-30108-7)].

Scarisbrick, J. J. Henry VIII. Univ. of California. [Univ. of California, paper, $14 (0-5200-1130-9)].

Seager, Allan. The Glass House: The Life of Theodore Roethke. McGraw-Hill. [Univ. of Michigan, $42.50 (0-472-09454-8); paper, $14.95 (0-472-06454-1)].

Servan-Schreiber, J. J. The American Challenge. Atheneum. [o.p.].

Solzhenitsyn, Aleksandr Isaevich. The First Circle (Novel). Harper, $10. [o.p.].

Taylor, Gordon Rattray. The Biological Time Bomb. World. [o.p.].

Troyat, Henri. Tolstoy. Doubleday. [o.p.].

Warner, Sylvia Townsend. T. H. White: A Biography. Viking. [o.p.].

Watson, James D. The Double Helix; A Personal Account of the Discovery of the Structure of DNA. Atheneum. [Macmillan, paper, $11.95 (0-689-70602-2); Norton, paper, $9.95 (0-393-95075-1)].

Westheimer, David. Song of the Young Sentry (Novel). Little, Brown. [o.p.].

Wolfe, Tom. The Electric Kool-Aid Acid Test. Farrar. [Bantam, paper, $6.50 (0-55-326491-5)].

Notable Books, 1967

Amado, Jorge. Shepherds of the Night (Novel). Knopf. [Avon, paper, $7.95 (0-380-75471-1)].

Amosov, Nikolai Mikhailovich. The Open Heart. Simon & Schuster. [o.p.].

Arciniegas, Germáu. Latin America: A Cultural History. Knopf. [o.p.].

Auden, Wystan Hugh. Collected Shorter Poems, 1927–1957. Random. [o.p.].

Barnes, Hazel Estella. An Existentialist Ethics. Knopf. [Univ. of Chicago, paper, $19.95 (0-22-603729-0)].

Becker, Stephen D. The Outcasts (Novel). Atheneum. [o.p.].

Bernstein, Jeremy. A Comprehensible World: On Modern Science and Its Origins. Random. [o.p.].

Bulgakov, Mikhail Afans'evich. The Master and Margarita (Novel). Harper. [Random, paper, $17 (0-679-41046-5)].

Carawan, Candie and **Carawan, Guy.** Ain't You Got a Right to the Tree of Life? The People of St. John's Island, South Carolina, Their Faces, Their Words, and Their Songs. Simon & Schuster. [Univ. of Georgia, $34.95 (0-8203-1132-4); paper, $19.95 (0-8203-1643-1)].

Ciardi, John. The Strangest Everything (Novel). Rutgers. [o.p.].

Cole, Ernest and **Flaherty, Thomas.** House of Bondage. Random. [o.p.].

Coles, Robert. Children of Crisis; A Study of Courage and Fear. Little, Brown. [o.p.].

Conot, Robert E. Rivers of Blood, Years of Darkness. Bantam. [o.p.].

Dickey, James. Poems, 1957–1967. Wesleyan Univ. [Univ. Press of New England, paper, $15.95 (0-8195-6055-3)].

Friendly, Fred W. Due to Circumstances beyond Our Control. Random. [o.p.].

Fulbright, James William. The Arrogance of Power. Random. [o.p.].

Galbraith, John Kenneth. The New Industrial State. Houghton. [NAL, paper, $4.95 (0-451-62440-8)].

Gold, Herbert. Fathers; A Novel in the Form of a Memoir. Random. [Penguin, paper, $12.95 (1-556-11314-5)].

Golding, William Gerald. The Pyramid (Novel). Harcourt. [Harcourt, paper, $3.95 (0-15-674703-0)].

Halle, Louis Joseph. The Cold War as History. Harper. [HarperCollins, paper, $12.95 (0-06-096888-5)].

Hartog, Jan de. The Captain (Novel). Atheneum. [Nautical & Aviation, $24.95 (0-933852-83-5)].

Hilsman, Roger. To Move a Nation: The Politics of Foreign Policy in the Administration of John F. Kennedy. Doubleday. [o.p.].

Johnson, Ronald. The Book of the Green Man (Poetry). Norton. [o.p.].

Kavanaugh, James J. A Modern Priest Looks at His Outdated Church. Trident. [Steven J. Nash, paper, $13.95 (1-87899-516-2)].

Kennan, George Frost. Memoirs, 1925–1950. Little, Brown. [Pantheon, paper, $18 (0-395-71624-8)].

Kerr, Walter. Tragedy and Comedy. Simon & Schuster. [Da Capo, paper, $9.95 (0-306-80249-X)].

Kozol, Jonathan. Death at an Early Age: The Destruction of the Hearts and Minds of Negro Children in the Boston Public Schools. Houghton. [NAL, paper, $11.95 (0-452-26292-5)].

Kuznetsov, Anatolii Petrovich. Babi Yar: A Documentary Novel. Dial. [o.p.].

Lowell, Robert. Near the Ocean (Poems). Farrar. [o.p.].

Massie, Robert K. Nicholas and Alexandra. Atheneum. [Simon & Schuster, $35 (0-689-10177-5); Bantam, paper, $7.99 (0-44-036358-6)].

Moore, Marianne. Complete Poems. Viking-Macmillan. [Buccaneer, $39.95 (1-56849-631-1); Penguin, paper, $12.95 (0-14-018851-7)].

Morison, Samuel Eliot. "Old Bruin": Commodore Matthew Perry, 1794–1858. Little, Brown. [o.p.].

Morris, Willie. North toward Home. Houghton. [Yoknapatawpha, paper, $14.95 (0-916-24216-1)].

Mumford, Lewis. The Myth of the Machine: Technics and Human Development. Harcourt. [o.p.].

Nabokov, Vladimir Vladimirovich. Speak, Memory: An Autobiography Revisited. Putnam. [Random, paper, $13 (0-679-72339-0)].

Neruda, Pablo. The Heights of Macchu Picchu (Poem). Farrar. [Farrar, paper, $10 (0-374-50648-5)].

Nicolson, Sir Harold. Diaries and Letters. v2., The War Years, 1939–1945. Atheneum. [o.p.].

Pinter, Harold. The Homecoming (Play). Grove. [Grove, paper, $7.95 (0-802-15105-1)].

Point, Nicolas. Wilderness Kingdom, Indian Life in the Rocky Mountains: 1840–1847; The Journals & Paintings of Nicolas Point. Holt. [o.p.].

Potok, Chaim. The Chosen: A Novel. Simon & Schuster. [Random, $30 (0-679-40222-5); Fawcett, paper, $5.95 (0-449-21344-7)].

Pritchett, Victor Sawdon. Dublin, A Portrait. Harper. [o.p.].

Reston, James Barrett. The Artillery of the Press; Its Influence on American Foreign Policy. Harper. [Books on Demand, $36.50 (0-8357-9150-5)].

Rheims, Maurice. The Flowering of Art Nouveau. Abrams. [o.p.].

Russell, Bertrand. Autobiography, 1872–1914. Little, Brown. [Routledge, paper, $16.95 (0-04-921022-X)].

Sachs, Nelly. O the Chimneys: Selected Poems, Including the Verse Play, Eli. Farrar. [o.p.].

Sack, John. M. New American Library. [Avon, paper, $5.99 (0-380-69866-8)].

Schell, Jonathan. The Village of Ben Suc. Knopf. [o.p.].

Schulberg, Budd, ed. From the Ashes: Voices of Watts. New American Library. [o.p.].

Shachtman, Max and others. As We Saw the Thirties: Essays on Social and Political Movements of a Decade. Univ. of Illinois. [Books on Demand, paper, $74.40 (0-7837-8088-5)].

Sichel, Pierre. Modigliani: A Biography of Amedeo Modigliani. Dutton. [o.p.].

Snow, Charles Percy. Variety of Men. Scribner. [o.p.].

Steel, Ronald. Pax Americana. Viking. [o.p.].

Stegner, Wallace Earle. All the Little Live Things (Novel). Viking. [Penguin, paper, $11.95 (0-14-015441-8).

Stoppard, Tom. Rosencrantz and Guildenstern are Dead (Play). Grove. [Grove, paper, $8.95 (0-8021-3275-8)].

Styron, William. The Confessions of Nat Turner (Novel). Random, $15.50 (0-685-70622-2).

Terkel, Studs. Division Street: America. Pantheon. [Peter Smith, $22.30 (0-8446-6741-2); New Press, paper, $12.95 (1-56584-075-5)].

Thomas, Piri. Down These Mean Streets. Knopf. [Random, paper, $11 (0-679-73238-1)].

Tillich, Paul. My Search for Absolutes. Simon & Schuster. [o.p.].

U.S. President's Commission on Law Enforcement. The Challenge of Crime in a Free Society. U.S. Govt. Print Office. [o.p.].

Weinberg, Alvin Martin. Reflections on Big Science. M.I.T. [Franklin, $81 (0-08-012545-X)].

Westin, Alan F. Privacy and Freedom. Atheneum. [o.p.].

Wilder, Thornton Niven. The Eighth Day (Novel). Harper [Amereon, $24.95 (0-8488-0669-7); Carroll & Graf, paper, $4.95 (0-8818-4339-3)].

Wilson, Angus. No Laughing Matter (Novel). Viking. [o.p.].

Woolf, Leonard Sidney. Downhill All the Way: An Autobiography of the Years 1919–1939. Harcourt. [Peter Smith, $20.05 (0-8446-6516-9); Harcourt, paper, $8.95 (0-15-626145-6)].

Yoors, Jan. The Gypsies. Simon & Schuster. [Waveland, paper, $10.95 (0-8813-3305-0)].

Notable Books, 1966

Albee, Edward. A Delicate Balance: A Play. Atheneum. [o.p.].

Aleichem, Sholom, (pseud. of Shalom Rabinowitz). Old Country Tales (Stories). Putnam. [o.p.].

Altizer, Thomas J. J. and **Hamilton, William.** Radical Theology and the Death of God. Bobbs-Merrill. [o.p.].

Anderson, Margaret. Children of the South. Farrar. [o.p.].

Ardrey, Robert. The Territorial Imperative: A Personal Inquiry into the Animal Origins of Property and Nations. Atheneum. [o.p.].

Ashton-Warner, Sylvia. Greenstone (Novel). Simon & Schuster. [o.p.].

Barth, John. Giles Goat-Boy; or, The Revised New Syllabus (Novel). Doubleday. [Bantam, paper, $15.95 (0-38-524086-4)].

Beadle, George Wells and **Beadle, Muriel.** The Language of Life: An Introduction to the Science of Genetics. Doubleday. [o.p.].

Beam, Philip C. Winslow Homer at Prout's Neck. Little, Brown. [o.p.].

Billington, James H. The Icon and the Axe: An Interpretive History of Russian Culture. Knopf. [Peter Smith, $26.55 (0-8446-6754-4); Random, paper, $20 (0-394-70846-6)].

Bird, Caroline. The Invisible Scar. McKay. [o.p.].

Bowen, Catherine Drinker. Miracle at Philadelphia: The Story of the Constitutional Convention, May to September 1787. Little, Brown. [Dercum, $49.95 (1-556-56060-5); Little, Brown, paper, $13.95 (0-316-10398-5)].

Carr, Donald Eton. Death of the Sweet Waters. Norton, $6.95 (0-393-06354-2).

Cirici, Aljandro Pellicer. Treasures of Spain from Charles V to Goya. Skira-World. [o.p.].

Colette, Sidonie Gabrielle. Earthly Paradise: An Autobiography. Farrar. [o.p.].

Cowley, Malcolm and **Faulkner, William.** The Faulkner-Cowley File: Letters and Memories, 1944–1962. Viking. [o.p.].

Crichton, Richard. The Secret of Santa Vittoria: A Novel. Simon & Schuster. [Buccaneer, $21.95 (1-56849-149-2); Carroll & Graf, paper, $3.95 (0-8818-4267-2)].

Danielsson, Bengt. Gauguin in the South Seas. Doubleday. [o.p.].

Eisenstaedt, Alfred. Witness to Our Time. Studio-Viking. [o.p.].

Fletcher, Joseph Francis. Situation Ethics: The New Morality. Westminster. [Westminster, paper, $12.99 (0-6642-4691-5)].

Glaze, Andrew. Damned Ugly Children: Poems. Trident. [o.p.].

Godden, Jon and **Godden, Rumer.** Two under the Indian Sun. Knopf & Viking. [Transaction, $15.95 (1-8505-9076-5)].

Graves, Robert. Collected Poems, 1966. Doubleday, Anchor. [o.p.].

The Guaranteed Income: Next Step in Economic Evolution? Ed. by Robert Theobald. Doubleday. [o.p.].

Hall, Donald. Henry Moore: The Life and Work of a Great Sculptor. Harper. [o.p.].

Hall, Edward Twitchell. The Hidden Dimension. Doubleday. [Peter Smith, $20 (0-8446-6552-5); Bantam, paper, $9.95 (0-385-08476-5)].

Hazzard, Shirley. The Evening of the Holiday (Novel). Knopf. [Penguin, paper, $6.95 (0-14-010451-8)].

Heilbroner, Robert L. The Limits of American Capitalism. Harper. [o.p.].

Hotchner, A. E. Papa Hemingway: A Personal Memoir. Random. [o.p.].

The Hours of Catherine of Cleves. Braziller. [o.p.].

Kaplan, Justin. Mr. Clemens and Mark Twain. Simon & Schuster. [Simon & Schuster, paper, $15 (0-671-74807-6)].

Lancaster, Richard. Piegan: A Look from within at the Life, Times, and Legacy of an American Indian Tribe. Doubleday. [o.p.].

Lekachman, Robert. The Age of Keynes. Random. [o.p.].

Lewis, Oscar. La Vida: A Puerto Rican Family in the Culture of Poverty–San Juan and New York. Random. [o.p.].

Lindsay, Jack. J. M. W. Turner: His Life and Work; A Critical Biography. New York Graphic Society. [o.p.].

Lloyd, Alan. The Making of the King, 1066. Holt. [Marboro, $19.95 (0-88029-473-6)].

Lorenz, Konrad. On Agression. Harcourt. [Harcourt, paper, $9.95 (0-15-668741-0)].

Luce, Gay Gaer and **Segal, Julius.** Sleep. Coward-McCann. [o.p.].

Malamud, Bernard. The Fixer (Novel). Farrar. [Penguin, paper, $9.95 (0-14-018515-1)].

Maurois, André. Prometheus: The Life of Balzac. Harper. [Carroll & Graf, paper, $11.95 (0-8818-4023-8)].

Mitford, Nancy. The Sun King. Harper. [Viking, paper, $19.95 (0-14-023967-7)].

Moore, Marianne. Tell Me, Tell Me; Granite, Steel, and Other Topics (Poems). Viking. [o.p.].

Nader, Ralph. Unsafe at Any Speed: The Designed-In Dangers of the American Automobile. Grossman. [o.p.].

Ogburn, Charlton. The Winter Beach. Morrow. [Parnassus, paper, $7.95 (0-688-07785-4)].

Oldenbourg, Zoé. The Crusades. Pantheon. [o.p.].

Parks, Gordon. A Choice of Weapons. Harper. [Minnesota Historical Society, paper, $10.95 (0-87351-202-2)].

Plath, Sylvia. Ariel (Poems). Harper. [Harper, paper, $10 (0-06-090890-4)].

Rexroth, Kenneth. An Autobiographical Novel. Doubleday. [Norton, paper, $14.95 (0-8112-1179-7)].

Roethke, Theodore. Collected Poems. Doubleday. [Doubleday, paper, $12.95 (0-385-08601-6)].

Sandoz, Mari. The Battle of the Little Bighorn. Lippincott. [Amereon, $18.95 (0-8919-0879-X); Univ. of Nebraska, paper, $7.95 (0-8032-9100-0)].

Scott, Paul. The Jewel in the Crown: A Novel. Morrow. [Avon, paper, $11 (0-380-71808-1)].

Singer, Isaac Bashevis. In My Father's Court. Farrar. [Farrar, paper, $12 (0-374-50592-6)].

Sontag, Susan. Against Interpretation and Other Essays. Farrar. [Bantam, paper, $9.95 (0-385-26708-8)].

Tillich, Paul. The Future of Religions. Harper. [Greenwood, $45 (0-8371-8861-X)].

Toland, John. The Last 100 Days. Random. [Bantam, paper, $6.95 (0-55-328640-4)].

Traven, B. The Night Visitor and Other Stories. Hill & Wang. [Ivan Dee, paper, $10.95 (1-5666-3039-8)].

Tuchman, Barbara (Wertheim). The Proud Tower: A Portrait of the World Before the War, 1890–1914. Macmillan, $60 (0-02-620300-6).

Warren, Robert Penn. Selected Poems, New and Old, 1923–1966. [o.p.].

West, Rebecca (pseud.). The Birds Fall Down (Novel). Viking. [o.p.].

Yadin, Yigael. Masada; Herod's Fortress and the Zealots' Last Stand. Random, $29.95 (0-394-43542-7).

Notable Books, 1965

Adler, Mortimer Jerome. The Conditions of the Philosophy: Its Checkered Past, Its Present Disorder, and Its Future Promise. Atheneum. [o.p.].

Ammons, A. R. Corson's Inlet: A Book of Poems. Cornell. [o.p.].

Bassani, Giorgio. The Garden of the Finzi-Continis (Novel). Atheneum. [Harcourt, paper, $7.95 (0-15-634570-6)].

Bell, Millicent. Edith Wharton & Henry James: The Story of Their Friendship. Braziller. [o.p.].

Bishop, Elizabeth. Question of Travel (Poems). Farrar. [o.p.].

Böll, Heinrich. The Clown (Novel). McGraw-Hill. [Penguin, $10.95 (0-14-018726-X)].

Borgstrom, Georg. The Hungry Planet: The Modern World at the Edge of Famine. Macmillan. [o.p.].

Brown, Claude. Manchild in the Promised Land. Macmillan, $40 (0-02-517320-0); NAL, paper, $4.95 (0-451-15741-9).

Buechner, Frederick. The Final Beast (Novel). Atheneum. [o.p.].

Clark, Kenneth Bancroft. Dark Ghetto: Dilemmas of Social Power. Harper. [Univ. Press of New England, paper, $16.95 (0-81956-226-2)].

Fussell, Edwin S. Frontier: American Literature and the American West. Princeton. [o.p.].

Grass, Günter. Dog Years. Harcourt. [Harcourt, paper, $12.95 (0-15-626112-X)].

Harding, Walter Roy. The Days of Henry Thoreau. Knopf. [Princeton, paper, $17.95 (0-69-102479-0)].

Harrington, Michael. The Accidental Century. Macmillan. [o.p.].

Hawkins, Gerald S. Stonehenge Decoded. Doubleday. [o.p.].

Jarrell, Randall. The Lost World (Poems). Macmillan. [o.p.].

Joannes, Pope XXIII. Journal of a Soul. McGraw-Hill. [o.p.].

Josephy, Alvin M. The Nez Perce Indians and the Opening of the Northwest. Yale. [Univ. of Nebraska, $35 (0-8032-2555-5); paper, $16.95 (0-8032-7551-X)].

Kael, Pauline. I Lost It at the Movies. Little, Brown. [Marion Boyars, paper, $18.95 (0-7145-2975-3)].

Kazantzakis, Nikos. Report to Greco. Simon & Schuster. [Simon & Schuster, paper, $12.95 (0-671-22027-6)].

Kazin, Alfred. Starting Out in the Thirties. Little, Brown. [Cornell Univ., paper, $9.95 (0-8014-9562-8)].

Lamont, Lansing. Days of Trinity. Atheneum. [o.p.].

Landowska, Wanda. Landowska on Music. Stein & Day. [Reprint Services, $59 (0-685-14898-X)].

Lapp, Ralph Eugene. The New Priesthood: The Scientific Elite and the Uses of Power. Harper. [o.p.].

Letters from Mississippi. Ed. by Elizabeth Sutherland. McGraw-Hill. [o.p.].

Lind, Jakow. Soul of Wood, & Other Stories. Grove. [o.p.].

Matthiessen, Peter. At Play in the Fields of the Lord (Novel). Random. [Peter Smith, $23.25 (0-8446-6636-X); Random, paper, $12 (0-679-73741-3)].

Moore, Brian. The Emperor of Ice-Cream (Novel). Viking. [o.p.].

Morris, Donald R. The Washing of the Spears: A History of the Rise of the Zulu Nation under Shaka and Its Fall in the Zulu War of 1879. Simon & Schuster. [Simon & Schuster, paper, $16.95 (0-671-62822-4)].

Morris, Richard Brandon. The Peacemakers: The Great Powers and American Independence. Harper. [o.p.].

Mydans, Shelley Smith. Thomas: A Novel of the Life, Passion, and Miracles of Becket. Doubleday. [o.p.].

Myrdal, Jan. Report from a Chinese Village. Pantheon. [o.p.].

O'Connor, Flannery. Everything That Rises Must Converge (Stories). Farrar. [Farrar, paper, $11 (0-374-50464-4)].

Paton, Alan. South African Tragedy: The Life and Times of Jan Hofmeyr. Scribner. [o.p.].

Roethke, Theodore. On the Poet and His Craft: Selected Prose. Univ. of Washington. [o.p.].

Roy, Jules. The Battle of Dienbienphu. Harper. [Carroll & Graf, paper, $10.95 (0-88184-034-3)].

Rudofsky, Bernard. The Kimono Mind: An Informal Guide to Japan and the Japanese. Doubleday. [o.p.].

Schlesinger, Arthur Meier. A Thousand Days: John F. Kennedy in the White House. Houghton. [Fawcett, paper, $6.95 (0-449-30021-8)].

Shaplen, Robert. The Lost Revolution: The Story of Twenty Years of Neglected Opportunities in Vietnam and of America's Failure to Foster Democracy There. Harper. [o.p.].

Sharp, Alan. A Green Tree in Gedde (Novel). New American Library. [o.p.].

Simpson, Louis Aston Marantz. Selected Poems. Harcourt. [o.p.].

Sorenson, Theodore C. Kennedy. Harper. [o.p.].

Stern, Richard G. Stitch (Novel). Harper. [o.p.].

Swanberg, W. A. Dreiser. Scribner. [o.p.].

Teale, Edwin Way. Wandering through Winter: A Naturalist's Record of a 20,000-Mile Journey through the North American Winter. Dodd. [St. Martin's, paper, $12.95 (0-312-04458-5)].

Tolson, Melvin Beaunorus. Harlem Gallery: Book 1, The Curator. Twayne. [o.p.].

Tomkins, Calvin. The Bride & the Bachelors: The Heretical Courtship in Modern Art. Viking. [Viking, paper, $11 (0-14-004313-6)].

Warren, Robert Penn. Who Speaks for the Negro? Random. [o.p.].

Weller, Jack. Yesterday's People: Life in Contemporary Appalachia. Univ. of Kentucky. [Univ. of Kentucky, paper, $8 (0-8131-0109-3)].

Weltfish, Gene. The Lost Universe, with a Closing Chapter on the Universe Regained. Basic. [Univ. of Nebraska, paper, $16.95 (0-8032-5871-2)].

Wiesner, Jerome Bert. Where Science and Politics Meet. McGraw-Hill. [o.p.].

Notable Books, 1964

Bardach, John E. Downstream: A Natural History of the River. Harper. [o.p.].

Barrett, William. What Is Existentialism? Grove. [o.p.].

Barzini, Luigi Giorgio. The Italians. Atheneum. [Peter Smith, $23.25 (0-8446-6146-5); Macmillan, paper, $13 (0-689-70540-9)].

Barzun, Jacques. Science: The Glorious Entertainment. Harper. [o.p.].

Bellow, Saul. Herzog (Novel). Viking. [Penguin, paper, $11 (0-14-007270-5)].

Berelson, Bernard and **Steiner, George Albert.** Human Behavior: An Inventory of Scientific Findings. Harcourt. [o.p.].

Brustein, Robert Sanford. The Theatre of Revolt: An Approach to the Modern Drama. Little, Brown. [Ivan Dee, paper, $13.95 (0-9295-8753-7)].

Capa, Robert. Images of War. Grossman. [o.p.].

Cichy, Bodo. The Great Ages of Architecture: From Ancient Greece to the Present Day. Putnam. [o.p.].

Clark, Eleanor. The Oysters of Locmariaquer. Pantheon. [Harper, paper, $10 (0-06-097488-5)].

Conant, James Bryant. Shaping Educational Policy. McGraw-Hill. [o.p.].

Ernst, Morris Leopold and **Schwartz, Alan U.** Censorship: The Search for the Obscene. Macmillan. [o.p.].

Farrell, Michael. Thy Years Might Cease (Novel). Knopf. [o.p.].

Fischer, Louis. The Life of Lenin. Harper. [o.p.].

Frost, Robert. Selected Letters. Holt. [o.p.].

Galbraith, John Kenneth. The Scotch. Houghton. [o.p.].

Gardner, John William. Self-Renewal: The Individual and the Innovative Society. Harper. [Norton, paper, $9.95 (0-393-30112-5)].

Giedion, Sigfried. The Eternal Present: v.2, The Beginnings of Architecture; A Contribution on Constancy and Change. Pantheon. [o.p.].

Gilot, François and **Lake, Carlton.** Life with Picasso. McGraw-Hill. [Doubleday, paper, $8.95 (0-385-26186-1)].

Gregory, Horace. Collected Poems. Holt. [o.p.].

Gruen, Victor. The Heart of Our Cities; The Urban Crisis: Diagnosis and Cure. Simon & Schuster. [o.p.].

Hamilton, Edith. The Ever-Present Past. Norton. [o.p.].

Hammarskjöld, Dag. Markings. Knopf. [Random, $23 (0-394-43532-X; Bantam, paper, $5.99 (0-34-532741-1)].

Handlin, Oscar. Fire-Bell in the Night: The Crisis in Civil Rights. Little, Brown. [o.p.].

Hartog, Jan de. The Hospital. Atheneum. [o.p.].

Hemingway, Ernest. A Moveable Feast. Scribner. [Macmillan, $35 (0-68-417340-9); paper, $5.95 (0-02-051960-5)].

Hochhuth, Rolf. The Deputy (Drama). Grove. [o.p.].

Hodgins, Eric. Episode: Report on the Accident inside My Skull. Atheneum. [o.p.].

Idyll, Clarence P. Abyss, the Deep Sea and the Creatures That Live in It. Crowell. [o.p.].

Jones, Howard Mumford. O Strange New World; American Culture: The Formative Years. Viking. [Greenwood, $52.50 (0-313-23494-4)].

Koestler, Arthur. The Act of Creation. Macmillan. [Penguin, paper, $12.95 (0-14-019191-7)].

Laurence, Margaret. The Stone Angel (Novel). Knopf. [Univ. of Chicago, paper, $10.95 (0-2264-6936-0)].

Laxalt, Robert. A Man in the Wheatfield (Novel). Harper. [Univ. of Nevada, $17.95 (0-8741-7130-X)].

Lewis, Anthony. Gideon's Trumpet. Random. [Random, paper, $10 (0-679-72312-9)].

Lowell, Robert. For the Union Dead (Poems). Farrar. [o.p.].

McGrady, Pat. The Savage Cell: A Report on Cancer and Cancer Research. Basic. [o.p.].

Meyer, Franz. Marc Chagall. Abrams. [o.p.].

New York Times. The Kennedy Years. Viking. [o.p.].

Overstreet, Harry Allen and **Overstreet, Bonaro Wilkinson.** The Strange Tactics of Extremism. Norton. [Norton, $5.95 (0-393-05268-0)].

Roethke, Theodore. The Far Field (Poems). Doubleday. [o.p.].

Sartre, Jean Paul. The Words. Braziller. [Random, paper, $10 (0-394-74709-7)].

Schaller, George B. The Year of the Gorilla. Univ. of Chicago. [Univ. of Chicago, paper, $16.95 (0-2267-3648-2)].

Schmutzler, Robert. Art Nouveau. Abrams. [o.p.].

Scott, Paul. The Corrida at San Feliu (Novel). Morrow. [Carroll & Graf, paper, $3.95 (0-88184-274-5)].

Selye, Hans. From Dream to Discovery: On Being a Scientist. McGraw-Hill. [Ayer, $35.95 (0-4050-6616-3)].

Shapiro, Karl Jay. The Bourgeois Poet (Poems). Random. [o.p.].

Silberman, Charles E. Crisis in Black and White. Random. [o.p.].

Silver, James Wesley. Mississippi: The Closed Society. Harcourt. [o.p.].

Smith, Page. The Historian and History. Knopf. [o.p.].

Stafford, Jean. Bad Characters (Short Stories). Farrar. [o.p.].

Teilhard de Chardin, Pierre. The Future of Man. Harper. [o.p.].

Van der Post, Laurens. A View of All the Russias. Morrow. [o.p.].

Werth, Alexander. Russia at War, 1941–1945. Dutton, $10. [Carroll & Graf, paper, $17.95 (0-8818-4084-X)].

Wind, Edgar. Art and Anarchy. Knopf. [Northwestern Univ., paper, $12.95 (0-8101-0662-0)].

Notable Books, 1963

Albee, Edward. Who's Afraid of Virgina Woolf? Atheneum. [Macmillan, paper, $10 (0-689-70565-4)].

Arendt, Hannah. Eichmann in Jerusalem: A Report on the Banality of Evil. Viking. [Peter Smith, $21.80 (0-8446-5977-0); Penguin, paper, $12.95 (0-14-018765-0)].

Ashton-Warner, Sylvia. Teacher. Simon & Schuster. [Simon & Schuster, paper, $9.95 (0-67-161768-0)].

Baldwin, James. The Fire Next Time. Dial. [Random, $12.50 (0-679-60151-1); paper, $8 (0-679-74472-X)].

Barth, Karl. Evangelical Theology. Holt. [o.p.].

Bazelon, David T. The Paper Economy. Random. [Greenwood, $75 (0-313-21001-2)].

Bowen, Catherine Drinker. Francis Bacon: The Temper of a Man. Little, Brown. [Fordham Univ., $30 (0-8232-1537-7); paper, $20 (0-8232-1538-5)].

Carlisle, Olga Andreyev. Voices in the Snow: Encounters with Russian Writers. Random. [o.p.].

Caudill, Harry M. Night Comes to the Cumberlands: A Biography of a Depressed Area. Little, Brown. [Little, Brown, paper, $14.95 (0-316-13212-8)].

Conant, James Bryant. The Education of American Teachers. McGraw-Hill. [o.p.].

Cousteau, Jacques Yves and **Dugan, James.** The Living Sea. Harper. [Lyons & Burford, paper, $12.95 (0-941130-73-8)].

De Mille, Agnes. The Book of the Dance. Golden. [o.p.].

Desroches-Noblecourt, Christiane. Tutankhamen: Life and Death of a Pharaoh. New York Graphic Society. [Penguin, paper, $17.95 (0-14-011665-6)].

Deutscher, Isaac. The Prophet Outcast: Trotsky, 1929–1940. Oxford. [o.p.].

Durrell, Lawrence and **Miller, Henry.** A Private Correspondence. Dutton. [o.p.].

Farb, Peter. Face of North America: The Natural History of a Continent. Harper. [o.p.].

Freyre, Gilberto. The Mansions and the Shanties (Sobrados e Mucambos); The Making of Modern Brazil. Knopf. [o.p.].

Grass, Günter. The Tin Drum (Novel). Pantheon. [Random, $20 (0-679-42033-9); paper, $15 (0-679-72575-X)].

Handlin, Oscar. The Americans: A New History of the People of the United States. Little, Nrown. [o.p.].

Heilbroner, Robert Louis. The Great Ascent: The Struggle for Economic Development in Our Time. Harper. [o.p.].

Hersey, John. Here to Stay. Knopf. [o.p.].

Hoffer, Eric. The Ordeal of Change. Harper. [Buccaneer, $23.95 (0-8996-6748-1)].

Hofstadter, Richard. Anti-Intellectualism in American Life. Knopf. (Random, paper, $14.95 (0-394-70317-0)].

Jeffers, Robinson. The Beginning & the End and Other Poems. Random. [o.p.].

Jung, Carl Gustav. Memories, Dreams, Reflections. Pantheon. [o.p.].

King, Martin Luther. Strength to Love. Harper. [Augsburg, paper, $9 (0-8006-1441-0)].

McGill, Ralph Emerson. The South and the Southerner. Little, Brown. [Univ. of Georgia, paper, $14.95 (0-8203-1443-9)].

Malamud, Bernard. Idiots First (Short Stories). Farrar. [Farrar, paper, $8.95 (0-374-52010-0)].

Mehta, Ved Parkash. Fly and the Fly-Bottle: Encounters with British Intellectuals. Little, Brown. [Columbia Univ., $50 (0-2310-5618-4); paper, $15.50 (0-2310-5619-2)].

Mitford, Jessica. The American Way of Death. Simon & Schuster. [Buccaneer, $25.95 (1-56849-159-X)].

Morison, Samuel Eliot. The Two-Ocean War, A Short History of the United States Navy in the Second World War. Little, Brown, $37.50 (0-316-58366-9); paper, $21.95 (0-316-58352-9).

Morris, James. The Road to Huddersfield: A Journey to Five Continents. Pantheon. [o.p.].

Muller, Herbert Joseph. Freedom in the Western World, from the Dark Ages to the Rise of Democracy. Harper. [o.p.].

Nabokov, Vladimir Vladimirovich. The Gift: A Novel. Putnam. [Random, paper, $11 (0-679-72725-6)].

Nelson, Jack and **Roberts, Gene.** The Censors and the Schools. Little, Brown. [Greenwood, $55 (0-8371-9687-6)].

North, Sterling. Rascal: A Memoir of a Better Era. Dutton, $14.99 (0-525-18839-8).

O'Donovan, Michael (Frank O'Connor, pseud.). The Lonely Voice: A Study of the Short Story. World. [o.p.].

Paris Review. Writers at Work: The Paris Review Interviews, Second Series. Viking. [o.p.].

Rock, John Charles. The Time Has Come; A Catholic Doctor's Proposals to End the Battle over Birth Control. Knopf. [o.p.].

Rugg, Harold. Imagination. Harper. [o.p.].

Rynne, Xavier (pseud.). Letters from Vatican City Vatican Council II, First Session. Farrar. [o.p.].

Sartre, Jean Paul. Saint Genet, Actor and Martyr. Braziller. [o.p.].

Steichen, Edward. A Life in Photography. Doubleday. [o.p.].

Swenson, May. To Mix with Time: New and Selected Poems. Scribner. [o.p.].

Tunnard, Christopher and others. Man-Made America: Chaos or Control? An Inquiry into Selected Problems of Design in the Urbanized Landscape. Yale. [o.p.].

Udall, Stewart L. The Quiet Crisis. Holt. [o.p.].

Updike, John. The Centaur (Novel). Knopf. [Random, $24.95 (0-394-41881-6); Fawcett, paper, $5.95 (0-449-21522-9)].

Wheelock, John Hall. What Is Poetry? Scribner. [o.p.].

Woodham Smith, Cecil Blanche Fitz Gerald. The Great Hunger: Ireland, 1845–1849. Harper. [Penguin, paper, $13.95 (0-14-014515-X)].

Yáñez, Augustín. The Edge of the Storm: A Novel. Univ. of Texas. [Univ. of Texas, paper, $16.95 (0-2927-0131-4)].

Notable Books, 1962

Amado, Jorge. Gabriela, Clove and Cinnamon: A Novel. Knopf. [Avon, paper, $12.50 (0-38-075470-3)].

Arms and Arms Control: A Symposium. Ed. by Ernest W. Lefever. Praeger. [o.p.].

Asimov, Isaac. Life and Energy. Doubleday. [o.p.].

Bolt, Robert. A Man for all Seasons: A Play in Two Acts. Random. [Random, paper, $8 (0-679-72822-8)].

Calisher, Hortense. Tale for the Mirror: A Novella and Other Stories. Little, Brown. [o.p.].

Canaday, John Edwin. Embattled Critic: Views on Modern Art. Farrar. [o.p.].

Carson, Rachel Louise. Silent Spring. Houghton. [Buccaneer, $27.95 (1-56849-552-8); Houghton Mifflin, paper, $10.95 (0-39-568329-7)].

Clavell, James. King Rat: A Novel. Little, Brown. [Dell, paper, $6.99 (0-440-14546-5)].

Clemens, Samuel Langhorne (Mark Twain, pseud.). Letters from the Earth. Harper. [Buccaneer, $21.95 (1-56849-069-0)].

Coon, Carleton Stevens. The Origin of Races. Knopf. [o.p.].

Daniels, Robert Vincent. The Nature of Communism. Random. [o.p.].

de Grazia, Sebastian. Of Time, Work, and Leisure. Twentieth Century Fund. [o.p.].

Dyson, James Lindsay. The World of Ice. Knopf. [o.p.].

Edel, Leon. Henry James: v.2, The Conquest of London, 1870–1881; v.3, The Middle Years, 1882–1895. Lippincott. [Avon, paper, each $2.95, v.2 (0-380-39651-3); v.3 (0-380-39669-6)].

Faulkner, William. The Reivers: A Reminiscence. Random. [Garland, $50 (0-8240-6834-3); Random, paper, $10 (0-679-74192-5)].

Frost, Robert. In the Clearing. Holt, $10.95 (0-8050-0625-7); paper, $9.95 (0-8050-0624-9).

Harrington, Michael. The Other America: Poverty in the United States. Macmillan. [Macmillan, paper, $9 (0-02-020763-8)].

Hayter, Stanley William. About Prints. Oxford. [o.p.].

Heidegger, Martin. Being and Time. Harper. [Harper, $27 (0-06-063850-8)].

Hughes, Richard Arthur Warren. The Fox in the Attic: A Novel. Harper. [o.p.].

Hyman, Stanley Edgar. The Tangled Bank: Darwin, Marx, Frazer and Freud as Imaginative Writers. Atheneum. [o.p.].

Jackson, Barbara (Ward) (Barbara Ward). The Rich Nations and the Poor Nations. Norton. [Norton, paper, $5.95 (0-393-00746-4)].

Kazin, Alfred. Contemporaries. Little, Brown. [o.p.].

Kuh, Katharine. The Artist's Voice: Talks with Seventeen Artists. Harper. [o.p.].

Küng, Hans. The Council, Reform, and Reunion. Sheed & Ward. [o.p.].

Luthuli, Albert John. Let My People Go. McGraw-Hill. [o.p.].

Macdonald, Dwight. Against the American Grain. Random. [Da Capo, paper, $9.95 (0-306-80205-8)].

Madariaga, Salvador de. Latin America between the Eagle and the Bear. Praeger. [Greenwood, $49.75 (0-8371-8423-1)].

Milne, Lorus Johnson and **Milne, Margery Joan (Greene).** The Senses of Animals and Men. Atheneum. [o.p.].

Nabokov, Vladimir Vladimirovich. Pale Fire: A Novel. Putnam. [Random, paper, $11 (0-679-72342-0)].

New Frontiers of Christianity. Ed. by Ralph C. Raughley. Association Press. [o.p.].

Porter, Katherine Anne. Ship of Fools: A Novel. Little, Brown. [Little, Brown, paper, $13.95 (0-31-671390-2)].

Powers, James Farl. Morte D'Urban: A Novel. Doubleday. [o.p.].

Price, Reynolds. A Long and Happy Life: A Novel. Atheneum. [Simon & Schuster, $20 (0-689-11947-X); paper, $4.95 (0-689-10224-0)].

Pritchett, Victor Sawdon. London Perceived. Harcourt. [Harcourt, paper, $3.95 (0-15-652970-X)].

Renoir, Jean. Renoir, My Father. Little, Brown. [Mercury, paper, $13.95 (0-9165-1539-7)].

Riessman, Frank. The Culturally Deprived Child. Harper. [o.p.].

Saarinen, Eero. Eero Saarinen on His Work: A Selection of Buildings Dating from 1947 to 1964. Yale. [o.p.].

Schreiber, William Ildephonse. Our Amish Neighbors. Univ. of Chicago. [o.p.].

Seven Plays of the Modern Theater. Intro. by Harold Clurman. Grove. [o.p.].

Singer, Isaac Bashevis. The Slave: A Novel. Farrar. [Farrar, paper, $12 (0-374-50680-9)].

Smith, Page. John Adams. 2v. Doubleday. [o.p.].

Stegner, Wallace Earle. Wolf Willow: A History, a Story, and a Memory of the Last Plains Frontier. Viking. [Univ. of Nebraska, $30 (0-8032-4109-7); Penguin, paper, $11.95 (0-14-013439-5)].

Taper, Bernard. Gomillion Versus Lightfoot: The Tuskegee Gerrymander Case. McGraw-Hill. [o.p.].

Trier, Eduard. Form and Space: Sculpture of the Twentieth Century. Praeger. [o.p.].

Tuchman, Barbara (Wertheim). The Guns of August. Macmillan, $19.95 (0-02-620311-1); Ballantine, paper, $14 (0-345-38623-X).

Turnbull, Andrew. Scott Fitzgerald. Scribner. [Macmillan, paper, $10.95 (0-02-040621-5)].

Wells, Donald A. God, Man, and the Thinker: Philosophies of Religion. Random. [o.p.].

White, Elwyn Brooks. The Points of My Compass: Letters from the East, the West, the North, the South. Harper. [o.p.].

Wilde, Oscar. The Letters of Oscar Wilde. Harcourt. [o.p.].

Williams, Edward Bennett. One Man's Freedom. Atheneum. [o.p.].

Williams, Emlyn. George: An Early Autobiography. Random. [o.p.].

Wilson, Edmund. Patriotic Gore: Studies in the Literature of the American Civil War. Oxford. [Peter Smith, $23.80 (0-8446-6851-6); Norton, paper, $15.95 (0-393-31256-9)].

Wohlstetter, Roberta. Pearl Harbor: Warning and Decision. Stanford Univ., $49.50 (0-804-70597-6)]; paper, $17.95 (0-804-70598-4).

Notable Books, 1961

Adams, John. Diary and Autobiography. 4v. Belknap Press of Harvard. [Random, $24.99 (0-517-39180-5)].

American Heritage. Book of Indians. Simon & Schuster. [o.p.].

Arms Control, Disarmament, and National Security. Ed. by Donald G. Brennan. Braziller. [o.p.].

Baldwin, James. Nobody Knows My Name: More Notes of a Native Son. Dial. [Random, paper, $10 (0-679-74473-8)].

Barbanson, Adrienne. Fables in Ivory: Japanese Netsuke and Their Legends. Tuttle. [o.p.].

Barr, Stringfellow. The Will of Zeus. Lippincott. [o.p.].

Burchard, John Ely and **Bush-Brown, Albert.** The Architecture of America; A Social and Cultural History. Little, Brown. [o.p.].

Camus, Albert. Resistance, Rebellion, and Death. Knopf. [Random, paper, $9 (0-394-71966-2)].

Conant, James Bryant. Slums and Suburbs: A Commentary on Schools in Metropolitan Areas. McGraw-Hill. [o.p.].

The Dawn of Civilization: The First World Survey of Human Cultures in Early Times. Ed. by Stuart Piggott. McGraw-Hill. [o.p.].

Dockstader, Frederick J. Indian Art in America: The Arts and Crafts of the North American Indian. New York Graphic Society. [o.p.].

Doderer, Heimito de. The Demos. 2v. Knopf. [Sun & Moon, paper, $29.95 (0-55713-030-2)].

Dumond, Dwight Lowell. Antislavery: The Crusade for Freedom in America. Univ. of Michigan. [o.p.].

Durant, William James and **Durant, Ariel.** The Age of Reason Begins. Simon & Schuster, $35 (0-67-101320-3).

Education for Public Responsibility. Ed. by Cyril Scott Fletcher. Norton. [o.p.].

Gann, Ernest Kellogg. Fate Is the Hunter. Simon & Schuster. [Simon & Schuster, paper, $12.95 (0-671-63603-0)].

Gardner, John William. Excellence, Can We be Equal and Excellent Too? Harper. [Norton, paper, $9.95 (0-393-31287-9)].

Gary, Romain. Promise at Dawn. Harper. [New Directions, paper, $10.95 (0-8112-1016-2)].

Greene, Graham. A Burnt-Out Case. Viking. [Penguin, paper, $9.95 (0-14-018539-9)].

Hindus, Maurice Gerschon. House without a Roof: Russia after Forty-three Years of Revolution. Doubleday. [o.p.].

Hogben, Lancelot Thomas. Mathematics in the Making. Doubleday. [o.p.].

The Horizon Book of the Renaissance. Ed. by the eds. of Horizon Magazine. American Heritage. [o.p.].

Jacobs, Jane. The Death and Life of American Cities. Random. [Random, paper, $17.50 (0-679-60047-7)].

Jaspers, Karl. The Future of Mankind. Univ. of Chicago. [o.p.].

Johnson, Gerald White. The Man Who Feels Left Behind. Morrow. [o.p.].

Kaufmann, Walter Arnold. The Faith of a Heretic. Doubleday. [o.p.].

Kennan, George Frost. Russia and the West under Lenin and Stalin. Little, Brown. [NAL, paper, $5.99 (0-45-162460-2)].

Kroeber, Theodora. Ishi in Two Worlds: A Biography of the Last Wild Indian in North America. Univ. of California, $35 (0-5200-0674-7); paper, $13 (0-5200-0675-5).

Landström, Björn. The Ship: An Illustrated History. Doubleday. [o.p.].

Lewis, Oscar. The Children of Sánchez: Autobiographyof a Mexican Family. Random. [Random, paper, $16 (0-394-70280-8).]

MacLeish, Archibald. Poetry and Experience. Houghton. [o.p.].

Malamud, Bernard. A New Life. Farrar. [Farrar, paper, $8.95 (0-374-52103-4)].

Maxwell, Gavin. Ring of Bright Water. Dutton. [Penguin, paper, $9.95 (0-14-003932-6)].

Maxwell, William. The Château. Knopf. [o.p.].

Moore, Ruth E. The Coil of Life: The Story of the Great Discoveries of the Life Sciences. Knopf. [o.p.].

Moorehead, Alan. The White Nile. Harper. [Adventure Library, $25 (1-885283-03-2)].

Mumford, Lewis. The City in History: Its Origins, Its Transformations, and Its Prospects. Harcourt. [Harcourt, paper, $22.95 (0-15-618035-9)].

Murchie, Guy. Music of the Spheres. Houghton. [Dover, paper, v.1, $8.95 (0-486-21809-0); v.2, $6.95 (0-486-21810-4)].

O'Connor, Edwin. The Edge of Sadness. Little, Brown. [Thomas More, $17.95 (0-8834-7259-7)].

O'Connor, Frank (Michael O'Donovan, pseud.). An Only Child. Knopf. [o.p.].

Paton, Alan. Tales from a Troubled Land. Scribner. [Simon & Schuster, $20 (0-684-15135-9); paper, $9 (0-684-82584-8)].

Salinger, J. D. Franny and Zooey. Little, Brown, $22.95 (0-3167-6954-1); paper, $4.99 (0-3167-6949-5).

Sanderson, Ivan Terence. The Continent We Live On. Random. [o.p.].

Schorer, Mark. Sinclair Lewis: An American Life. McGraw-Hill. [Books On Demand, $25 (0-7837-2867-0)].

Statler, Oliver. Japanese Inn. Random. [Univ. of Hawaii, paper, $9.95 (0-8248-0818-5)].

Swanberg, W. A. Citizen Hearst: A Biography of William Randolph Hearst. Scribner. [Simon & Schuster, paper, $7.95 (0-684-17147-3)].

Thomas, Hugh. The Spanish Civil War. Harper. [Simon & Schuster, $20 (0-671-75876-4)].

Toynbee, Arnold Joseph. Reconsiderations. Oxford. [o.p.].

Tynan, Kenneth. Curtains: Selections from the Drama Criticism and Related Writings. Atheneum. [o.p.].

White, Theodore Harold. The Making of a President, 1960. Atheneum. [Buccaneer, $24.95 (1-56849-143-3); Simon & Schuster, paper, $14.95 (0-689-70803-3)].

Notable Books, 1960

Adams, Ansel Easton and **Newhall, Nancy (Wynne).** This Is the American Earth. Sierra Club, $50 (0-8715-6557-9).

Adamson, Joy. Born Free: A Lioness of Two Worlds. Pantheon. [Random, $11.95 (0-679-56141-2); paper, $15 (0-394-74635-X)].

American Heritage. The American Heritage Picture History of the Civil War. Doubleday. [o.p.].

Asimov, Isaac. The Intelligent Man's Guide to Science. 2v. Basic. [o.p.].

Baruch, Bernard Mannes. Baruch: The Public Years. Holt. [Buccaneer, $24.95 (1-56849-096-8)].

Bates, Marston. The Forest and the Sea: A Look at the Economy of Nature and the Ecology of Man. Random. [Lyons & Burford, paper, $11.95 (1-55821-009-1)].

Berckelaers, Ferdinand Louis (Michel Seuphor, pseud.). The Sculpture of This Century. Braziller. [o.p.].

Berenson, Bernard. The Passionate Sightseer: From the Diaries, 1947–1956. Simon & Schuster. [o.p.].

Blake, Peter. The Master Builders. Knopf. [Norton, paper, $12.95 (0-393-00796-0)].

Bowen, Elizabeth. A Time in Rome. Knopf. [Peter Smith, $18.50 (0-8446-6537-1)].

Brown, Robert McAfee and **Weigel, Gustave.** An American Dialogue: A Protestant Looks at Catholicism and a Catholic Looks at Protestantism. Doubleday. [o.p.].

Catton, Bruce. Grant Moves South. Little, Brown. [Little, Brown, paper, $16.95 (0-31-613244-6)].

Copland, Aaron. Copland on Music. Doubleday. [o.p.].

Cousins, Norman. Dr. Schweitzer of Lambaréné. Harper. [o.p.].

Durrell, Lawrence. Clea: A Novel. Dutton. [Penguin, paper, $10.95 (0-14-015322-5)].

Eiseley, Loren. The Firmament of Time. Atheneum. [Macmillan, paper, $9 (0-689-70068-7)].

Frankfurter, Felix. Felix Frankfurter Reminisces, Recorded in Talks with Harlan B. Phillips. Reynal. [Greenwood, $35 (0-313-20466-7)].

Gombrich, Ernst Hans Josef. Art and Illusion: A Study in the Psychology of Pictorial Representation. Pantheon. [Princeton, $63 (0-69-109785-2); paper, $19.95 (0-69-101750-6)].

Graves, John. Goodbye to a River, a Narrative. Knopf. [Random, $22.50 (0-394-42690-8); Gulf, paper, $8.95 (0-9320-1275-2)].

Grout, Donald Jay. A History of Western Music. Norton, $47.95 (0-393-95629-6).

Heilbroner, Robert L. The Future as History. Harper. [o.p.].

Hersey, John Richard. The Child Buyer. Knopf. [o.p.].

Kahn, Herman. On Thermonuclear War. Princeton. [Greenwood, $95 (0-313-20060-2)].

Knowles, John. A Separate Peace: A Novel. Macmillan. [Simon & Schuster, $40 (0-02-564850-0); Bantam, paper, $4.99 (0-55-328041-4)].

Kobler, John. The Reluctant Surgeon: A Biography of John Hunter. Doubleday. [o.p.].

Lampedusa, Guiseppe Di. The Leopard. Pantheon. [Random, $15 (0-679-40757-X); paper, $12 (0-679-73121-0)].

Lee, Harper. To Kill a Mockingbird. Lippincott. [HarperCollins, $17 (0-06-017322-X); Warner, paper, $4.99 (0-44-631078-6)].

Lewis, Clive Staples. The Four Loves. Harcourt, $18.50 (0-15-132916-8); paper, $6.95 (0-15-632930-1).

McGinley, Phyllis. Times Three: Selected Verse from Three Decades. Viking. [o.p.].

Mauriac, François. The Son of Man. World. [o.p.].

Morison, Elting Elmore. Turmoil and Tradition: A Study of the Life and Times of Henry L. Stimson. Houghton. [o.p.].

Nowell, Elizabeth. Thomas Wolfe: A Biography. Doubleday. [Greenwood, $38.50 (0-8371-6519-9)].

Pope-Hennessy, James. Queen Mary, 1867–1953. Knopf. [o.p.].

Priestly, John Boynton. Literature and Western Man. Harper. [o.p.].

Read, Conyers. Lord Burghley and Queen Elizabeth. Knopf. [o.p.].

Rostow, Walt Whitman. Stages of Economic Growth: A Non-Communist Manifesto. Cambridge, $59.95 (0-52-140070-8); paper, $19.95 (0-52-140928-4).

Schlesinger, Arthur Meier. The Age of Roosevelt: v.3, The Politics of Upheaval. Houghton. [Houghton, paper, $11.95 (0-395-48904-0)].

Schwarz-Bart, André. The Last of the Just. Atheneum. [Robert Bentley, $22 (0-83760-456-7); Simon & Schuster, paper, $15.95 (0-689-70365-1)].

Sergeant, Elizabeth Shepley. Robert Frost: The Trial by Existence. Holt. [o.p.].

Shapiro, Karl Jay. In Defense of Ignorance. Random. [o.p.].

Shirer, William Lawrence. The Rise and Fall of the Third Reich: A History of Nazi Germany. Simon & Schuster, $17.95 (0-671-08912-9); paper, $16 (0-671-72868-7).

Snow, Sir Charles Percy. The Affair. Scribner. [o.p.].

Snow, Sir Charles Percy. The Two Cultures and the Scientific Revolution. Cambridge. [Cambridge, paper, $9.95 (0-521-45730-0)].

Teale, Edwin Way. Journey Into Summer: A Naturalist's Record of a 19,000-Mile Journey through the North American Summer. Dodd. [o.p.].

Thelen, Herbert Arnold. Education and the Human Quest. Harper. [o.p.].

Williams, Vinnie. Walk Egypt. Viking. [o.p.].

Notable Books of the 1950s

Notable Books, 1959

Amrine, Michael. The Great Decision: The Secret History of the Atomic Bomb. Putnam. [o.p.].

Anderson, William R. and **Blair, Clay.** Nautilus 90 North. World. [o.p.].

Ashton-Warner, Sylvia. Spinster, A Novel. Simon & Schuster. [o.p.].

Barzun, Jacques. The House of Intellect. Harper. [Greenwood, $55 (0-313-20071-8)].

Bernstein, Leonard. The Joy of Music. Simon & Schuster. [Doubleday, paper, $14.95 (0-385-47201-3)].

Bowen, Catherine Drinker. Adventures of a Biographer. Little, Brown. [o.p.].

Bridgman, Percy Williams. The Way Things Are. Harvard. [o.p.].

Brinton, Clarence Crane. A History of Western Morals. Harcourt. [Paragon, paper, $14.95 (1-55778-370-5)].

Bruckberger, Raymond Léopold. Image of America. Viking. [o.p.].

Canaday, John Edwin. Mainstreams of Modern Art. Simon & Schuster. [Harcourt, paper, $44 (0-03-057638-5)].

Carter, Hodding. The Angry Scar: The Story of Reconstruction. Doubleday. [Greenwood, $49.75 (0-8371-7022-2)].

Conant, James Bryant. The Child, the Parent, and the State. Harvard. [o.p.].

Cordell, Alexander. The Rape of the Fair Country. Doubleday [o.p.].

Davis, Burke. To Appomattox: Nine April Days, 1865. Rinehart. [Eastern Acorn, paper, $4.25 (0-915992-17-5)].

Drury, Allen. Advise and Consent. Doubleday. [Buccaneer, $45.95 (1-56849-060-7)].

Eliot, Alexander. Sight and Insight. McDowell, Obolensky. [o.p.].

Fleming, Peter. The Siege of Peking. Harper. [Marboro, $19.95 (0-88029-462-0); Oxford, paper, $11.95 (0-19-583735-5)].

Gray, Jesse Glenn. The Warriors: Reflections on Men in Battle. Harcourt. [Harper, paper, $18.25 (0-06-131294-0)].

Griffith, Thomas. The Waist-High Culture. Harper. [Greenwood, $35 (0-8371-6645-4)].

Guérard, Albert Léon. France: A Modern History. Univ. of Michigan. [o.p.].

Guthrie, Tyrone. A Life in the Theatre. McGraw-Hill. [AMS, $32.50 (0-404-20114-8)].

Hart, Moss. Act One; An Autobiography. Random. [Buccaneer, $27.95 (1-56849-558-7); St. Martin's, paper, $14.95 (0-312-03272-2)].

Howells, William White. Mankind in the Making: The Story of Human Evolution. Doubleday. [o.p.].

Jackson, Barbara (Ward). Five Ideas That Changed the World. Norton. [Norton, paper, $6.95 (0-393-09438-3)].

Jenkins, Elizabeth. Elizabeth the Great. Coward-McCann. [o.p.].

Karsh, Yousuf. Portraits of Greatness. Nelson. [o.p.].

Kieran, John. A Natural History of New York City, a Personal Report after Fifty Years of Study & Enjoyment of Wildlife within the Boundaries of Greater New York. Houghton. [Fordham Univ., paper, $17.50 (0-8232-1086-3)].

Krutch, Joseph Wood. Human Nature and the Human Condition. Random. [Greenwood, $55 (0-313-21010-1)].

Lansing, Alfred. Endurance: Shackleton's Incredible Voyage. McGraw-Hill. [Louisiana State Univ., $25 (1-885283-00-8); Carroll & Graf, paper, $9.95 (0-88184-178-1)].

Laurence, William Leonard. Men and Atoms: The Discovery, the Uses, and the Future of Atomic Energy. Simon & Schuster. [o.p.].

Leech, Margaret. In the Days of McKinley. Harper. [o.p.].

McCarthy, Mary Therese. The Stones of Florence. Harcourt, $49.95 (0-15-185079-8); paper, $19.95 (015-685081-8).

MacLennan, Hugh. The Watch That Ends the Night. Scribner. [o.p.].

Mann, Thomas. Last Essays. Knopf, $4.50. [o.p.].

Matthiessen, Peter. Wildlife in America. Viking. [Viking, paper, $12.95 (0-14-004793-X)].

Mattingly, Garrett. The Armada. Houghton. [Houghton, paper, $13.95 (0-395-08366-4)].

Meeker, Oden. The Little World of Laos. Scribner. [o.p.].

Michener, James Albert. Hawaii. Random, $45 (0-394-42797-1); Fawcett, paper, $6.99 (0-449-21335-8).

Morison, Samuel Eliot. John Paul Jones: A Sailor's Biography. Little, Brown. [Naval Institute, $32.95 (0-87021-323-7); Northeastern Univ., paper, $18.95 (0-930350-70-7)].

Ogburn, Charlton. The Marauders. Harper. [Morrow, paper, $6.25 (0-688-01625-1)].

Rama Rau, Santha. My Russian Journey. Harper. [o.p.].

Read, Sir Herbert Edward. A Concise History of Modern Painting. Praeger. [Thames & Hudson, paper, $14.95 (0-500-20141-2)].

Russell, Bertrand Russell. Wisdom of the West: A Historical Survey of Western Philosophy in Its Social and Political Setting. Doubleday. [Random $17.99 (0-517-69041-1)].

Schlesinger, Arthur Meier. The Age of Roosevelt: v.2, The Coming of the New Deal. Houghton. [Houghton Mifflin, paper, $15.95 (0-395-48905-9)].

Tharp, Louise (Hall). Adventurous Alliance: The Story of the Agassiz Family of Boston. Little, Brown. [o.p.].

Thomas, Elizabeth Marshall. The Harmless People. Knopf. [Random, paper, $12 (0-679-72446-X)].

Thurber, James. The Years with Ross. Little, Brown. [Amereon, $22.95 (0-89190-257-0)].

Ustinov, Peter. Add a Dash of Pity. Little, Brown. [o.p.].

West, Morris L. The Devil's Advocate. Morrow. [Morrow, $17.95 (0-688-01453-4)].

Notable Books, 1958

Ashmore, Harry S. An Epitaph for Dixie. Norton. [o.p.].

Boorstin, Daniel Joseph. The Americans: v.1, The Colonial Experience. Random. [3v. set, Random, $114.95 (0-394-49588-8); McGraw-Hill, v.1, paper, $8.95 (0-07-553700-1)].

Brittain, Robert Edward. Rivers, Man, and Myths. Doubleday. [o.p.].

Capote, Truman. Breakfast at Tiffany's, a Short Novel and Three Stories. Random, $12.50 (0-679-60085-X); NAL paper, $3.50 (0-451-15644-7).

Churchill, Sir Winston. A History of the English-speaking Peoples: v.4, The Great Democracies. Dodd. [Buccaneer, $29.96 (1-56849-507-2)].

cummings, e. e. 95 Poems. Harcourt. [o.p.].

Del Castillo, Michel. Child of Our Time. Knopf. [o.p.].

Dermout, Maria. The Ten Thousand Things, a Novel. Simon & Schuster. [Univ. of Massachusetts, $32.50 (0-87023-384-X)].

Djilas, Milovan. Land without Justice. Harcourt. [o.p.].

Dowdey, Clifford. Death of a Nation: The Story of Lee and His Men at Gettysburg. Knopf. [Butternut & Blue, paper, $12.95 (0-935523-15-4)].

Duncan, David Douglas. The Private World of Pablo Picasso. Harper. [o.p.].

Durrell, Lawrence. Bitter Lemons. Dutton. [Amereon, $20.95 (0-8488-0480-5); Penguin, paper, $9 (0-14-015318-7)].

Eiseley, Loren. Darwin's Century: Evolution and the Men Who Discovered It. Doubleday. [o.p.].

Ferguson, Charles Wright. Naked to Mine Enemies: The Life of Cardinal Wolsey. Little, Brown. [o.p.].

Fortune. The Exploding Metropolis. Doubleday. [Greenwood, $55 (0-8371-8823-7); Univ. of California, paper, $12 (0-520-08090-4)].

Freuchen, Peter and **Salomonsen, Finn.** The Arctic Year. Putnam. [o.p.].

Galbraith, John Kenneth. The Affluent Society. Houghton. [NAL, paper, $4.95 (0-451-62394-0)].

Gary, Romain. The Roots of Heaven. Simon & Schuster. [o.p.].

Gavin, James Maurice. War and Peace in the Space Age. Harper. [o.p.].

Gogh, Vincent Van. Complete Letters. 3v. NY Graphic Society. [Bulfinch, $125 (0-8212-0735-0)].

Golden, Harry Lewis. Only in America. World. [Greenwood, $67.50 (0-8371-6607-1)].

Gunther, John. Inside Russia Today. Harper. [o.p.].

Hays, Hoffman Reynolds. From Ape to Angel: An Informal History of Social Anthropology. Knopf. [Greenwood, $79.50 (0-313-21235-X)].

Joyce, Stanislaus. My Brother's Keeper: James Joyce's Early Years. Viking. [o.p.].

Jung, Carl Gustav. The Undiscovered Self. Little, Brown. [Little, Brown, paper, $9.95 (0-316-47694-3)].

Kazantzakis, Nikos. The Odyssey: A Modern Sequel. Simon & Schuster. [o.p.].

King, Martin Luther. Stride toward Freedom: The Montgomery Story. Harper. [Harper, paper, $10 (0-06-250490-8)].

MacLeish, Archibald. J. B., a Play in Verse. Houghton. [Houghton, paper, $10.95 (0-395-08353-2)].

Marek, Kurt W. (C. W. Ceram, pseud.). The March of Archaeology. Knopf. [o.p.].

Maxwell, Gavin. People of the Reeds. Harper. [o.p.].

Montgomery, Bernard Law Montgomery. Memoirs of Field Marshall Montgomery. World. [Da Capo, paper, $10.95 (0-306-80173-6)].

Moraes, Francis Robert. Yonder One World: A Study of Asia and the West. Macmillan. [o.p.].

Overstreet, Harry Allen and **Overstreet, Bonaro Wilkinson.** What We Must Know about Communism. Norton. [o.p.].

Pasternak, Boris Leonidovich. Doctor Zhivago. Knopf $20 (0-679-40759-6); Pantheon, paper, $15 (0-679-73123-7).

Redding, Jay Saunders. The Lonesome Road: The Story of the Negro's Part in America. Doubleday [o.p.].

Renault, Mary. The King Must Die. Pantheon. [Random, paper, $10 (0-394-75104-3)].

Ross, Ishbel. First Lady of the South: The Life of Mrs. Jefferson Davis. Harper. [o.p.].

Saarinen, Aline Bernstein. The Proud Possessors. Random. [o.p.].

Snow, Charles Percy. The Conscience of the Rich. Scribner. [o.p.].

Snow, Edgar. Journey to the Beginning. Random. [o.p.].

Swanberg, W. A. First Blood: The Story of Fort Sumter. Scribner. [Marboro, $19.95 (0-88029-461-2)].

Tillion, Germaine. Algeria: The Realities. Knopf. [o.p.].

Van Doren, Mark. Autobiography. Harcourt. [o.p.].

Wagenknecht, Edward Charles. The Seven Worlds of Theodore Roosevelt. Longmans. [o.p.].

White, Theodore Harold. The Mountain Road. Sloane. [o.p.].

Wister, Owen. Owen Wister Out West: His Journals and Letters. Univ. of Chicago. [o.p.].

Writers at Work: The Paris Review Interviews. Ed. by Malcolm Cowley. Viking. [o.p.].

Notable Books, 1957

Agar, Herbert. The Price of Power: America since 1945. Univ. of Chicago. [Univ. of Chicago, paper, $1.95 (0-226-00937-8)].

Agee, James. A Death in the Family. McDowell, Obolensky. [Bantam, paper, $5.99 (0-553-27011-7)].

Allen, Robert Porter. On the Trail of Vanishing Birds. McGraw-Hill. [o.p.].

Bedford, Sybille. A Legacy: A Novel. Simon & Schuster. [o.p.].

Bone, Edith. 7 Years' Solitary. Harcourt. [o.p.].

Bowen, Catherine Drinker. The Lion and the Throne: The Life and Times of Sir Edward Coke (1552–1634). Little, Brown. [Little, Brown, paper, $12.95 (0-685-45399-5)].

Brooks, Van Wyck. Days of the Phoenix: The Nineteen-Twenties I Remember. [o.p.].

Burlingame, Roger. The American Conscience. Knopf. [o.p.].

Chase, Mary Ellen. The Edge of Darkness. Norton. [o.p.].

Church, Richard. The Golden Sovereign: A Concusion to Over the Bridge. Dutton. [o.p.].

Churchill, Sir Winston. A History of the English-Speaking Peoples: v.3, The Age of Revolution. Dodd. [Buccaneer, $29.95 (1-56849-506-4)].

Coit, Margaret L. Mr. Baruch. Houghton. [o.p.].

Connell, Brian. A Watcher on the Rhine: An Appraisal of Germany Today. Morrow. [o.p.].

Coon, Carleton Stevens. The Seven Caves: Archaeological Explorations in the Middle East. Knopf. [o.p.].

Cozzens, James Gould. By Love Possessed. Harcourt. [Buccaneer, $21.95 (1-56849-549-8)].

Djilas, Milovan. The New Class: An Analysis of the Communist System. Praeger. [Harcourt, paper, $8.95 (0-15-665489-X)].

Durant, William James. The Story of Civilization: v.6, The Reformation: A History of European Civilization from Wyclif to Calvin: 1300–1564. Simon & Schuster, $35 (0-671-61050-3).

Farre, Rowena. Seal Morning. Rinehart. [o.p.].

Flanner, Janet. Men and Monuments. Harper. [Ayer, paper, $23.95 (0-8369-1876-2)].

Hamilton, Edith. The Echo of Greece. Norton. [Norton, paper, $9.95 (0-393-00231-4)].

Highet, Gilbert. Poets in a Landscape. Knopf. [Akadine, $35 (1-888173-02-5)].

Jackson, Barbara Ward. The Interplay of East and West: Points of Conflict and Cooperation. Norton. [Norton, paper, $1.75 (0-393-00162-8)].

Janson, Horst Woldemar and **Janson, Dora Jane.** The Picture History of Painting, from Cave Painting to Modern Times. Abrams. [o.p.].

Johnson, Gerald White. The Lunatic Fringe. Lippincott. [Greenwood, $38.50 (0-8371-6680-2)].

Kissinger, Henry Alfred. Nuclear Weapons and Foreign Policy. Harper. [o.p.].

Lea, Tom. The King Ranch. Little, Brown, $125 (0-316-51745-3).

Lerner, Max. America as a Civilization: Life and Thought in the United States Today. Simon & Schuster. [Holt, paper, $19.95 (0-8050-0355-X)].

Life (Chicago). The World's Great Religions. Time. [o.p.].

Low, David. Autobiography. Simon & Schuster. [o.p.].

Mehta, Ved Parkash. Face to Face: An Autobiography. Little, Brown. [o.p.].

Michener, James Albert. The Bridge at Andau. Random. [Fawcett, paper, $5.99 (0-449-21050-2)].

Mowat, Farley. The Dog Who Wouldn't Be. Little, Brown, $18.95 (0-316-58636-6); Bantam, paper, $5.99 (0-7704-2265-9)].

Packard, Vance Oakley. The Hidden Persuaders. McKay. [o.p.].

Stewart, Sidney. Give Us This Day. Norton. [Avon, paper, $3.95 (0-380-76076-2)].

Thiel, Rudolph. And There Was Light: The Discovery of the Universe. Knopf. [o.p.].

Vandiver, Frank Everson. Mighty Stonewall. McGraw-Hill. [Texas A & M Univ., $27.50 (0-89096-384-3); paper, $16.95 (0-89096-391-6)].

Walters, Raymond. Albert Gallatin: Jeffersonian Financier and Diplomat. [o.p.].

White, William Smith. Citadel: The Story of the U.S. Senate. Harper. [o.p.].

Woodring, Paul. A Fourth of a Nation. McGraw-Hill. [o.p.].

Wright, Frank Lloyd. A Testament. Horizon. [o.p.].

Wylie, Laurence William. Village in the Vaucluse. Harvard. [Harvard, paper, $15.95 (0-674-93936-0).

Notable Books, 1956

Anderson, Marian. My Lord, What a Morning. Viking. [Univ. of Wisconsin, $17.95 (0-299-13390-7); paper, $12.95 (0-299-13394-X)].

Bemis, Samuel F. John Quincy Adams and the Union. Knopf. [o.p.].

Bowers, Faubion. Theatre in the East. Nelson. [o.p.].

Brooks, Van Wyck. Helen Keller. Dutton. [o.p.].

Brown, J. M. Through These Men. Harper. [Ayer, $23.95 (0-8369-2756-7)].

Burns, J. M. Roosevelt: The Lion and the Fox. Harcourt. [Harcourt, paper, $16.95 (0-156-78870-5)].

Catton, Bruce. This Hallowed Ground. Doubleday. [o.p.].

Chafee, Zechariah. The Blessings of Liberty. Lippincott. [o.p.].

Churchill, Winston. A History of the English-Speaking Peoples. v.1, The Birth of Britain. v.2, The New World. Dodd. [v.1, Buccaneer, $29.95 (1-56849-504-8); v.2, Buccaneer, $29.95 (1-56849-506-6)].

Daiches, David. Two Worlds. Harcourt. [Univ. of Alabama, paper, $12.50 (0-817-30417-7)].

Donovan, R. J. Eisenhower: The Inside Story. Harper. [o.p.].

Ervine, St. J. G. Bernard Shaw: His Life, Work, and Friends. Morrow. [o.p.].

Forester, C. S. The Age of Fighting Sail. Doubleday. [Chapman Billies, paper, $17.85 (0-939218-06-2)].

Gesell, A. L. and others. Youth: The Years from Ten to Sixteen. Harper. [o.p.].

Hersey, John R. A Single Pebble. Knopf. [Random, paper, $11 (0-39-475697-5)].

Huddleston, Trevor. Naught for Your Comfort. Doubleday. [o.p.].

Hulme, K. C. The Nun's Story. Little, Brown. [o.p.].

Kendall, P. M. Richard the Third. Norton. [Norton, paper, $16.95 (0-39-300785-5)].

Kennedy, John F. Profiles in Courage. Harper. [Harper, paper, $6 (0-06-080698-2)].

Kirby, R. S. and others. Engineering in History. McGraw-Hill. [Dover, paper, $13.95 (0-486-26412-2)].

La Farge, Oliver. Behind the Mountains. Houghton. [Charles, paper, $12 (0-912880-07-4)].

Marek, Kurt W. The Secret of the Hittites, by C. W. Ceram (pseud.). Knopf. [o.p.].

Maughan, A. M. Harry of Monmouth. Sloane. [o.p.].

Maurois, André. Olympio: The Life of Victor Hugo. Harper. [o.p.].

Mead, Margaret. New Lives for Old. Morrow. [o.p.].

Millis, Walter. Arms and Men. Putnam. [Rutgers Univ., paper, $15 (0-8135-0931-9)].

Mills, C. Wright. The Power Elite. Oxford. [Oxford, paper, $15.95 (0-19-500680-1)].

Moore, R. E. The Earth We Live On. Knopf. [o.p.].

Moorehead, Alan. Gallipoli. Harper. [Noontide, $18.95 (0-939482-35-5); Ballantine, paper, $5.99 (0-345-33088-9)].

Moraes, F. R. Jawaharlal Nehru. Macmillan. [o.p.].

Muir, Edwin. One Foot in Eden. Grove. [o.p.].

O'Connor, Edwin. The Last Hurrah. Little, Brown. [Little, Brown, paper, $12.95 (0-316-62659-7)].

Olson, S. F. The Singing Wilderness. Knopf. [Knopf, $24.95 (0-394-44560-0)].

O'Neill, Eugene G. Long Day's Journey into Night. Yale. [Yale Univ., $18.50 (0-300-04600-6); paper, $8 (0-300-04601-4)].

Rossiter, C. L. The American Presidency. [Johns Hopkins, paper, $13.95 (0-8018-3545-3)].

Rowan, C. T. The Pitiful and the Proud. [o.p.].

Russell, Bertrand R. Portraits from Memory and Other Essays. Simon & Schuster. [o.p.].

Seldes, Gilbert V. The Public Arts. Simon & Schuster. [Transaction, paper, $12.95 (1-56000-748-6)].

Teale, Edwin Way. Autumn across America. Dodd. [St. Martin, paper, $12.95 (0-312-04455-0)].

Tharp. Louise. Three Saints and a Sinner. Little, Brown. [o.p.].

Toynbee, Arnold J. An Historian's Approach to Religion. Oxford. [o.p.].

Warren, Robert Penn. Segregation: The Inner Conflict in the South. Random. [Univ. of Georgia, paper, $9.95 (0-8203-1670-9)].

Notable Books, 1955

Allen, Gay W. The Solitary Singer. Macmillan. [o.p.].

Anderson, Erica. The World of Albert Schweitzer. Harper. [o.p.].

Barth, Alan. Government by Investigation. Viking. [Augustus Kelley, $29.50 (0-6780-3150-9)].

Bates, Marston. The Prevalence of People. Scribner. [o.p.].

Bishop, J. A. The Day Lincoln Was Shot. Harper. [Harper, paper, $6.50 (0-06-080005-4)].

Bourlière, François. Mammals of the World. Knopf. [o.p.].

Bowles, Chester. The New Dimensions of Peace. Harper. [o.p.].

Bridgeman, William and **Hazard, Jacqueline.** The Lonely Sky. Holt. [Ayer, $30.95 (0-40512-148-2)].

Burrows, Millar. The Dead Sea Scrolls. Viking. [o.p.].

Carson, Rachel L. The Edge of the Sea. Houghton. [Houghton, $11.95 (0-395-28519-4)].

Chase, Gilbert. America's Music: From the Pilgrims to the Present. McGraw-Hill. [Univ. of Illinois, paper, $24.95 (0-252-06275-2)].

Chase, Mary Ellen. Life and Language in the Old Testament. Norton. [o.p.].

Clifford, J. L. Young Sam Johnson. McGraw-Hill. [o.p.].

Davenport, R. W. The Dignity of Man. Harper. [o.p.].

De Santillana, George. The Crime of Galileo. Univ. of Chicago. [Univ. of Chicago, paper, $21 (0-226-73481-1)].

De Voto, Bernard A. The Easy Chair. Houghton. [Ayer, $23.95 (0-8369-2433-9)].

Fine, Benjamin. 1,000,000 Delinquents. World. [o.p.].

Fromm, Erich. The Sane Society. Rinehart. [Holt, paper, $12.95 (0-8050-1402-0)].

Goodenough, E. R. Toward a Mature Faith. Prentice-Hall. [Univ. Press of America, paper, $20 (0-819-16791-6)].

Gunther, John. Inside Africa. Harper. [Ayer, $49.95 (0-8369-8197-9)].

Hachiya, Michihiko. Hiroshima Diary. Univ. of North Carolina. [Univ. of North Carolina, paper, $14.95 (0-8078-4044-0)].

Hanson, Lawrence and **Hanson, Elisabeth.** Noble Savage. Random. [o.p.].

Herberg, Will. Protestant, Catholic, Jew. Doubleday. [Univ. of Chicago, paper, $12.95 (0-226-32734-5)].

Hoyle, Fred. Frontiers of Astronomy. Harper. [o.p.].

Irvine, William. Apes, Angels, and Victorians. McGraw-Hill. [o.p.].

Jackson, R. H. The Supreme Court in the American System of Government. Harvard. [o.p.].

Life (Chicago). The World We Live In. Simon & Schuster. [o.p.].

Lindbergh, Anne (M.). Gift from the Sea. Pantheon. [Random, $16 (0-679-40683-2); paper, $7 (0-679-73241-1)].

Luethy, Herbert. France against Herself. Praeger. [o.p.].

MacGowan, Kenneth. The Living Stage. Prentice-Hall. [o.p.].

Millar, G. R. A Crossbowman's Story of the First Exploration of the Amazon. Knopf. [o.p.].

Niebuhr, Reinhold. The Self and the Dramas of History. Scribner. [o.p.].

Oldenbourg, Zoé. The Cornerstone. [o.p.].

Peterson, R. T. Wild America. Houghton. [o.p.].

Phillips, Wendell. Qataban and Sheba. Harcourt. [o.p.].

Reischauer, Edwin O. Wanted: An Asian Policy. Knopf. [o.p.].

Steichen, Edward, comp. The Family of Man. Simon & Schuster. [Simon & Schuster, paper, $18.50 (0-671-55411-5)].

Taylor, K. (P.). (Kamala Markandaya, pseud.) Nectar in a Sieve. Day. [NAL, paper, $5.99 (0-451-16836-4)].

Tenzing, Norgay. Tiger of the Snows. Putnam. [o.p.].

Trilling, Lionel. The Opposing Self. Viking. [Harcourt, $15.25 (0-15-170068-0); paper, $3.95 (0-15-670065-4)].

Tunnard, Christopher. American Skyline. Houghton. [o.p.].

Van Der Post, Laurens. The Dark Eye in Africa. Morrow. [o.p.].

Walker, R. L. China under Communism. Yale. [o.p.].

Weeks, Edward. The Open Heart. Little, Brown. [o.p.].

West, Rebecca, pseud. A Train of Powder. Viking. [o.p.].

White, W. F. How Far the Promised Land? Viking. [o.p.].

Notable Books, 1954

Abrahams, Peter. Tell Freedom. Knopf. [Faber, $9.95 (0-571-11777-5)].

Arnow, Harriette L. S. The Dollmaker. Macmillan. [Avon, paper, $6.50 (0-380-00947-1)].

Barzun, Jacques. God's Country and Mine. Little, Brown. [Greenwood, $35 (0-8371-6860-0)].

Basso, Hamilton. The View from Pompey's Head. Doubleday. [Buccaneer, $24.95 (1-56849-557-9)].

Bowles, Chester. Ambassador's Report. Harper. [o.p.].

Brooks, Van Wyck. Scenes and Portraits. Dutton. [o.p.].

Buck, Pearl S. My Several Worlds. Day. [Buccaneer, $27.95 (0-8996-6987-5)].

Carson, Gerald. The Old Country Store. Oxford. [o.p.].

Catton, Bruce. U.S. Grant and the American Military Tradition. Little, Brown. [Amereon, $18.95 (0-8488-0279-9)].

Commager, Henry Steele. Freedom, Loyalty, Dissent. Oxford. [o.p.].

Coon, Carleton S. The Story of Man. Knopf. [o.p.].

Davis, E. H. But We Were Born Free. Bobbs-Merrill. [Greenwood, $55 (0-8371-5784-6)].

Dodson, Kenneth. Away All Boats. Little, Brown. [Naval Institute, $32.95 (1-55750-173-4)].

Gheerbrant, Alain. Journey to the Far Amazon. Simon & Schuster. [o.p.].

Gouzenko, Igor. The Fall of a Titan. Norton. [o.p.].

Hagedorn, Hermann. The Roosevelt Family of Sagamore Hill. Macmillan. [o.p.].

Harrer, Heinrich. Seven Years in Tibet. Dutton. [Putnam, paper, $10.95 (0-874-77217-6)].

Highet, Gilbert. Man's Unconquerable Mind. Columbia Univ., $34 (0-231-02016-3); paper, $12 (0-231-08501-X).

Horgan, Paul. Great River. Rinehart. [Univ. Press of New England, paper, $24.95 (0-8195-6251-3)].

Howells, W. W. Back of History. Doubleday. [o.p.].

Hunt, Sir John. The Conquest of Everest. Dutton. [o.p.].

Krutch, Joseph Wood. The Measure of Man. Bobbs-Merrill. [Peter Smith, $22.80 (08446-0749-5)].

La Farge, John. The Manner Is Ordinary. Harcourt. [o.p.].

Lie, Trygve. In the Cause of Peace. Macmillan. [o.p.].

Murchie, Guy. Song of the Sky. Houghton. [o.p.].

Robertson, R. B. Of Whales and Men. Knopf. [o.p.].

St. John, Robert. Through Malan's Africa. Doubleday. [o.p.].

Smith, Lillian E. The Journey. World. [o.p.].

Stegner, Wallace E. Beyond the Hundredth Meridian. Houghton. [Penguin, paper, $12.95 (0-14-015994-0)].

Thomas, N. M. The Test of Freedom. Norton. [o.p.].

Ward, Barbara. Faith and Freedom. Norton. [o.p.].

White, E. B. The Second Tree from the Corner. Harper. [Harper, paper, $12 (0-14-001278-8)].

Whitehead, A. N. Dialogues, as Recorded by Lucien Price. Little, Brown. [Greenwood, $72.50 (0-8371-9341-9)].

Woodham Smith, Cecil B. F. The Reason Why. McGraw-Hill. [Penguin, paper, $11.95 (0-14-001278-8)].

Woolf, Virginia S. A Writer's Diary. Harcourt. [Harcourt, paper, $13 (0-15-698380-X)].

Notable Books, 1953

Anderson, Sherwood. Letters. [o.p.].

Bartlett, Vernon. Struggle for Africa. [o.p.].

Bellow, Saul. The Adventures of Augie March. [Penguin, paper, $11.95 (0-14-007272-1)].

Brown, E. K. Willa Cather: A Critical Biography. [Univ. of Nebraska, paper, $9.95 (0-8032-6084-9)].

Catton, Bruce. A Stillness at Appomattox. [Peter Smith, $22.80 (0-84466-550-9)].

Churchill, Winston. Triumph and Tragedy. v.6 of The Second World War. [Houghton Mifflin, paper, $14.95 (0-395-41060-6)].

Chute, Marchette. Ben Johnson of Westminster. [o.p.].

Cousins, Norman. Who Speaks for Man? [o.p.].

Cousteau, J. Y. and **Dumas, Frederic.** The Silent World. [o.p.].

A Critical History of Children's Literature. Ed. by C. L. Meigs. [o.p.].

Dean, G. E. Report on the Atom. [o.p.].

Durant, William. The Renaissance. pt.5 of The Story of Civilization. [Simon & Schuster, $35 (0-671-61600-5)].

Fisher, D. F. C. Vermont Tradition. [o.p.].

Florinsky, M. T. Russia: A History and an Interpretation. [o.p.].

Heilbroner, R. L. The Worldly Philosophers. [Simon & Schuster, paper, $14 (0-671-63318-X)].

Herzog, Maurice. Annapurna. [o.p.].

Highet, Gilbert. People, Places, and Books. [o.p.].

Holmes, Oliver Wendell and **Laski, H. J.** Holmes-Laski Letters. 2v. [o.p.].

Hulme, K. C. The Wild Place. [o.p.].

Ickes, H. L. The Secret Diary of Harold Ickes: The First Thousand Days, 1933–1936. Da Capo, $175 (0-2067-0628-8).

Jones, Ernest. The Life and Work of Sigmund Freud. v.1. [Basic, $40 (0-685-00711-1)].

Kirk, Russell. The Conservative Mind. [Regnery, paper, $24.95 (0-89526-724-1)].

Kouwenhoven, J. A. Columbia Historical Portrait of New York. [o.p.].

Lamming, George. In the Castle of My Skin. [Univ. of Michigan, $47.50 (0-472-09468-8); paper, $15.95 (0-472-06468-1)].

Latourette, Kenneth S. A History of Christianity. [Harper, v.1, paper, $21 (0-06-064952-6); v.2, $21 (0-06-064953-4)].

Lewis, Meriwether and **Clark, William.** Journals. Ed. by Bernard De Voto. [Houghton, paper, $15.95 (0-395-08380-X)].

Lincoln, Abraham. Collected Works. [2v. Library of America, $70 (0-940450-68-2)].

Lindbergh, Charles A. The Spirit of St. Louis. [Buccaneer, $33.95 (0-89966-793-7)].

Malraux, André. The Voices of Silence. [Princeton Univ., $95 (0-691-09941-3); paper, $24.95 (0-691-01821-9)].

Maritain, Jacques. Creative Intuition in Art and Poetry. [o.p.].

Maurois, André. Lélia: The Life of George Sand. [o.p.].

May, Rollo. Man's Search for Himself. [Dell, paper, $13.95 (0-38-528617-1)].

Michener, James A. The Bridges at Toko-ri. [Fawcett, paper, $5.95 (0-44-920651-3)].

Paton, Alan. Too Late the Phalarope. [Amereon, $21.95 (0-8919-0392-5); Macmillan, paper, $5.95 (0-68-418500-8)].

Randall, R. P. Mary Lincoln: Biography of a Marriage. [o.p.].

Raverat, G. M. Period Piece. [Univ. of Michigan, paper, $15.95 (0-472-06475-4)].

Richter, Conrad. The Light in the Forest. [Random, $23 (0-394-43314-9)].

Rommel, Erwin. The Rommel Papers. [o.p.].

Ruggles, Eleanor. Prince of Players: Edwin Booth. [Amereon, $25.95 (0-89190-565-0)].

Sandburg, Carl. Always the Young Strangers. [Harcourt, paper, $12.95 (0-15-604765-9)].

Sneider, V. J. A Pail of Oysters. [o.p.].

Stevens, L. C. Russian Assignment. [o.p.].

Tharp, Louise H. Until Victory: Horace Mann and Mary Peabody. [Greenwood, $65 (0-8371-9653-1)].

Thomas, Dylan. Collected Poems. [Norton, paper, $9.95 (0-8112-0205-4)].

Tolstaia, A. L. Tolstoy: A Life of My Father. [o.p.].

Uris, Leon M. Battle Cry. [Bantam, paper, $6.99 (0-55-325983-0)].

Wechsler, J. A. The Age of Suspicion. [Donald Fine, paper, $10.95 (0-917657-38-1)].

Wheeler-Bennett, J. W. The Nemesis of Power. [o.p.].

White, T. H. Fire in the Ashes: Europe in Mid-Century. [o.p.].

Wright, Frank Lloyd. The Future of Architecture. [o.p.].

Young, Jefferson. A Good Man. [o.p.].

Notable Books, 1952

Agar, Herbert. A Declaration of Faith. [o.p.].

Allen, Frederick. The Big Change. [Greenwood, $35 (0-313-23791-3); Harper paper, $14 (0-06-132082-X)].

Behrman, S. N. Duveen. [o.p.].

Berenson, Bernard. Rumor and Reflection. [o.p.].

Bible. The Holy Bible. Revised Standard Version. [Now New Revised Standard Version in many editions]

Brooks, Van Wyck. The Confident Years: 1885–1915. [o.p.].

Castro, Josue. The Geography of Hunger. [o.p.].

Chambers, Whittaker. Witness. [Regnery, $21.95 (0-89526-571-0); paper, $14.95 (0-89526-789-6)].

Clark, Eleanor. Rome and a Villa. [Harper, paper, $12 (0-06-097589-3)].

Conrad, Barnaby. Matador. [o.p.].

Cooke, Alistair. One Man's America. [o.p.].

De Voto, Bernard A. The Course of Empire. [o.p.].

Dewey, Thomas Edmund. Journey to the Far Pacific. [o.p.].

Dobie, James Frank. The Mustangs. [Univ. of Texas, paper, $10.95 (0-292-75081-1)].

Douglas, P. H. Ethics in Government. [Greenwood, $39.75 (0-8371-5579-7)].

Douglas, William O. Beyond the High Himalayas. [o.p.].

Eliot, T. S. Complete Poems and Plays. [Harcourt, $27.95 (0-15-121185-X)].

Ellison, Ralph. Invisible Man. [Random, $17.50 (0-679-60015-9); paper, $11 (0-679-72313-7)].

Frank, Anne. The Diary of a Young Girl. [Many editions available].

Freeman, Douglas. George Washington. v.5, Victory with the Help of France. [Augustus Kelley, $50 (0-6780-2831-1)].

Grew, Joseph C. Turbulent Era. [Ayer, $96.95 (0-8369-5284-7)].

Hand, Learned. The Spirit of Liberty. [o.p.].

Hart-Davis, Rupert. Hugh Walpole. [o.p.].

Hemingway, Ernest. The Old Man and the Sea. [Macmillan, $13.95 (0-68-410245-5); paper, $6.95 (0-68-471805-7)].

Hoover, Herbert. Memoirs. v.2, The Cabinet and the Presidency; v.3, The Great Depression. [o.p.].

Howard, Joseph Kinsey. Strange Empire. [Minnesota Historical Society, paper, $16.95 (0-87351-298-7)].

Killilea, Marie. Karen. [Buccaneer, $27.95 1-5684-9098-4)].

King, Ernest J. and Whitewall, W. Fleet Admiral King: A Naval Record. [Da Capo, $74.50 (0-3067-0772-1)].

Koestler, Arthur. Arrow in the Blue. [o.p.].

Krutch, Joseph Wood. The Desert Year. [Univ. of Arizona, paper, $13.95 (0-8165-0923-9)].

Latourette, Kenneth S. The American Record in the Far East, 1945–1951. [o.p.].

Lubell, Samuel. The Future of American Politics. [Greenwood, $41.50 (0-313-24377-8)].

MacLeish, Archibald. Collected Poems, 1917–1952. [o.p.].

Millay, Edna St. Vincent. The Letters of Edna St. Vincent Millay. [o.p.].

Niebuhr, Reinhold. The Irony of American History. [Macmillan, $30 (0-68-417602-5)].

O'Donovan, Frank. The Stories of Frank O'Connor, by Frank O'Connor, pseud. [Knopf, $20 (0-394-51602-8); paper, $18 (0-394-71048-7)].

Philbrick, Herbert Arthur. I Led 3 Lives. [o.p.].

Porter, Katherine Anne. The Days Before. [Ayer, $21.95 (0-8369-2066-X)].

Prescott, H. F. M. The Man on a Donkey. [o.p.].

Remarque, Erich Maria. Spark of Life. [o.p.].

Rowan, Carl T. South of Freedom. [o.p.].

Shaw, George Bernard. Bernard Shaw, and Mrs. Patrick Campbell, Their Correspondence. [AMS, $36.50 (0-4042-0233-0)].

Shirer, William L. Midcentury Journey. [Buccaneer, $27.95 (0-56849-429-7)].

Simon, Edith. The Golden Hand. [o.p.].

Stevenson, Adlai E. Speeches of Adlai Stevenson. [o.p.].

Strong, George Templeton. The Diary of George Templeton Strong. [Univ. of Washington, $35 (0-295-96511-8); paper, $17.50 (0-295-96512-6)].

Thomas, Benjamin P. Abraham Lincoln. [Random, $18 (0-394-60468-7)].

Vandenberg, Arthur H. The Private Papers of Senator Vandenberg. [o.p.].

Vining, Elizabeth Gray. Windows for the Crown Prince. [Tuttle, paper, $12.95 (0-8048-1604-2)].

Webb, Walter Prescot. The Great Frontier. [Univ. of Nebraska, paper, $9.95 (0-8032-9711-4)].

Wecter, Dixon. Sam Clemens of Hannibal. [AMS, $36 (0-404-15328-3)].

Wilmot, Chester. The Struggle for Europe. [Greenwood, $43 (0-8371-5711-0)].

Wilson, Edmund. The Shores of Light. [Northeastern Univ., paper, $16.95 (0-9303-5068-5)].

Notable Books, 1951

Aldridge, John W. After the Lost Generation: A Critical Study of the Writers of the Two Wars. [Ayer, $23.95 (0-8369-2141-0)].

Asch, Sholem. Moses. [o.p.].

Ashley-Montagu, M. F. Statement on Race. Greenwood, $55 (0-313-22793-X)].

Auden, Wystan Hugh. Nones. [o.p.].

Barth, Alan. Loyalty of Free Men. [o.p.].

Berger, Meyer. Story of the New York Times, 1851–1951. [Ayer, $21.95 (0-4050-1652-2)].

Bradley, Omar Nelson. A Soldier's Story. [o.p.].

Carson, Rachel L. The Sea around Us. [Oxford, $24.95 (0-19-506186-1); paper, $10.95 (0-19-506997-8)].

Churchill, Winston. Closing the Ring. [Houghton Mifflin, paper, $14.95 (0-395-41059-2)].

Conant, James B. Science and Common Sense. [o.p.].

Costain, Thomas B. The Magnificent Century. [Buccaneer, $37.95 (1-56849-371-1)].

Davidson, Marshall B. Life in America. [o.p.].

Douglas, William O. Strange Lands and Friendly People. [o.p.].

Forrestal, James. The Forrestal Diaries. [o.p.].

Freeman, Douglas. George Washington: v.3, Planter and Patriot; v.4, Leader of the Revolution. [o.p.].

Harrod, Roy F. Life of John Maynard Keynes. [Norton, paper, $14.95 (0-393-30024-2)].

Hoover, Herbert. Memoirs: Years of Adventure, 1874–1920. [o.p.].

Hulburd, David. This Happened in Pasadena. [o.p.].

The Interpreter's Bible. v.7. [New Interpreter's Bible now in process, Abingdon, 1994].

Johnson, Gerald W. This American People. [o.p.].

Kefauver, Estes. Crime in America. [Greenwood, $38.50 (0-8371-0126-3)].

Kennan, George Frost. American Diplomacy, 1900–1950. [Univ. of Chicago, paper, $8.95 (0-2264-3147-9)].

Lagerkvist, Par. Barabbas. [Random, paper, $8 (0-679-72544-X)].

Life Magazine. Life's Picture History of Western Man. [o.p.].

Living Ideas in America. Ed. by Henry Steele Commager. [o.p.].

Lorant, Stephan. The Presidency. [o.p.].

McDonald, James G. My Mission to Israel, 1948–1951. [o.p.].

Malone, Dumas. Jefferson and the Rights of Man; v.2. [Little, Brown, $27.50 (0-31-654473-6)].

Mann, Thomas. Holy Sinner. [Univ. of California, $30 (0520-07672-9); paper, $13 (0-520-07671-0)].

Marek, Kurt (Ceram, pseud.). Gods, Graves and Scholars: The Story of Archaeology. [Random, paper, $10 (0-394-74319-9)].

Michener, James. Voice of Asia. [o.p.].

Mizener, Arthur. The Far Side of Paradise. [o.p.].

Monsarrat, Nicholas. The Cruel Sea. [Naval Institute, $32.95 (0-87021-055-6)].

Mumford, Lewis. The Conduct of Life. [o.p.].

Pusey, Merlo J. Charles Evans Hughes. [o.p.].

Robb, David M. The Harper History of Painting. [o.p.].

Roosevelt, Theodore. Letters of Theodore Roosevelt; v.1–4. [Harvard Univ., $75 (0-685-02130-0)].

Salinger, J. D. Catcher in the Rye. [Little, Brown, $22.95 (0-316-76953-3); paper, $4.99 (0-316-76948-7)].

Santayana, George. Dominations and Powers. [Augustus Kelley, $45 (0-6780-2775-7)].

Teale, Edwin Way. North with the Spring. [St. Martin's, paper, $12.95 (0-31-204457-7)].

Trueblood, Elton. The Life We Prize. [o.p.].

Van Der Post, Laurens. Venture to the Interior. [o.p.].

Ward, Barbara. Policy for the West. [o.p.].

Waters, Ethel. His Eye Is on the Sparrow. [Greenwood, $45 (0-313-20201-X)].

Welles, Sumner. Seven Decisions that Shaped History. [o.p.].

Williams, Peggy Eileen Arabella. Autobiography. [o.p.].

Wilson, Donald P. My Six Convicts. [o.p.].

Woodham-Smith, Cecil. Florence Nightingale. [o.p.]

Wouk, Herman. The Caine Mutiny. [Naval Institute, $32.95 (0-87021-010-6)]; Little, Brown, paper, $10.95 (0-316-95510-8)].

Notable Books, 1950

Appleton, Le Roy H. Indian Art of the Americas. [As *American Indian Design & Decoration,* Dover, paper, $9.95 (0-486-22704-9)].

Bainton, Roland H. Here I Stand. [Peter Smith, $18 (0-8446-6225-9); Abingdon, paper, $5.95 (0-6871-6895-3)].

Barzun, Jacques. Berlioz and the Romantic Century. [o.p.].

Boswell, James. London Journal, 1762–1763. [Yale, paper, $16 (0-300-05735-0)].

Bowen, Catherine. John Adams and the American Revolution. [o.p.].

Brinton, Clarence Crane. Ideas and Men. [o.p.].

Christensen, Edwin O. Index of American Design. [o.p.].

Churchill, Winston. Grand Alliance. [Houghton Mifflin, paper, $14.95 (0-395-41057-6)].

Churchill, Winston. Hinge of Fate. [Houghton Mifflin, paper, $14.95 (0-395-41058-4)].

Chute, Marchette Gaylord. Shakespeare of London. [o.p.].

Coit, Margaret L. John C. Calhoun. [Univ. of South Carolina, $49.95 (0-87249-774-7); paper, $14.95 (0-87249-775-5)].

Commanger, Henry Steele. American Mind. [Yale Univ., $17 (0-300-00046-4)].

Douglas, William O. Of Men and Mountains. [o.p.].

Durant, William James. Age of Faith. [Simon & Schuster, $35 (0-671-01200-2)].

Faulkner, William. Collected Stories. [o.p.].

Fischer, Louis. Life of Mahatma Gandhi. [Greenleaf, paper, $18 (0-934676-79-8)].

Fry, Christopher. Lady's Not for Burning. [Oxford, paper, $6.95 (0-19-519916-2)].

Gebler, Ernest. Plymouth Adventure. [o.p.].

Goodspeed, Edgar J. Life of Jesus. [o.p.].

Hart, James D. Popular Book: A History of America's Popular Taste. [Univ. of California, paper, $12 (0-520-00538-4)].

Hersey, John. The Wall. [Random, $25 (0-394-45092-2); paper, $14 (0-394-75696-7)].

Heyerdahl, Thor. Kon-Tiki. [Buccaneer, $35.95 (1-56849-010-0)].

Highet, Gilbert. Art of Teaching. [Random, paper, $10 (0-679-72314-5)].

Jefferson, Thomas. Papers. [Princeton Univ., 28v. available so far].

Johnson, Gerald W. Incredible Tale. [o.p.].

Kelly, Amy Ruth. Eleanor of Aquitaine. [o.p.].

Lewis, Lloyd. Captain Sam Grant. [Little, Brown paper, $13.95 (0-316-52348-8)].

McCune, George M. Korea Today. [Greenwood, $69.50 (0-313-23446-9)].

Menaboni, Athos and **Menaboni, Sarah.** Menaboni's Birds. [o.p.].

Millikan, Robert A. Autobiography. [Ayer, $29.95 (0-405-12558-5)].

Nevins, Allan. Emergence of Lincoln. [o.p.].

Payne, Pierre Stephen Robert. Mao Tse-Tung. [o.p.].

Perkins, Maxwell E. Editor to Author. [Cherokee, $29.95 (0-8779-7229-X)].

Sandburg, Carl. Complete Poems. [o.p.].

Schulberg, Budd. The Disenchanted. [Donald Fine, paper, $8.95 (1-55611-027-8)].

Seldes, Gilbert Vivian. Great Audience. [o.p.].

Tharp, Louise Hall. Peabody Sisters of Salem. [Little, Brown, paper, $8.95 (0-316-83919-1)].

Trilling, Lionel. Liberal Imagination. [o.p.].

Van Doren, Carl. Jane Mecom. [o.p.].

Wiener, Norbert. Human Use of Human Beings: Cybernetics and Society. [Da Capo, paper, $11.95 (0-306-80320-8)].

Notable Books of the 1940s

Notable Books, 1949

Allen, Frederick Lew. The Great Pierpont Morgan. [Marboro, $19.95 (0-88029-453-1].

Arnold, H. H. Global Mission. [Ayer, $37.95 (0-405-03750-3].

Arnow, Harriette Lou. Hunter's Horn. [o.p.].

Asch, Sholem. Mary. [o.p.].

Barr, Stringfellow. The Pilgrimage of Western Man. [Greenwood, $35 (0-8371-6152-5)].

Beebe, William. High Jungle. [o.p.].

Bell, Bernard. Crisis in Education. [o.p.].

Bemis, Samuel Flagg. John Quincy Adams and the Foundation of American Foreign Policy. [o.p.].

Blanshard, Paul. American Freedom and Catholic Power. [Greenwood, $79.50 (0-313-24620-3)].

Brown, Lloyd Arnold. The Story of Maps. [Dover, paper, $10.95 (0-4862-3873-3)].

Bush, Vannevar. Modern Arms and Free Men. [Greenwood, $65 (0-313-24985-7)].

Carr, John D. The Life of Sir Arthur Conan Doyle. [Amereon, $25.95 (0-8919-0973-7); Carroll & Graf, paper, $8.95 (0-8818-4372-5)].

Chapman, F. Spencer. The Jungle Is Neutral. [o.p.].

Churchill, Winston L. Their Finest Hour. [Houghton Mifflin, paper, $11.95 (0-395-4106-8)].

Clark, Walter Van Tilburg. The Track of the Cat. [Univ. of Nevada, paper, $14.95 (0-8741-7230-6)].

Deutscher, Isaac. Stalin. [Oxford, paper, $17.95 (0-19-500273-3)].

Dulles, Foster Rhea. Labor in America. [Harlan Davidson, paper, $24.95 (0-8829-5900-X)].

Frazier, Edward Franklin. The Negro in the United States. [o.p.].

Frost, Robert. Complete Poems of Robert Frost, 1949. [Many editions available].

Gunther, John. Behind the Curtain. [o.p.].

Gunther, John. Death Be Not Proud. [Borgo, $23 (0-8095-9101-4); Harper, paper, $6.50 (0-06-080973-6)].

Guthrie, A. B. The Way West. [Buccaneer, $32.95 (0-89968-305-3); Houghton, paper, $10.95 (0-395-65662-1)].

Hogben, Lancelot. From Cave Painting to Comic Strip. [o.p.].

Kluckhohn, Clyde. Mirror for Man: The Relation of Anthropology to Modern Life. [Univ. of Arizona, paper, $17.95 (0-8165-0919-0)].

Kohn, Hans. The Twentieth Century. [o.p.].

Lattimore, Owen. The Situation in Asia. [o.p.].

Lea, Tom. The Brave Bulls. [o.p.].

Lilienthal, David E. This I Do Believe. [o.p.].

Marquand, John P. Point of No Return. [Academy Chicago, paper, $12 (0-8973-3174-5)].

Maugham, W. Somerset. A Writer's Notebook. [Penguin, paper, $10.95 (0-14-018601-8)].

Mead, Margaret. Male and Female. [o.p.].

Miller, Arthur. Death of a Salesman. [Amereon, $17.95 (0-89190-729-7); Penguin, paper, $14.95 (0-14-024773-4)].

Muntz, Hope. The Golden Warrior. [o.p.].

Orwell, George. Nineteen Eighty-Four. [Many editions available]

Overstreet, Harry Al. The Mature Mind. [o.p.].

Pearson, Hesketh. Dickens. [o.p.].

Roosevelt, Eleanor. This I Remember. [Greenwood, $85 (0-8371-7702-2)].

Rusk, Ralph L. The Life of Ralph Waldo Emerson. [o.p.].

Schlesinger, Arthur. The Vital Center. [Da Capo, $32.50 (0-306-76280-3); paper, $10.95 (0-306-80323-2)].

Sheean, Vincent. Lead, Kindly Light. [o.p.].

Sheen, Fulton. Peace of Soul. [Liguori, $10.95 (0-89243-915-7)].

Smith, Howard K. The State of Europe. [o.p.].

Smith, Lillian. Killers of the Dream. [Norton, paper, $9.95 (0-393-31160-0)].

Stettinius, Edward R. Roosevelt and the Russians. [Greenwood, $35 (0-8371-2976-1)].

Stuart, Jesse. The Thread That Runs So True. [Simon & Schuster, $40 (0-684-15160-X); paper, $9.95 (0-684-71904-5)].

U.S. Commission on Organization of the Executive Branch of the Government. The Hoover Commission Report. [o.p.].

Van Doren, Mark. Nathaniel Hawthorne. [Greenwood, $59.75 (0-8371-6552-0)].

Weizmann, Chaim. Trial and Error: The Autobiography of Chaim Weizmann. [Greenwood, $35 (0-8371-6166-5)].

Welty, Eudora. The Golden Apples. [Harcourt, paper, $10 (0-15-636090-X)].

Williams, Kenneth. Lincoln Finds a General. [Indiana Univ., $27.95 (0-253-33437-3); paper, $6.95 (0-253-20359-7)].

Notable Books, 1948

Bradley, David J. No Place to Hide. [Univ. Press of New England, paper, $13.95 (0-8745-1275-1)].

Camus, Albert. The Plague. [Random, $23 (0-394-44061-7)].

Chase, Stuart. The Proper Study of Mankind. [Greenwood, $35 (0-313-20261-3)].

Churchill, Winston. The Gathering Storm. [Houghton, paper, $16.95 (0-395-41055-X)].

Conant, James. Education in a Divided World. [Greenwood, $35 (0-8371-2548-0)].

Crankshaw, Edward. Russia and the Russians. [o.p.].

Eisenhower, Dwight D. Crusade in Europe. [Da Capo, $45 (0-306-70768-3); paper, $14.95 (0-306-80109-4)].

Evatt, Herbert V. The United Nations. [o.p.].

Fairbank, John King. The United States and China. [o.p.].

Faulkner, William. Intruder in the Dust. [Random, $13.95 (0394-43074-3); paper, $9 (0-679-73651-4)].

Freeman, Douglas S. George Washington, 2v. [Abridged ed., Simon & Schuster, paper, $18.95 (0-684-18354-4)].

Gandhi, Mohandas Karamchand. Gandhi's Autobiography. [Greenleaf, $12 (0-934676-40-2); paper, $5 (0-934676-68-2)].

Giedion, Sigfried. Mechanization Takes Command. [Norton, paper, $16.95 (0-39-300489-9)].

Greene, Graham. The Heart of the Matter. [Viking, $9.95 (0-14-018496-1); paper, $5.95 (0-14-001789-5)].

Hamilton, Edith. Witness to the Truth: Christ and His Interpreters. [o.p.].

Hull, Cordell. The Memoirs of Cordell Hull. [Reprint Services, $150 (0-7812-4811-6)].

Joy, Charles F. and **Arnold, Melvin.** The Africa of Albert Schweitzer. [o.p.].

Kinsey, Alfred Charles and others. Sexual Behavior in the Human Male. [o.p.].

Krutch, Joseph W. Henry David Thoreau. [Greenwood, $35 (0-8371-6587-3)].

La Guardia, Fiorello. The Making of an Insurgent: An Autobiography. [Greenwood, $55 (0-313-22769-1)].

Laski, Harold J. The American Democracy. [Augustus Kelley, $57.50 (0-678-03165-7)].

LeCompte Du Nouy. The Road to Reason. [o.p.].

Literary History of the United States. Ed. by Robert E. Spiller. [o.p.].

Lockridge, Ross Jr. Raintree Country. [Buccaneer, $49.95 (0-89966-865-8); Penguin, paper, $18.95 (0-14-023666-X)].

Lomax, John A. and **Lomax, Alan.** Folk Song U.S.A. [o.p.].

McWilliams, Carey. A Mask for Privilege. [Greenwood, $59.75 (0-313-20880-8)].

Mailer, Norman. The Naked and the Dead. [Holt, $30 (0-8050-1273-7); paper, $14.95 (0-8050-05218)].

Malone, Dumas. Jefferson and his Time (v.1). [Little, Brown, $29.95 (0-316-54474-4); paper, $15.95 (0-316-54472-8)].

Mann, Thomas. Dr. Faustus. [Random, $18.50 (0-679-60042-6); paper, $13 (0-679-73905-X)].

Mearns, David C. The Lincoln Papers. [o.p.].

Merton, Thomas. The Seven Storey Mountain. [Harcourt, $17 (0-15-181354-X); paper, $12 (0-15-680679-7)].

Paton, Alan. Cry, the Beloved Country. [Simon & Schuster, $35 (0-684-15559-1); paper, $12 (0-684-81894-9)].

Plivier, Theodore. Stalingrad. [o.p.].

Russell, Bertrand. Human Knowledge. [Routledge, paper, $22.95 (0-4150-8302-8)].

Sandburg, Carl. Remembrance Rock. [Harcourt, paper, $19.95 (0-15-676390-7)].

Shaw, Irwin. The Young Lions. [o.p.].

Sherwood, Robert Emmet. Roosevelt and Hopkins. [o.p.].

Sitwell, Osbert. Laughter in the Next Room. [Greenwood, $35 (0-8371-6042-1)].

Stewart, George Ripp. Fire. [Univ. of Nebraska, paper, $7.95 (0-8032-9138-8)].

Stilwell, Joseph W. The Stilwell Papers. [AMS, $44.50 (0-404-20247-0); Da Capo, paper, $14.95 (0-306-80428-X)].

Stimson, Henry L. On Active Service in Peace and War. [o.p.].

Taylor, Francis H. The Taste of Angels. [o.p.].

Toynbee, Arnold J. Civilization on Trial. [o.p.].

Van Doren, Carl C. The Great Rehearsal. [Greenwood, $65 (0-313-23492-2)].

Vogt, William. Road to Survival. [o.p.].

Ward, Barbara. The West at Bay. [o.p.].

Wecter, Dixon. The Age of the Great Depression, 1929–1941. [AMS, $42.50 (0-4042-0283-7)].

Welles, Sumner. We Need Not Fail. [o.p.].

White, Walter Francis. A Man Called White: A Biography. [Ayer, $35.95 (0-405-01906-8); Univ. of Georgia, paper, $17.95 (0-8203-1698-9)].

Wilder, Thornton. The Ides of March. [Buccaneer, $24.95 (1-56849-445-9)].

Notable Books, 1947

Brace, G. W. The Garretson Chronicle. [Norton, paper, $1.65 (0-39-300272-1)].

Brooks, Van Wyck. The Times of Melville and Whitman. [o.p.].

Burns, John Horne. The Gallery. [o.p.].

Butterfield, Roger Place. The American Past. [o.p.].

Byrnes, James Francis. Speaking Frankly. [o.p.].

Canby, Henry S. American Memoir. [o.p.].

Colum, Mary G. Life and the Dream. [o.p.].

Commission on Freedom of the Press. A Free and Responsible Press. [o.p.].

Conant, James B. On Understanding Science. [o.p.].

Crum, Bartley Cavanaugh. Behind the Silken Curtain: A Personal Account of Anglo-American Diplomacy. [Milah, $24.95 (0-9646886-1-1)].

Dallin, David J. Forced Labor in Soviet Russia. [o.p.].

Davidson, David A. The Steeper Cliff. [o.p.].

Dean, Vera. The United States and Russia. [o.p.].

De Voto, Bernard A. Across the Wide Missouri. [Houghton Mifflin, paper, $12.95 (0-39-508374-5)].

Duncan, Thomas W. Gus the Great. [o.p.].

Fischer, Louis. Gandhi and Stalin. [o.p.].

Frost, Robert. Steeple Bush. [o.p.].

Gunther, John. Inside U.S.A. [o.p.].

Guthrie, A. B. The Big Sky. [Houghton Mifflin, paper, $12.95 (0-39-561153-9)].

Haines, William. Command Decision. [Dramatists Play Service, paper, $4.75 (0-8222-0233-6)].

Hobson, Laura. Gentleman's Agreement. [Amereon, $20.95 (0-88411-845-2)].

Johnson, Hewlett. Soviet Russia Since the War. [Greenwood, $69.50 (0-313-20865-4)].

Johnson, Walter. William Allen White's America. [o.p.].

Kantor, Mackinlay. But Look, the Morn. [o.p.].

Keith, Agnes N. Three Came Home. [o.p.].

Lauterbach, Richard E. Danger from the East. [o.p.].

LeCompte Du Nuoy. Human Destiny. [o.p.].

Levi, Carlo. Christ Stopped at Eboli. [Farrar, paper, $10 (0-374-50316-8)].

Levin, Meyer. My Father's House. [o.p.].

Lewis, Sinclair. Kingsblood Royal. [o.p.].

Lundberg, Ferdinand. Modern Woman: The Lost Sex. [o.p.].

Matthiessen, Francis Otto. The James Family. [o.p.].

Mauldin, Bill. Back Home. [o.p.].

Meyer, Cord. Peace or Anarchy. [o.p.].

Millis, Walter. This Is Pearl! [Greenwood, $65 (0-8371-5795-1)].

Morison, Samuel E. The Battle of the Atlantic. [Little, Brown, $50 (0-316-58301-4).

Mott, Frank L. Golden Multitudes. [o.p.].

Murphy, Robert C. Logbook for Grace. [o.p.].

Nevins, Allan. Ordeal of the Union, 2v. [Macmillian, $25 (0-02-035442-9)].

Paul, Elliot H. Linden on the Saugus Branch. [Reprint Services, $99 (0-7812-8609-3)].

President's Committee on Civil Rights. To Secure These Rights. [o.p.].

Roberts, Kenneth Lew. Lydia Bailey. [o.p.].

Shirer, William L. End of a Berlin Diary. [Buccaneer, $27.95 (1-56849-428-9)].

Spence, Hartzell. Vain Shadow. [o.p.].

Stone, Irving. Adversary in the House. [o.p.].

Taylor, Edmund L. Richer by Asia. [o.p.].

Toynbee, Arnold. A Study of History (abridged). [Oxford, paper, $15.95 (0-19-505081-9)].

Walker, Mildred. The Quarry. [Univ. of Nebraska, paper, $14 (0-8032-9779-3)].

West, Rebecca. The Meaning of Treason. [o.p.].

Williams, Ben Ames. House Divided. [o.p.].

Notable Books, 1946

Barbour, Thomas. A Naturalist's Scrapbook. [o.p.].

Beard, Mary R. Woman as Force in History. [Persea, paper, $12.95 (0-89255-113-5)].

Bridge, Ann. Singing Waters. [o.p.].

Bulosan, Carlos. America Is in the Heart. [Univ. of Washington, paper, $13.95 (0-295-9528-9)].

Butcher, Harry C. My Three Years with Eisenhower. [o.p.].

Chute, Marchette Gaylord. Geoffrey Chaucer of England. [o.p.].

Clapper, Olive. Washington Tapestry. [o.p.].

Corbett, Jim. Man-Eaters of Kumaon. [Buccaneer, $25.95 (0-8996-6574-8); Oxford, paper, $8.95 (0-19-562255-3)].

Crow, John. Epic of Latin America. [4th ed., Univ. of California, $60 (0-520-07868-3); paper, $18 (0-520-07723-7)].

Dean, Vera. Four Cornerstones of Peace. [o.p.].

Dos Passos, John. Tour of Duty. [o.p.].

Dreiser, Theodore. The Bulwark. [o.p.].

Fast, Howard. The American. [o.p.].

Fowler, Gene. A Solo in Tom-toms. [o.p.].

Gould, Ralph E. Yankee Storekeeper. [Reprint Services, $69 (0-7812-8535-6)].

Greenslet, Ferris. The Lowells and Their Seven Worlds. [o.p.].

Halsey, Margaret. Color Blind. [o.p.].

Hersey, John. Hiroshima. [Knopf, $21 (0-394-54844-2); Random, paper, $4.50 (0-679-72103-7)].

Howe, Helen H. We Happy Few. [o.p.].

Hughes, Lora Wood. No Time for Tears. [Univ. of Nebraska, $30 (0-8032-2336-6); paper, $7.95 (0-8032-7229-4)].

Hume, Edward H. Doctors East, Doctors West. [o.p.].

Hutton, Graham. Midwest at Noon. [Northern Illinois Univ., paper, $14 (0-8758-0550-7)].

Ingersoll, Ralph M. Top Secret. [o.p.].

Jackson, R. H. The Case against the Nazi War Criminals. [o.p.].

Kravchenko, Victor. I Chose Freedom. [Transaction, paper, $24.95 (0-8873-8754-3)].

La Farge, Christopher. The Sudden Guest. [o.p.].

Lamb, Harold. Alexander of Macedon. [o.p.].

Liebman, Joshua Loth. Peace of Mind. [Carol, $9.95 (0-8065-1496-5)].

Logan, Spencer. Negro's Faith in America. [o.p.].

McWilliams, Vera. Lafcadio Hearn. [o.p.].

Moore, Ruth. Spoonhandle. [Blackberry, paper, $10.95 (0-9423-9649-9)].

Perkins, Frances. The Roosevelt I Knew. [o.p.].

Pyle, Ernest. Last Chapter. [o.p.].

Quezon, Manuel L. The Good Fight. [AMS, $49.50 (0-4040-9036-2)].

Richter, Conrad. The Fields. [Ohio Univ., paper, $12.95 (0-8214-0979-4)].

Roosevelt, Elliott. As He Saw It. [o.p.].

Schmitt, Gladys. David, the King. [o.p.].

Seagrave, Gordon S. Burma Surgeon Returns. [o.p.].

Sevareid, Eric. Not So Wild a Dream. [o.p.].

Sharp, Margery. Britannia Mews. [o.p.].

Sheean, Vincent. This House against This House. [o.p.].

Starling, Edmund W. Starling of the White House. [o.p.].

Stowe, Leland. While Time Remains. [o.p.].

Van Paassen, Pierre. Earth Could be Fair. [o.p.].

Wainwright, Jonathan M. General Wainwright's Story. [Greenwood, $35 (0-8371-2972-9)].

Ward, Mary Jane. Snake Pit. [Buccaneer, $21.95 (0-8996-6260-9)].

Welty, Eudora. Delta Wedding. [Harcourt, $15.95 (0-15-124774-9); paper, $8.95 (0-15-625280-5)].

White, Vaughan. Our Neighbors, the Chinese. [o.p.].

White, William A. Autobiography of William Allen White. [Univ. Press of Kansas, $35 (0-7006-0470-7); paper, $12.95 (0-7006-0471-5)].

Williams, Oscar. Little Treasury of Modern Poetry. [o.p.].

Notable Books, 1945

Adamic, Louis. A Nation of Nations. [o.p.].

Adams, Samuel H. A. Woollcott. [Ayer, $25.95 (0-8369-5518-8)].

Auden, W. H. The Collected Poetry of W. H. Auden. [Many editions available]

Barzun, Jacques. Teacher in America. [Liberty, $14 (0-9139-6678-9); paper, $6 (0-9139-6679-7)].

Bowers, Claude G. The Young Jefferson, 1743–1789. [o.p.].

Bromfield, Louis. Pleasant Valley. [Amereon, $24.95 (0-8841-1504-6)].

Caruso, Dorothy. Enrico Caruso, His Life and Death. [Greenwood, $62.50 (0-313-25377-3)].

Costain, Thomas B. The Black Rose. [o.p.].

Dickinson, Emily. Bolts of Melody. [o.p.].

Dobie, James Frank. A Texan in England. [Univ. of Texas, paper, $11.95 (0-292-78034-6)].

Du Bois, W. E. B. Color and Democracy. [Kraus, $10 (0-5272-5290-5)].

Eskelund, Karl. My Chinese Wife. [o.p.].

Harvard University. General Education in a Free Society. [o.p.].

Hobart, Alice Tisdale. The Peacock Sheds His Tail. [o.p.].

James, Marquis. The Cherokee Strip. [Univ. of Oklahoma, paper, $14.95 (0-8061-2537-3)].

Langley, Adria. A Lion Is in the Streets. [o.p.].

Lattimore, Owen. Solution in Asia. [AMS, $31.50 (0-4041-0635-8)].

Lauterbach, Richard E. These Are the Russians. [o.p.].

Lewis, Sinclair. Cass Timberlane. [Amereon, $17.95 (0-8488-1411-8)].

MacDonald, Betty. The Egg and I. [Amereon, $21.95 (0-8919-0959-1); Harper paper, $12 (0-06-091428-9)].

Marshall, Bruce. The World, the Flesh, and Father Smith. [o.p.].

Mauldin, Bill H. Up Front. [Norton, $21.95 (0-393-03053-9)].

Mencken, Henry L. The American Language. First Supplement. [Knopf, paper, $25 (0-394-73315-0)].

Norris, George W. Fighting Liberal. [Univ. of Nebraska, paper, $14.95 (0-8032-8365-2)].

Papashvily, George. Anything Can Happen. [o.p.].

Peattie, Donald C. Immortal Village. [o.p.].

Pinckney, Josephine. Three O'Clock Dinner. [o.p.].

Rama Rau, Santha. Home to India. [o.p.].

Robeson, Eslanda C. African Journey. [Greenwood, $35 (0-8371-6222-X)].

Russell, Bertrand. A History of Western Philosophy. [Simon & Schuster, paper, $22 (0-67-120158-1)].

Santayana, George. The Middle Span. [v1. & v.2, Simon & Schuster, $35 (0-684-16830-8)].

Schlesinger, Arthur. The Age of Jackson. [Little, Brown, $22.50 (0-316-77344-1); paper, $15.95 (0-316-77343-3)].

Shaw, Lau. Rickshaw Boy. [o.p.].

Shellabarger, Samuel. Captain from Castile. [o.p.].

Simonov, Konstantin M. Days and Nights. [o.p.].

Smyth, Henry De Wolf. Atomic Energy for Military Purposes. [Da Capo, $35 (0-306-70767-5); Stanford Univ., paper, $13.95 (0-8047-1722-2)].

Snow, Edgar. The Pattern of Soviet Power. [o.p.].

Stegner, Wallace E. One Nation. [o.p.].

Steinbeck, John. Cannery Row. [Penguin, $9.95 (0-14-018737-5)].

Stewart, George R. Names on the Land. [o.p.].

Ullman, James Ramsey. The White Tower. [o.p.].

U.S. War Dept. Chief of Staff. General Marshall's Report. [o.p.].

Wallace, Henry A. Sixty Million Jobs. [o.p.].

Welles, Sumner. An Intelligent American's Guide to the Peace. [o.p.].

Wescott, Glenway. Apartment in Athens. [o.p.].

Willison, George F. Saints and Strangers. [Parnassus, paper, $12.50 (0-94016-019-6)].

Wise, James W. The Springfield Plan. [o.p.].

Woodward, William E. Tom Paine: America's Godfather, 1737–1809. [o.p.].

Wright, Richard. Black Boy. [Buccaneer, $21.95 (1-56849-067-4); Harper paper, $6.50 (0-06-081250-8)].

Yank. The Army Weekly. The Best from Yank. [o.p.].

Notable Books, 1944

Adams, James D. The Shape of Books to Come. [Ayer, $20.95 (0-8369-2479-7)].

Adams, James T. Album of American History. v.1. [3v. Simon & Schuster, $295 (0-684-16848-0)].

Adler, Mortimer J. How to Think about War and Peace. [Fordham Univ., $30 (0-8232-1642-X); paper, $18 (0-8232-1643-8)].

Allen, Hervey. Bedford Village. [o.p.].

Becker, Carl L. How New Will the Better World Be? [Ayer, $23.95 (0-8369-2482-7)].

Benét, Stephen Vincent. America. [o.p.].

Best, Herbert. Young'un. [o.p.].

Bodmer, Frederick. The Loom of Language. [Norton, paper, $16.95 (0-393-0034-X)].

Botkin, B. A. A Treasury of American Folklore. [o.p.].

Bourke-White, Margaret. They Call It "Purple Heart Valley." [o.p.].

Bowen, Catherine D. Yankee from Olympus. [o.p.].

Brooks, Van Wyck. The World of Washington Irving. [o.p.].

Brown, Harry. A Walk in the Sun. [Carroll & Graf, $3.95 (0-8818-4117-X)].

Brown, John Mason. Many a Watchful Night. [o.p.].

Carrighar, Sally. One Day on Beetle Rock. [Univ. of Nebraska, paper, $6.95 (0-8032-6301-5)].

Chase, Mary Ellen. The Bible and the Common Reader. [o.p.].

Cronin, Archibald Joseph. The Green Years. [o.p.].

Davenport, Russell Wheeler. My Country. [o.p.].

Duffus, Robert. The Valley and Its People. [o.p.].

Fast, Howard Melvin. Freedom Road. [o.p.].

Fowler, Gene. Good Night, Sweet Prince: The Life and Times of John Barrymore. [Mercury, paper, $12.95 (0-916515-56-7)].

Grew, Joseph C. Ten Years in Japan. [Ayer, $40.95 (0-4050-4600-6)].

Hatcher, Harlan H. The Great Lakes. [o.p.].

Hazard, Paul. Books, Children & Men. [Horn Book, paper, $11.95 (0-87675-059-5)].

Helmericks, Constance. We Live in Alaska. [o.p.].

Hersey, John R. A Bell for Adano. [Random, $22.95 (0-394-41660-0); paper, $11 (0-394-75695-9)].

Jaffe, Bernard. Men of Science in America. [Ayer, $68.95 (0-4051-2551-8)]

Johnston, Eric A. America Unlimited. [o.p.].

Karski, Jan. Story of a Secret State. [o.p.].

Krutch, Joseph W. Samuel Johnson. [o.p.].

Landon, Margaret. Anna and the King of Siam. [Buccaneer, $29.95 (0-89966-753-8)].

Lippmann, Walter. U.S. War Aims. [o.p.].

McWilliams, Carey. Prejudice: Japanese-Americans. [o.p.].

Myrdal, Gunnar. An American Dilemma. [Transaction, paper, $29.95 (1-56000-857-1)].

Porter, Katherine Anne. The Leaning Tower. [o.p.].

Pyle, Ernest. Brave Men. [Greenwood, $35 (0-8371-7368-X)].

Santayana, George. Persons and Places. [Simon & Schuster, $35 (0-684-16830-8)].

Sherrod, Robert. Tarawa: The Story of a Battle. [Admiral Nimitz Foundation, $15 (0-934841-06-3); paper, $9.95 (0-934841-14-4)].

Shotwell, James T. The Great Decision. [o.p.].

Shute, Nevil. Pastoral. [Amereon, $20.95 (0-8841-1322-1)].

Smith, Lillian. Strange Fruit. [Buccaneer, $24.95 (1-56849-420-3)].

Snow, Edgar. People on Our Side. [o.p.].

Stettinius, Edward R. Lend-lease: Weapon for Victory. [o.p.].

Stone, Irving. Immortal Wife. [o.p.].

Stowe, Leland. They Shall Not Sleep. [o.p.].

Straus, Nathan. The Seven Myths of Housing. [Ayer, $28.95 (0-405-05426-2)].

U.S. National Gallery of Art. Masterpieces of Painting. [o.p.].

Waller, Willard W. The Veteran Comes Back. [o.p.].

Welles, Sumner. The Time for Decision. [o.p.].

Woodward, William E. The Way Our People Lived. [o.p.].

Author Index

Rheims, Maurice. 104.
Rhodes, Richard. 27.
Rich, Adrienne. 65.
Richter, Conrad. 142, 159.
Riessman, Frank. 119.
Rivabella, Omar. 30.
Robb, David M. 147.
Roberts, Gene. 117.
Roberts, Kenneth Lew. 157.
Robertson, R. B. 140.
Robeson, Eslanda C. 161.
Robinson, David. 33.
Robinson, Marilynne. 51.
Rock, John Charles. 117.
Rockwell, John. 42.
Rodriguez, Richard. 47.
Roethke, Theodore. 108, 111, 114.
Rogers, Thomas. 90.
Rommel, Erwin. 142.
Roosevelt, Eleanor. 152.
Roosevelt, Elliott. 159.
Roosevelt, Theodore. 147.
Rosengarten, Theodore. 30, 82.
Ross, Ishbel. 131.
Rossiter, C. L. 136.
Rossner, Judith. 78.
Rosten, Leo Calvin. 101.
Rostow, Walt Whitman. 125.
Roszak, Theodore. 30.
Roth, Philip. 14, 60, 99.
Rowan, Carl T. 136, 145.
Roy, Jules. 111.
Rudofsky, Bernard. 99, 111.
Ruesch, Hans. 86.
Rugg, Harold. 117.
Ruggles, Eleanor. 142.
Rukeyser, Muriel. 74.
Rush, Norman. 30.
Rushdie, Salman. 42.
Rusk, Ralph L. 152.
Russell, Bertrand. 104, 129, 136, 155, 162.
Russell, Ross. 86.
Russo, Richard. 7.
Ryan, Cornelius. 60.
Ryan, Kathryn Morgan. 60.
Rynne, Xavier (pseud.). 117.
Saarinen, Aline Bernstein. 131.
Saarinen, Eero. 119.
Sachs, Nelly. 105.
Sack, John. 105.
Sagan, Carl. 69.
Sajer, Guy. 94.
Sakurai, Atsushi. 37.
Salinger, J. D. 123, 147.
Salisbury, Harrison. 65, 99.
Salomonsen, Finn. 130.
Sampson, Anthony. 69.
Sandburg, Carl. 142, 149, 155.
Sanderson, Ivan Terence. 123.
Sandoz, Mari. 108.
Santayana, George. 147, 162, 164.
Santoli, Al. 51.
Sarton, May. 65, 101.

Sartre, Jean Paul. 114, 117.
Savage, Thomas. 69.
Scarisbrick, J. J. 102.
Schaeffer, Susan Fromberg. 19.
Schaller, George B. 8, 86, 114.
Scheffer, Victor B. 99.
Schell, Jonathan. 47, 105.
Schell, Orville. 34.
Schlesinger, Arthur M. 65, 86, 111, 125, 129, 152, 162.
Schmitt, Gladys. 160.
Schmutzler, Robert. 114.
Schorer, Mark. 123.
Schreiber, William Ildephonse. 119.
Schulberg, Budd. 105, 149.
Schulman, Audrey. 4.
Schumacher, Julie. 1.
Schwartz, Alan U. 112.
Schwartz-Nobel, Loretta. 51.
Schwarz-Bart, Andre. 86, 125.
Scott, Paul. 70, 79, 108, 114.
Scott, Rachel. 82.
Scully, Vincent. 79.
Seager, Allan. 102.
Seagrave, Gordon S. 160.
Seagrave, Sterling. 34.
Secrest, Meryle. 82.
Segal, Julius. 108.
Seldes, G. V. 136, 149.
Selye, Hans. 114.
Selzer, Richard. 11, 70.
Sergeant, Elizabeth Shepley. 125.
Servan-Schreiber, J. J. 102.
Sevareid, Eric. 160.
Sewall, Richard B. 79.
Sexton, Anne. 79, 99.
Sexton, Linda Gray. 22.
Shachtman, Max. 105.
Shapiro, Judith. 41.
Shapiro, Karl. 65, 114, 125.
Shaplen, Robert. 111.
Sharansky, Natan. 24.
Sharp, Alan. 111.
Sharp, Margery. 160.
Shaw, George Bernard. 145.
Shaw, Irwin. 65, 155.
Shaw, Lau. 162.
Shawcross, William. 60.
Sheaffer, Louis. 87.
Sheean, Vincent. 153, 160.
Sheehy, Gail. 74.
Sheen, Fulton. 153.
Shellabarger, Samuel. 162.
Shelton, Richard. 11.
Sherrod, Robert. 164.
Sherwood, Robert Emmet. 155.
Shilts, Randy. 27.
Shipler, David K. 30.
Shirer, William L. 38, 126, 145, 158.
Shotwell, James T. 164.
Shreve, Susan Richards. 70.
Shute, Nevil. 164.
Sichel, Pierre. 105.
Silberman, Charles E. 65, 97,

114.
Silk, Leonard. 55.
Silk, Mark. 55.
Silver, James Wesley. 114.
Silverman, Jonathan. 42.
Simon, Edith. 145.
Simonov, Konstantin M. 162.
Simpson, Eileen. 47.
Simpson, Louis Aston Marantz. 111.
Simpson, Mona. 25.
Singer, Isaac Bashevis. 47, 90, 108, 120.
Sitwell, Osbert. 155.
Skinner, Burrhus Frederic. 94.
Smedley, Agnes. 74.
Smiley, Jane. 11.
Smith, Adam. 51.
Smith, Aileen M. 79.
Smith, Hedrick. 74.
Smith, Howard K. 153.
Smith, Lee. 16, 22.
Smith, Lillian. 140, 153, 164.
Smith, Page. 79, 114, 120.
Smith, W. Eugene. 79.
Smyth, Henry De Wolf. 162.
Sneider, V. J. 142.
Snow, Charles Percy. 105, 126, 131.
Snow, Edgar. 131, 162, 164.
Solzhenitsyn, Aleksandr Isaevich. 90, 102.
Song, Cathy. 43.
Sontag, Susan. 65, 109.
Sorenson, Theodore C. 111.
Soyinka, Wole. 47.
Spark, Muriel. 22, 74.
Speer, Albert. 97.
Spence, Hartzell. 158.
Spence, Jonathan D. 38, 51.
Spencer, Elizabeth. 51.
Spencer, Scott. 61.
Spender, Stephen, ed. 79.
Sperber, A. M. 30.
St. John, Robert. 140.
Stafford, Jean. 114.
Stansky, Peter. 90.
Starling, Edmund W. 160.
Statler, Oliver. 123.
Steegmuller, Francis. 97.
Steel, Ronald. 55, 105.
Stegner, Wallace. 16, 25, 105, 120, 140, 162.
Steichen, Edward. 117, 138.
Steinbeck, John. 162.
Steiner, George Albert. 112.
Steinfels, Peter. 61.
Stern, Richard G. 111.
Stettinius, Edward R. 153, 164.
Stevens, L. C. 142.
Stevenson, Adlai E. 145.
Stewart, George Ripp. 155, 162.
Stewart, Sidney. 134.
Stilwell, Joseph W. 155.
Stimson, Henry L. 155.
Stone, Irving. 158, 165.

Title Index

Bolts of Melody. 161.
Book of Daniel, The. 92.
Book of Indians. 121.
Book of the Dance, The. 115.
Book of the Green Man, The. 103.
Books, Children & Men. 164.
Born Free, a Lioness of Two Worlds. 123.
Born on the Fourth of July. 73.
Bound to Violence. 93.
Bounds Out of Bounds. 48.
Bourgeois Poet, The. 124.
Brave Bulls, The. 152.
Brave Men. 164.
Breakfast at Tiffany's. 130.
Breaks of the Game, The. 49.
Breathing Lessons. 23.
Bricktop. 39.
Bride & the Bachelors, The. 112.
Bridge at Andau, The. 134.
Bridges at Toko-ri, The. 142.
Bright Book of Life. 85.
Britannia Mews. 160.
Broken Cord, The. 20.
Broken Vessels. 12.
Bronislava Nijinska: Early Memoirs. 50.
Brothers and Keepers. 38.
Brothers K., The. 9.
Bruno's Dream. 99.
Buffalo Afternoon. 19.
Bulwark, The. 158.
Burma Surgeon Returns. 160.
Burnt-Out Case, A. 121.
Burr. 87.
Bury My Heart at Wounded Knee. 91.
But Look, the Mourn. 157.
But We Were Born Free. 139.
Butterfly Ward, The. 53.
By Love Possessed. 133.
Cab at the Door, A. 101.
Cage, The. 4.
Cal. 41.
Calcutta. 90.
Cancerqueen and Other Stories. 93.
Canine Mutiny, The. 148.
Cannery Row. 162.
Cannibals and Kings. 68.
Captain From Castile. 162.
Captain Sam Grant. 149.
Captain, The. 103.
Carnival in Romans. 59.
Case Against the Nazi War Criminals, The. 159.
Case Worker, The. 80.
Cass Timberlane. 161.
Catcher in the Rye. 147.
Cathedral. 39.
Catherine the Great. 55.
Catholics. 85.
Cat's Eye. 17.
Censors and the Schools, The. 117.

Censorship: The Search for the Obscene. 112.
Centaur, The. 117.
Chaplin: His Life and Art. 33.
Charles Darwin: A Man of Enlarged Curiosity. 48.
Charles Evans Hughes, 2v. 147.
Chateau, The. 122.
Cheer, The. 54.
Cherokee Strip, The. 161.
Chicken Book, The. 79.
Child Buyer, The. 124.
Child of Our Time. 130.
Child, the Parent, and the State, The. 127.
Children of Crisis volume one. 103.
Children of Crisis volumes two and three. 89.
Children of Light. 30.
Children of Pride, The. 88.
Children of Sanchez, The. 122.
Children of the Dream, The. 98.
Children of the Holocaust. 57.
Children of the South. 106.
Children of the Sun. 72.
China Men. 54.
China Under Communism. 138.
Chip: How Two Americans Invented the Microchip and Launched a Revolution, The. 33.
Choice of Weapons, A. 108.
Chosen, The. 104.
Christ Stopped at Eboli. 157.
Chronicle of a Death Foretold. 40.
Chronicle of the Lodz Ghetto, 1941-1944, The. 35.
Circles on the Water. 46.
Citadel, the Story of the U.S. Senate. 134.
Cities and the Wealth of Nations. 36.
Citizen Hearst. 123.
City in History, The. 122.
City Life. 95.
City of Joy, The. 32.
Civil Wars. 35.
Civilization on Trial. 155.
Clea. 124.
Clear Light of Day. 53.
Clocks of Columbus, The. 89.
Closing the Ring. 146.
Clown, The. 109.
Cocteau: A Biography. 97.
Coil of Life, The. 122.
Cold War as History, The. 103.
Collected Essays, Journalism and Letters 4v. 101.
Collected Poems (Theodore Roethke). 108.
Collected Poems (Horace Gregory). 113.

Collected Poems (Dylan Thomas). 142.
Collected Poems (Carl Sandburg). 149.
Collected Poems (James Wright). 94.
Collected Poems: 1940-1977 (Karl Shapiro). 65.
Collected Poems, 1917-1952 (Archibald MacLeish). 144.
Collected Poems, 1951-1971 (A. R. Ammons). 87.
Collected Poems, 1966 (Robert Graves). 107.
Collected Poems of Langston Hughes, The. 2.
Collected Poems of W. H. Auden. 71.
Collected Poems, The (Sylvia Plath). 51.
Collected Poetry of W. H. Auden, The. 160.
Collected Shorter Poems, 1927-1957 (Wystan Hugh Auden). 102.
Collected Stories (William Faulkner). 148.
Collected Stories (Frank O'Connor). 50.
Collected Stories of Elizabeth Bowen, The. 48.
Collected Stories of Eudora Welty, The. 56.
Collected Stories of Isaac Bashevis Singer, The. 47.
Collected Stories of Wallace Stegner. 16.
Collected Stories, The (Grace Paley). 4.
Collected Works (Abraham Lincoln). 142.
Color and Democracy. 161.
Color Blind. 159.
Colored People. 5.
Columbia Historical Portrait of New York. 141.
Coming Alive: China after Mao. 49.
Coming into the Country. 69.
Coming of Age, The. 88.
Coming of Post-Industrial Society, The. 83.
Coming To. 76.
Command Decision. 157.
Commission on Freedom of the Press. 156.
Common Ground. 33.
Compleat Naturalist: A Life of Linnaeus, The. 91.
Complete Letters (Vincent Van Gogh). 130.
Complete Poems (Marianne Moore). 104.
Complete Poems and Plays (T. S. Eliot). 144.
Complete Poems of Robert Frost, 1949. 152.

179

Death of God. 106.
Ragtime. 76.
Rain or Shine. 29.
Raintree County. 154.
Ramains of the Day, The. 18.
Rape of the Fair Country, The. 127.
Rascal: A Memoir of a Better Era. 117.
Real West Marginal Way, The. 28.
Realms of Gold, The. 76.
Reason Why, The. 140.
Reckoning, A. 65.
Reconsiderations. 123.
Red Grooms: A Retrospective, 1956-1984. 28.
Redesigning the American Dream. 36.
Reflections of Nature. 36.
Reflections on Big Science. 105.
Regulating the Poor. 94.
Regulating the Poor. 94.
Reivers, A Reminiscence, The. 118.
Reluctant Surgeon, The. 125.
Remembering America. 23.
Remembering Babylon. 7.
Remembering Poets. 63.
Remembrance Rock. 155.
Renaissance, The. 141.
Renoir, My Father. 119.
Report by the U.S. National Advisory Commission on Civil Disorders. 101.
Report from a Chinese Village. 111.
Report on the Atom. 141.
Report to Greco. 110.
Requiem for a Woman's Soul. 30.
Resistance, Rebellion, and Death. 121.
Restless Earth, The. 88.
Rich Nations and the Poor Nations, The. 119.
Richard the Third. 135.
Richer by Asia. 158.
Rickshaw Boy. 162.
Right Stuff, The. 61.
Ring of Bright Water. 122.
Rise and Fall of the Third Reich, The. 126.
Rise of Theodore Roosevelt, The. 60.
River. 36.
Rivers, Man, and Myths. 130.
Rivers of Blood, Years of Darkness. 103.
Road from Coorain, The. 20.
Road to Huddersfield, The. 116.
Road to Reason, The. 154.
Road to Survival. 155.
Robert Capa: A Biography. 34.
Robert Frost: The Trial by Exist-

ence. 125.
Robert Kennedy and His Times. 65.
Robert Louis Stevenson. 78.
Roll, Jordan, Roll. 81.
Romance of American Communism, The. 63.
Romantic Education, A. 49.
Rome and a Villa. 143.
Rommel Papers, The. 142.
Roosevelt: The Lion and the Fox. 134.
Roosevelt: The Soldier of Freedom. 95.
Roosevelt and Hopkins. 155.
Roosevelt and the Russians. 153.
Roosevelt Family of Sagamore Hill, The. 139.
Roosevelt I Knew, The. 159.
Roots: The Saga of an American Family. 73.
Roots of Heaven, The. 130.
Rosenberg File, The. 42.
Rosencrantz and Guildenstern Are Dead. 105.
Royal Charles: Charles II and the Restoration. 58.
Rug Merchant, The. 24.
Rumor and Reflection. 143.
Rumor of War, A. 67.
Running in the Family. 46.
Russia: A History and an Interpretation. 141.
Russia and the Russians. 153.
Russia and the West under Lenin and Stalin. 122.
Russia at War, 1941-1945. 114.
Russian Assignment. 142.
Russians, The. 74.
Sadness. 87.
Sage of Monticello, The (Jefferson and His Time, v.6). 50.
Saint Genet, Actor and Martyr. 117.
Saints and Strangers. 162.
Saints and Strangers. 27.
Sal Si Puedes. 99.
Salmon. 37.
Salvador. 39.
Salvation on Sand Mountain. 2.
Sam Clemens of Hannibal. 145.
Samuel Johnson (Joseph W. Krutch). 164.
Samuel Johnson (Walter Jackson Bate). 67.
Samuel Johnson (John Wain). 79.
Sane Society, The. 137.
Sarajevo Daily. 2.
Sartre: A Life. 26.
Savage Cell, The. 114.
Savage God, The. 87.
Savage Inequalities. 13.

Scar Tissue. 4.
Scenes and Portraits. 139.
Science: The Glorious Entertainment. 112.
Science and Common Sense. 146.
Scientific Temperaments. 41.
Scotch, The. 113.
Scott Fitzgerald. 120.
Scrap of Time, A. 24.
Sculpture of This Century, The. 124.
Sea around Us, The. 146.
Sea, the Sea, The. 65.
Seal Morning. 133.
Searching for Caleb. 74.
Second Coming, The. 55.
Second Flowering, A. 84.
Second Tree from the Corner, The. 140.
Secret Diary of Harold Ickes, The. 141.
Secret of Santa Vittoria, The. 107.
Secret of the Hittites, The. 135.
Segregation, the Inner Conflict in the South. 136.
Selected Letters (Robert Frost). 113.
Selected Poems (Louis Aston Marantz Simpson). 111.
Selected Poems (Mark Strand). 55.
Selected Poems, New and Old, 1923-1966 (Robert Penn Warren). 109.
Selected Stories (Andre Dubus). 21.
Self and the Dramas of History, The. 138.
Self-Portrait: U.S.A. 98.
Self-Renewal. 113.
Senses of Animals and Men, The. 119.
Sent for You Yesterday. 43.
Separate Peace, A. 125.
Seven Arrows. 90.
Seven Caves, The. 133.
Seven Decisions That Shaped History. 147.
Seven Myths of Housing, The. 165.
Seven Plays of the Modern Theatre. 120.
Seven Worlds of Theodore Roosevelt, The. 132.
Seven Years in Tibet. 139.
Seventh Heaven. 15.
Seventh Storey Mountain, The. 155.
Sex and Destiny. 36.
Sexual Behavior in the Human Male. 154.
Sexual Politics. 97.
Shadow Train. 48.
Shah of Shahs. 32.
Shakespeare of London. 148.

DATE DUE

Text designed by Ben Segedin
Cover designed by Marcia Lange

Text printed on 50 lb Finch Opaque White
and bound in 12-point cover stock
by IPC Publishing Services